Crossing Jerusalem

Crossing Jerusalem

Journeys at the Centre of the World's Trouble

by
Nicholas Woodsworth

First Published in Great Britain in 2010 by
The Armchair Traveller
an imprint of Haus Publishing
4 Cinnamon Row
London SW11 3TW
www.hauspublishing.com

ISBN 978-1-906598-82-2
e-ISBN 978-1-909961-46-3

Typset in Garamond by MacGuru Ltd

Printed and bound in the UK by
CPI Mackays, Chatham ME5 8TD

A CIP catalogue for this book is available from the British Library

To Howard Polowin

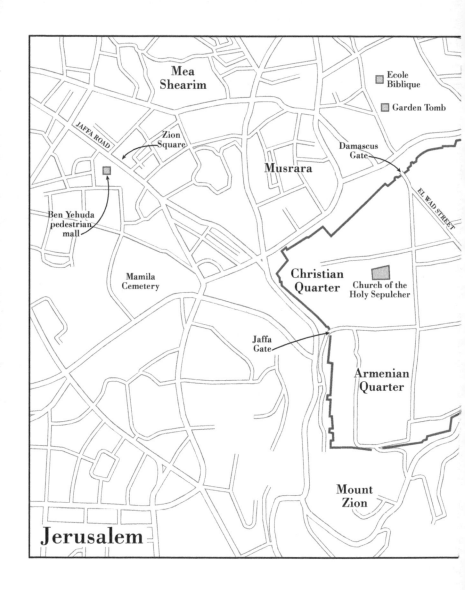

Mea
Shearim

Ecole
Biblique

Garden Tomb

JAFFA ROAD

Zion
Square

Musrara

Damascus
Gate

EL WAD STREET

Ben Yehuda
pedestrian
mall

Christian
Quarter

Church of the
Holy Sepulcher

Mamila
Cemetery

Jaffa
Gate

Armenian
Quarter

Mount
Zion

Jerusalem

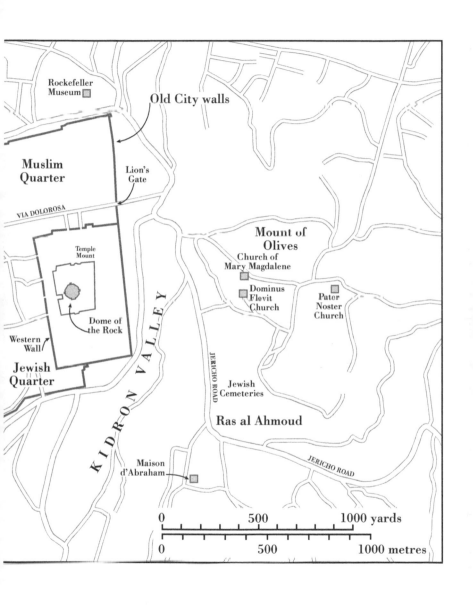

Rockefeller
Museum

Old City walls

Muslim
Quarter

Lion's
Gate

VIA DOLOROSA

Temple
Mount

Mount of
Olives

Church of
Mary Magdalene

Dominus
Flevit
Church

Pater
Noster
Church

Dome of
the Rock

Western
Wall

Jewish
Quarter

K I D R O N   V A L L E Y

JERICHO ROAD

Jewish
Cemeteries

Ras al Ahmoud

Maison
d'Abraham

JERICHO ROAD

0		500		1000 yards

0		500		1000 metres

One

They say the more time you spend in Jerusalem the less you understand it. After months you have answers, after years you don't. It's only a week since my arrival, and I don't have any answers at all. Even the questions are beginning to look shaky.

They also say there's nothing like the larger view. What I need to do is stand some distance from the city to get perspective on it. But right away there's a problem. There can't be many other places in the world where you'd find it as difficult to step back without risking a drop into the void. Only in the desert cartoon-world of the Roadrunner does that kind of thing happen more often. From a cliff-top Wile E. Coyote steps confidently backwards and – poof! – suddenly vanishes. Plummeting like a stone to the floor of the canyon far below, he presently totters out of a cloud of billowing dust looking flatter than a pancake. The arid Judean landscape surrounding Jerusalem is almost as rugged, but it isn't nearly as funny. The entire land about is so constricted, so cluttered with hazardous obstacles, that getting the city in perspective is an uncertain exercise. What they say is true. In Jerusalem you can listen all you like to infinitely complex reasoning, to elegant, lighter-than-air glosses on rights and wrongs seen from one perspective or another. But in the end everyone here slams hard into the ground and nobody walks blithely away from clouds of billowing dust. You can try it again and again – from wherever you stand near the city at the centre of the world's trouble it's almost impossible to make out anything at all.

It's not as though there are a lot of choices. If, while keeping your gaze firmly fixed on the city's soaring domes and spires, you start stepping carefully backwards towards the west you'll find yourself in no time floundering deep in the salt waves of the Mediterranean. Try moving to the north, and you'll finish by pricking your posterior on the barbed-wire borders of Lebanon and Syria. Back away southwards and Gaza waits. Above all, you shouldn't even think of trying to get a better view by reversing in an easterly direction. In just a matter of metres your shoulders will smack up against a wall of concrete twenty-five feet high. And from the other side of the wall, of course, the city can't be seen at all. For the people living behind the separation barrier the city barely exists – except, of course, in that dangerous place, the imagination. And there it never stops growing.

This is the irony of Jerusalem. This is the reason no one can agree on it. It may be a city of vast global scale, a metropolis that towers monumentally in the world's vision when seen from anywhere else. But up close it is shoehorned into a place too tight, too contested, too fraught for it even to be adequately seen.

What choice, in these straitened circumstances, do Jerusalem's inhabitants have? There is nowhere else to go but up. Denied the wide-angle, panoramic view, Jerusalemites choose the vertical one instead – they see their city as a function of what lies above it. Perhaps it's not such a privation after all. Given the city's ongoing trials one may question the wisdom of the choice, but this is the reason they built high up in these bare and flinty hills in the first place. Jerusalem is Jerusalem because it lies closer to God than anywhere else on earth.

Or just about. In reality, with a little effort you can actually get a view from high enough above the city – an elevation of several hundred additional feet – that you can look down over the top of the crenellated Turkish walls and gaze upon Jerusalem and all its works. Nor do you need wings to take a God's-eye view of the place. It's easily done on foot. You simply leave the Old City by the Lion's Gate and walk to the Garden of Gethsemane on the far side of the Kidron Valley; from behind the Garden you head up the road that leads towards the summit of the Mount of

Olives. It's steep, but in all not much more than half an hour's hike. And it's worth every step. No prospect of the city, whether viewed from Mount Scopus, Mount Zion or any of the other bone-dry hills that ring Jerusalem, is quite as fine.

And so I find myself, one bright autumn morning, puffing along under a hot sun and hoping for a little enlightenment above. I suppose that's why most people come this way. The Mount of Olives isn't the kind of place you'd visit for everyday things. There are no shops here, no cafés or bakeries or vegetable markets. There are no men standing behind stalls stuffing pitta bread at lightning speed with balls of deep-fried chickpea and pickled peppers. There *is* an appetite that people come here to satisfy, but it is slower and more patient, a long-term kind of craving. They are waiting for the End of Days.

For believers of a Messianic bent, there can be no better vantage point than the Mount of Olives from which to usher in time's last spectacular paroxysms and the final shutting down of history. I'm not sure it's the kind of show I'd wait in line for overnight. But it's said the spiritual rewards resulting from such patience are unbeatable – it's like finding yourself with front-row seats for a last-ever appearance of unimaginable cosmic dimension.

Up to the present day no devout Orthodox Jew will consider setting foot in the raised precinct where the Ark of the Covenant was once housed in the heart of Jerusalem; it has always been sacred ground permitted only to Jewish priests. But from the slopes of the Mount of Olives, clearly visible through the thin hill air, that holy of holies – the Temple Mount upon which the Muslim Dome of the Rock now rests – sits no distance away. From here nothing but the narrow confines of the Kidron Valley, in reality no more than a deep ravine, separates the worshipper from the object of his desires.

The valley holds a certain morbid fascination. Even today, a wasteland of sun-scorched grass and plastic bags flapping on thorn bushes in the hot wind, it remains more or less empty. But this desolate place, much evoked in the age of biblical prophecy, will not stay uncluttered forever. Zechariah, Isiah, Micah, Ezekiel and other fierce prophets of that time knew it as the Valley of Jehosaphat, and all warned that it was here that earthly life would come to an end. For a brief space of time the Kidron Valley, it's foresaid, will see such a rush of heaven-bound traffic as to put all the combined congestion of man's terrestrial highways to shame.

It will happen, said the prophets, after the Jewish Messiah has at last descended to earth, after the war of Gog and Magog and Israel's total defeat. Even Jerusalem, the final stronghold of the righteous, will be conquered. It is only then that God will join in battle. Sending down pestilence and rain, fire and stones, he will destroy Israel's enemies – their corpses will be strewn about in such numbers that it will take seven months to bury them. It is only after their destruction that the disposal of undeserving souls will begin. It is then that God, sitting high on his Judgment Throne, will preside over the divine trial that decides on the dispatch of all men to their final destination.

A miraculous bridge, spanning the space between the Mount of Olives and the Temple Mount, will stand revealed in the Kidron Valley. The dead will be raised from their burial places and all the human beings who have ever lived, Jews and Gentiles alike, will cross it. Not all, naturally, will get to the far end – only the righteous will arrive safely at the Temple Mount and from there proceed directly heavenwards to God's kingdom.

That, at least, is the simple version of events. A second Judaic version has it that there will be two bridges, the first built of paper and the second of iron. Sinners sent by God across the iron bridge will die when it collapses. But those who cross on the bridge of paper, carrying no weight of sin, will survive. No matter the version – all agree that those who have offended God will be hurled earthward to spend eternity in the lake of hellfire which will open up beneath them on the Kidron Valley floor.

So, at any rate, I read in my guide to Jerusalem, a volume that gives me the excuse every now and then to stop, consult, and rest. It's a hefty little tome to bring on such a climb, but I don't regret it for a moment. A guide to the sites around which the city's religious and cultural history is built, it may be earnest in intent, but it's also hugely entertaining. It's so chock-a-block with tales of the miraculous and the diabolical, the uplifting and the down-crushing, the weird and the wonderful, that I can only marvel that a single city can possibly merit so staggering a compilation of rare goings-on.

Most of the lower part of this steep road is bounded on both sides by the walls of churches and monasteries, for many of the events of Jesus' own final days are said to have taken place on the Mount of Olives. But presently I come to a break in the barrier and find a pleasant bit of shade to sit in. I read on. From here the Kidron Valley looks calm enough, at least for the moment. The only constructions I have seen in the valley below are two ancient monuments: the stone-carved burial site of Jehosaphat himself, and the oddly shaped Absolom's Pillar, a tomb that looks like an inverted funnel and houses, it's believed, the remains of the son of King David. So far, so quiet. But eventually, when the end of time finally comes, there can only be a frantic construction-boom here. For not only is it Jews who are planning to use the Kidron as an escape route to heaven. So are the world's Christians, and its Muslims too.

This is the penalty incurred by three religions for sharing a common progenitor, Abraham, for holding the same monotheistic traditions, and for listening to similar end-of-the-world messages. Inevitably, there is sibling rivalry right up to the last minute of mankind's allotted time on earth – Christian doomsday enthusiasts, not to be outdone by their Jewish counterparts, claim an even more lurid end to worldly existence.

There will be seven years of Tribulation, a period of great suffering, in which an Antichrist will arrive to deceive the world. There will be death by famine, by wild beasts and earthquake. Boils and pestilence will be humanity's common lot. Howling banshee horsemen will pursue men and women to the ends of the earth, forcing them to live in caves and rocky places. Hail and fire will rain down from the heavens. The sea and the moon turn red with blood. A poisonous star will fall from space, contaminating all sources of fresh water. Mountains and islands will be dislodged. The sky will roll up, light will fail and the world will go dark.

The most appalling mayhem ceases only with the Second Coming; Jesus Christ, the Christian Messiah, returns to earth from heaven. And although various branches of Millenarians cannot agree whether the Rapture happens before, after or during the Tribulation, all concur that the dead shall be resurrected and rise up from their graves. Then the righteous and the wicked, the living and the dead, will be gathered on the lip of the Kidron Valley for Christ's judgement. But if many are called, few are chosen – for Christian backsliders as for Jewish, it's the long-drop straight to Hell.

Muslim fundamentalists are not to be upstaged by the other Peoples of the Book. Their version of these last days on earth is no less cataclysmic. It, too, has its own divine messenger: the *Mahdi*, or 'Guided One,' sometimes believed to be a descendent of the prophet Mohammed himself. There are natural catastrophes: the ground caves in; smoke and fog cover the skies; a darkness lasts three days and nights; the sun rises in the west. The Beast of the Earth arrives to place his fearful mark on people's faces. There is the same ferocious and bloody slaughter that Jews and Christians anticipate, and then the total defeat of Islam's enemies. But if the gods of all faiths are unstinting in their bloodletting, the Muslim god is not as generous in theatrical arrangement. Come the Day of Judgement, there is no magnificent soaring bridge for the passage of the Just. What Allah slings across the Kidron Valley to the Dome of the Rock is merely a thin rope. He lays on something else, however – winged angels. They are the aid-givers, the balancers, one on each side, who help countless terrified mortals inch their way over the valley floor. The righteous are helped the entire way across; sinners, of course, are let go of at the halfway point and plunge to eternal damnation below.

The End of Days, as drawn by my guidebook, is all fine stuff – colourful, dramatic, stagey and spectacular. Nobody takes such stories literally, for that is exactly what they are – stories. Such myths of final completion act as counterpoints to other myths of original creation, and for centuries they have allowed people to find their place in an inexplicable cosmos. They are part of an early world literature that has enriched us all for centuries, and to understand them otherwise would be a nonsense. Take your pick – in any of these tales the prophecies of universal chaos and a last great crescendo of mega-death and extinction are delivered in the grand, apocalyptic style of a Charles Manson. Taken literally, what else could they be but the ravings of madmen caught in the grip of collective homicidal delusion?

The sun moving higher into the sky, my shade fast disappearing, I read over the accounts again. Could I be reading them wrong? Without the sanction of religious tradition, surely there's enough extreme psychopathology on display here to put any serious end-of-the-worlder away in a padded cell for good.

But the trouble is that Jerusalem is like no place else on earth – this is a city where religious sanction for all sorts of nonsense can be found by the bucket-load. Here the most ordinary of lives are transformed every day by the most extraordinary of ideologies.

There exist in Jerusalem, of course, as there exist in isolated groups around the globe, radical Islamist terrorists who are literally dying to go to heaven. But they've hardly cornered the market on zealotry. Not far away in the leafy suburb of Rehavia on the west side of the city sits a well-financed evangelical Christian mission bent on kick-starting the Day of Judgement. Its ends may be spiritual, but its means are temporal. Supported by Protestant fundamentalists from around the world, it is the mission of the International Christian Embassy Jerusalem to abet political Zionism and the territorial expansion of Israel – by doing so it will ensure the fulfillment of Old Testament divination and thus the Messiah's return.

But in this city I don't have to seek out explosives caches or ersatz embassies to see that scriptural prophecy still has fervent believers here – as I sit gazing across the Mount of Olives, there is no need for me even to get to my feet.

For cascading downwards from the summit of the hill, in tier after tier of blocky, stone-built tombs, stretches the largest Jewish cemetery in the world. With the sun now high overhead and light bouncing harshly off quarry-hewn Jerusalem limestone, the cemetery looks like a vast glacier gleaming in the sun. Stark and treeless it may be, but there can be no doubt of the prestige of Jewish burial here. These tombs have always been prized for their placement – when the dead are brought to life and the Judgement begins, their residents shall be first in line to proceed to the Temple Mount, and from there to heaven.

Nor have these sleeping souls been abandoned by the living descendants who one day will follow right behind them. Braving perilous territory – for the Mount of Olives now lies in what is Arab East Jerusalem – a group of Ultra-Orthodox Jews moves slowly through the cemetery. Hatted, heavily bearded, dressed in black suits and silhouetted starkly against the broad white expanse of tombs, they proceed upwards in winding single file. At this distance they look like an expedition of old-fashioned alpinists threading their way over the crevasses and up the coulees of an ice-field. They halt to make base-camp behind an iron railing on a broad stone terrace, then spread out to tend tombstones and commemorate their departed ancestors with prayer and Torah reading.

I, too, continue to make my way up the steep slope, but do not stop for rituals of any kind. Beyond the Jewish cemetery Christian and Muslim sites, too, lie scattered over the hillside. But I'm not interested. In my mind I have conjured up images of paper bridges and tightropes and winged angels and falling bodies and sulphurous lakes of fire, and for one morning that is quite enough. Who knows what further mystery lies in Dominus Flevit, where Franciscans honour the rock over which Jesus wept for Jerusalem? Or what interfaith confusion awaits in the Muslim Mosque of the Ascension, where a footprint of Isa – none other than that selfsame Jesus in his guise as a prophet of Islam – remains marked on another piece of stone? Enough of sacred rocks. Enough of guilt, enough of bearded prophets in ash and sack-cloth, enough of epic myth-making. I simply want a view and a little quiet contemplation from the top of a high hill.

Instead I am taken for Lawrence of Arabia. Not far from the summit, I come to a junction where a larger road that follows the crest of the hill leads to a spectacular lookout above the Old City. There is a tour-company mini-van parked nearby and half a dozen foreign visitors admiring the panorama, but the viewpoint is still more or less peaceful. It is the standing-back place I have been hoping for, the spot to get the broad perspective that further down and closer in seems impossible.

I sit on a parapet and gaze citywards. From here, in one sweep, I can see the things that from below in narrow alleys and crowded passageways I haven't been able to see at all. Dominated by the gleaming gold cupola of the Dome of the Rock, everything in the four quarters of the city is on view, from the shrines of Sufi saints to the Tower of David to the spires of the Holy Sepulcher. Before me sits medieval Jerusalem, compact but complete, key in the dispute and bitterness that has spilled out over these old city walls and around the world.

Does some sort of answer lie inside those walls? I have no idea and no time to think about it. For I am not the only ruminator here. From down the road, led on a cord and wooden plug passed through its wide, flat nostrils, I am joined by a camel. His jaw works from side to side and his beautiful, liquid amber eyes are complimented above and below by graceful, curving eyelashes. This is no drab, run-of-the-mill nomad's camel. This is a flamboyant, show-dromedary decked out in bright Bedouin trappings. His saddle is embroidered, his saddlebags of woven cloth are capacious enough for a month-long crossing of the Empty Quarter, and his bridle is hung about with fluffy woolen tassels in the Arab colours of red, green and black. Altogether he is a proud beast, worthy of an Arabian Hollywood romance. And he is all mine.

'Just twenty shekels – sit on him for photo,' urges the man leading the camel, tapping it on the foreleg with a stick until with a groan the animal sinks to its knees on the ground. The camel-man doesn't look like a prince of the desert. At least he's an Arab, I think – his mustache is magnificent and he's as brown as a berry. But he's dressed in jeans and running shoes, and he's got on a pink sweatshirt that reads 'Pookie's LateNite DiscoBar.'

I decline his offer. He rummages around in the saddlebags and pulls out a long robe and a red and white *keffiyeh* head-dress. 'Ah,' I think, 'last call at Pookie's. Time for the day job.' But the gear is not for him. It's for me.

'Just thirty shekels – you get camel photo *and* look like star,' he inveigles me.

He tugs at the end of his lustrous mustache. 'Who am I? I, I am maybe only Omar Sharif. But you, you are Peter O'Toole.' I resist his entreaties. He shrugs, goes back to the saddlebag and delves about in it. Resistance, the gleam in his eye is telling me, is useless. With a flourish he pulls out the clincher, the object he is convinced will make me dress up in funny clothes and sit on a camel with the walls of Jerusalem as a backdrop. It is an oversized Bedouin ceremonial dagger, its blade broad and curved upward at the end, its scabbard studded with cheap rhinestones. I've never seen such a phony-looking prop.

I shake my head again. He is crestfallen, but only for a moment. 'O.K. Just forty shekels,' he says, going for his best, most alluring deal. 'You get camel photo, Peter O'Toole look and ride to Tomb of the Prophets and back. Special offer – Arafat's birthday. I lose money, never mind.'

It's a proposition a chunky young American sitting not far away eventually takes up, and I stay long enough to watch him get dressed in robe and *keffiyeh*. He looks like an off-duty soldier, perhaps a marine on leave from an U.S. base somewhere in the Gulf. The Lawrence of Arabia look is marred by the wraparound, silver-reflecting sunglasses he continues wearing. But the dagger the camel-man belts around his waist does him proud. Off he's led, departing on some desperate, glory-filled mission to save lost American honour in the Middle East.

Soon he disappears around a corner, and I do, too. More and more taxis and tour-vehicles are showing up and the place is getting crowded. But it's been a tough climb and I'm not ready to go down yet. I also want some relief from a sun growing hotter by the minute. So instead I follow the road along the hill's crest and stick my nose into the door of the first public site I come to. It happens to be Christian, the Church of the Pater

Noster. More important, its attractive cloister, planted with palms and other greenery, is cool and shady. So I pay my admission and stroll around.

The Pater Noster commemorates a cave where Jesus is thought to have taught his disciples the Lord's Prayer. The place has inspired Byzantine queens to raise churches here, Crusaders to construct oratories, and the 19th-century Princesse de la Tour d'Auvergne to build a Carmelite convent and have herself buried on the site. There is the little cave itself to visit down dark stairs beneath the church, but a far more cheerful attraction is the collection of large, florally-decorated ceramic panels that sit on the walls around the Gothic arched cloister. In Fon, Samaritan, Bariba, Isindibele, Edwardo, Biak, Moore, Helgoland, Grurien and dozens of other languages I've never heard of the panels record the prayer beginning, 'Our Father, who art in Heaven...

A Etanè waha nyo a lè a loo
joo joo li bè la ebegè
Likanyè joo li so
Nsom woo a bonbe a si aka a lè a loo

So begins the Lord's Prayer in the language of Mpoo, and as I stand there reading it lightens my mood. Mpoo, to judge by its short, trip-along monosyllables, kicky consonants and long, smooth vowels, is a happy and serendipitous tongue. The people who speak it, I get the feeling, are not the kind to be naturally filled with the dread and recrimination of patri-archally-revealed religion, wherever they live. Unless they were taught it by misguided missionaries, I doubt they could conceive of any cosmic menace as dark and foreboding as a Judgement Day. Leave them be, I think, in their dugout canoes – let them go on worshipping lava-spewing volcanoes, headless chickens or whatever it is they bow down before in their own small corner of the world. They're better off with it. Nothing could be as bad as taking your daily marching orders from a lunatic deity who promises humanity the death of the universe should it put a foot wrong. Personally I'd as soon be thrown into a cannibal's iron pot as hurled by God off a high bridge into a lake of fire. It's a shorter drop. And, nutritionally speaking any rate, at least you'd be doing somebody some good.

But there are, of course, wiser, gentler forms of religion, and as I make my way to the exit of the church I encounter their human embodiment. The Pater Noster still houses a Carmelite convent today, and in the little shop by the doorway out – a place where the nuns supplement their income by the sale of rosaries, crucifixes and other religious regalia – I meet a genuine doer of good.

As in the Maison d'Abraham, the Dominican-run hospice where I am staying, there are not enough nuns at Pater Noster to keep the place going. Being married to Christ doesn't have the same attractions these days as it used to, and young nuns are growing ever rarer. And so here, as in other such institutions in Jerusalem, foreign volunteers step in to give their time and energy. Usually they are women, widowed or retired, and although their children have long grown up and left home the maternal instinct is still strong in them. Above all they are possessed of a certain force of character – if you're working long hours in an unpredictable environment for no material reward it's a basic requirement.

Such character soon shows in this meeting. Browsing, I come across a carved wooden object which for Christian pilgrims has become a symbol of the city – the Jerusalem Cross. It is like other Christian crosses, but has four smaller crosses posed at its interstices. It makes a neat and regular geometrical tangle. As I pay for it I fall to chatting. The volunteer behind the counter is somewhere in her mid-seventies and comes from Alsace in north-eastern France. She is small, white-haired and blue-eyed, and as lively and energetic as a teenager. She is not overly pious or sanctimonious, but if Christianity means the observation of that simple precept, doing to others as you'd have done to you, she's a keen practitioner. She has been a volunteer for the Carmelite nuns several times in the past, and what strikes me most is her obvious love for this place – over the years she has learned to care deeply for Jerusalem, its people and its fate. Sweet and gentle, she is a model of that ever-scarcer virtue, Christian charity.

But the conversation soon turns to a troubled matter, the ongoing trials of Gaza, and immediately I see a steely light creep into those kind blue eyes. The gaze that was maternal is soon replaced by an ice-cold indignation. What has taken place there, I am told in no uncertain terms, amounts to crimes of war. Plainly criminal, too, is the man who brought Gaza to its dreadful state of suffering in the first place, Ariel Sharon. Not only was he an early instigator of Israeli military occupation, I'm told, he is also responsible for the state of limbo that prevails there now. When the Israelis were in charge there, they at least bore a legal responsibility for the material welfare of Gaza's population. With Sharon's decision to pull out came the abdication of even that responsibility. Gaza, my diminutive new acquaintance fulminates, is nothing more than a vast internment camp, cut off from the rest of the world by wire and guard towers, containing a million and a half people deprived of the most basic requirements of life. Why, she demands to know in a voice turned hard and fierce, is there no medicine for sick children there?

'You know, *Monsieur*,' she continues in French, 'we are quite familiar with military occupation in Alsace. It was French until the war of 1870, then German until 1918, then French again until 1939; I myself lived through Nazi occupation in the Second World War. It was difficult for everyone, but those who had the hardest time were our young men. We all knew of the exactions, the imprisonments, the summary justice the Nazis handed out to them. And still Frenchmen joined the Resistance – it was the only course of action left to them. Israel wonders today why young Palestinians resist their occupation. I, for myself, don't wonder at all! What other choice do they have?'

I am uncomfortable seeing a once serene individual become so anguished so quickly. Her voice is shaky, her fingers trembling. I mention that Ariel Sharon no longer has anything to do with Gaza; he's been lying deep in a coma for a very long time. The comment only pushes the Carmelite helper to new levels of wrath.

'In some small way,' she says in a clenched voice, 'God is now giving Ariel Sharon a taste of what he has given to hundreds of thousands of others. They are prisoners in Gaza, and he is now a prisoner in his own body. I hope with all my heart he is conscious inside it. I hope he is learning the wisdom he failed to show in his treatment of others. I hope he regrets his life. If he does, God at least has found one way, however minor, of rendering justice. He has his methods.'

I stumble from the Church of the Pater Noster into the hard glare of noon outside. It may just be the heat, but I am a little breathless and uncertain on my feet. I feel struck down, assaulted by the unexpected. From what hidden, unanticipated source deep inside this gentle woman has such thirst for vengeance arisen? This is not the compassionate discourse of an aid-giver. This is not a turning of the other cheek. This is a call for biblical justice, an evening of scores. We are back to the Old Testament. This is an eye for an eye.

I walk back down the hill, past the Jewish cemetery, towards the city. The camel in all his bright finery has vanished, the Orthodox Jews in their beards and black suits have disappeared. Gone, too, is any idea that I might so easily have stepped back from Jerusalem for a better view. I can handle the towering retribution called down upon endless seething crowds on the Day of Judgement. But I am less good at coping with the flesh-and-blood requital of a single, aging woman not much more than five feet tall. The city is no more understandable now than it was before my attempt at a better view of it. Like other hopefuls before me, I have without warning stepped backwards off a ledge. It is still a perfectly clear, calm day, so it's with some surprise that I find myself returning to Jerusalem, feeling flattened, in what seems like a billowing cloud of dust.

Two

At precisely seven o'clock each evening a weighty hand-bell is agitated by the vigorous and untiring arm of Soeur Marta as she stands outside the refectory in the Maison d'Abraham. Its strident clanging mounts the stone staircases, bounces along three floors of dimly-lit, high-ceilinged hallways, and finally penetrates narrow rooms whose regularly-spaced doors recede into the gloom as if placed there for the edification of students of Renaissance perspective.

Despite occasional bits of furniture and the odd gangly and sun-starved potted plant, there is an inescapable atmosphere of the institutional about these corridors – in fact theological study has been the primary concern of the inhabitants of these sparse and modest quarters from the beginning. Long ago, when the Maison d'Abraham was a French priory dedicated to Saint Benedict, woolen-gowned Benedictine monks lived out entire lives in study and silent contemplation in these thick-walled chambers. They are no longer present. Nor are the devout young seminarians, soutaned and serious, who followed them in a later century; they spent their early adulthood here, studying the rites and canons of the Syrian Catholic Church before their ordination and dispatch to obscure Christian corners of the Levant.

The constant flow of guests who now occupy these rooms usually do so only for a matter of days. But they, too, are students of a kind. Visitors from around the world, they have arrived in Jerusalem with a purpose. Parisians or Montevideans, New Yorkers or Marseillais, they come alone or in groups, well-heeled or near-indigent, as confirmed believers or as doubters wracked by hesitation. Some, like me, are even frank and long-confirmed disbelievers. But all are more than simple holidaying tourists bent on taking in the sights, for each has come to the city on some sort of quest. They are, for want of a more modern word, Jerusalem pilgrims.

Compared to the sweetness of a thousand other bells in Jerusalem, the jangle of Soeur Marta's dinner-bell might well sound somewhat harsh. But it is far from unwelcome. For if the Maison d'Abraham's final purpose in Jerusalem is to put pilgrims in touch with a higher power, their physical needs are not ignored. In accordance with the generally Gallic atmosphere that reigns here – the Maison d'Abraham is run under the auspices of France's *Secours Catholique* – the chef in the kitchen opposite the refectory has learned to cook in the French manner. To put it simply, the Maison d'Abraham offers by far and away the best dining of any hospice, monastery, convent, abbey, friary, nunnery or pilgrim's hostel in town. It may not approach the pricy sophistication of *haute cuisine*, for one of the Maison d'Abraham's directives is to provide affordable bed and board to pilgrims of all backgrounds and incomes. But in what other religious institution in Jerusalem can you get a decent *creme de potiron* soup, herb-sprinkled *tomates Provençales* and a fragrant *poulet basquaise* for dinner? So when the bell rings, it is astonishing quite how quickly, whatever the nature of their personal reflections, hungry pilgrims clatter down the stairs to take their place in the stone-pillared refectory. Father Michael jokes that it's a good thing that so few embassies have chosen to relocate from Tel Aviv to Jerusalem. Their choice may be political and secular, but it has positive consequences for the Church – not yet pinched by some unscrupulous housewife from the diplomatic corps, it has allowed the much-admired cook at the Maison d'Abraham to carry on cooking in the service of God and his hungry faithful.

Father Michael O'Sullivan is the director of the Maison d'Abraham. There isn't much Gallic sophistication in that particular name – Father Michael comes instead from the damp green landscape of County Clare in the west of Ireland. But he's certainly no cardboard cut-out Irish country priest. The idea of Father Michael weaving his way across the bog on a squeaky bicycle is not just homely and parochial, it's impossible. Decades have gone by since he's passed time in any damp green place at all. He is an Arabist, and has spent most of his career in uncertain, not to say downright dodgy, places on the very edges of Christianity. He has lived for almost a decade deep in the deserts of southern Algeria – 'Foucault country' as he calls it, after the Trappist missionary, part mystic, part anthropologist, who was killed there by Touareg tribesmen in the early 1900s. But in this part of the world you don't have to go back that far to see missionaries caught up in violence. Father Michael was well acquainted with the French monks of the Tibhirine Monastery in Algeria, seven of whom had their heads removed in the 1990s – to this day no one knows if their killers were Islamist radicals or *agents provocateurs* of the Algerian state. Perhaps more perilous still for zealous missionaries in the present century, Father Michael has spent long years working with Christian converts in the slums of Khartoum. When he needs a break from it all he pursues Arab studies in Rome or takes a retreat in an isolated monastery in northern Lebanon. Father Michael, his face ruddy, his white hair clipped short, is a kindly, concerned cleric with an easy laugh. But he's also astute, a man with that inborn sense of negotiated compromise needed for survival in tricky places, and nobody's fool.

When I knock on the door of his little office, a cluttered place where religious texts compete for space with invoices, receipts and bank statements, Father Michael is on the telephone and in full Arabic spate. As a new arrival to the Maison d'Abraham, I have come to introduce myself, chat, and get a little advice from a wise old head. Guttural and full of soft little explosions, Father Michael's words now come fast and furious, and as is often the case when I hear Arabic I cannot tell if the conversation is full of anger or merely hearty. It must be the latter, I conclude as he waves me into a chair, for the exchange ends with laughter and *Oualakoum Saalam*s. Peace and God's blessing has been wished upon us.

'Heavens,' says Father Michael, ballooning his cheeks and expelling air from them in a gesture of fatigue and relief at the end of a long, trying day. 'If you only knew how difficult it is to get the simplest thing done in a country where no one can agree on working hours. The Muslims take Fridays off, the Jews Saturday and the Christians Sunday. What's left of the week is mayhem. I have a party of thirty UN observers arriving from the Egyptian border tonight and an even larger group of Bombay and Goa pilgrims needing transport to the Sea of Galilee tomorrow. The staff were supposed to be paid yesterday. Our oldest employee – Om Jemal, the little Palestinian cleaning-lady who mops the halls every day – has lost her husband and needs funeral expenses immediately. If I can't get a cheque cleared in the next 24 hours we might as well close up shop altogether.'

Of course Father Michael won't close up shop; he's got any number of people depending on him far into the weeks and months ahead. Welcoming garden-variety pilgrims is just the beginning of his work. More demanding are the rarer exotics – the poor, who are hosted on *voyages d'esperance*, 'journeys of hope'; inspection visits by church officials; academic conferences; group retreats; soldier's R-and-R weekends; tented youth camps; specialist religious familiarisation tours for diplomats and NGOs. Why, says Father Michael to me in wonder, there's even a group coming shortly who want to know about Holy Land olive-oil production, everything from biblical pressing techniques to Internet marketing. So he's had to brush up on that, too. There are times, the Irish priest tells me, when he feels as if he's running some sort of 24-hour celestial travel agency. These days the Maison d'Abraham can even be found listed on a Holy Land website called travelujah.com.

It sounds a far cry from the lonely places of the desert or the self-imposed exile of the Sudanese slums. But that's why he enjoys it, says Father Michael. There is nothing quiet or self-effacing about Christianity in Jerusalem – there is too much competition for souls here. Even as a matter between different branches of the same Christian belief it's a brash, in-your-face business. But as old Europe continues to lose its appetite for God, as proselytization shifts the Christian centre of gravity to Africa,

Asia and Latin America, Jerusalem has become an ever more important focal point for the widely scattered faithful. Father Michael tells me he likes to think of the city as '*les tripes du monde*' – the gut of the earth. This is the place where all currents meet, where everything started and where, like tsunami waves propelled outwards on a prolonged circumnavigation of the globe, everything eventually ripples back again.

As a lifelong student of the Arab world, Father Michael, of course, has a preoccupation with the major fault-line on which Jerusalem sits; if you're interested in watching the tectonic plates of world religion collide and grind together, this is the place to be. And Father Michael has direct professional interests not far away on the other side of the line. He has strong ties with the Catholic churches of the Middle East, and travels often to the Gulf states, where Christianity, he tells me, is growing by leaps and bounds.

'Imagine,' he says, 'there are new multi-million dollar churches out there that beggar anything built in Europe in the last half-century. There are regular church congregations of Christian Arabs that now pass the 1,000 mark. Even Christian parking lots are getting bigger there – there are churches in Doha with parking spaces outside for 800 cars! And they are all taken! Can you picture 800 cars outside a church in France or England on a Sunday morning? It's wide open, anyone's game.'

But in the end, his enthusiasm for congregational car-parking aside, I suspect Father Michael enjoys Jerusalem for the same reasons he enjoyed Algeria and Sudan – once again he finds in the negotiations of Church life here a certain element of smoky back-room bargaining. It is the natural result of too many religious institutions competing with each other on too little turf. It is a delicate game of tactical gamesmanship, sectarian horse-trading and the subtle, secret wielding of power and influence. Requiring skills of discretion and dissimulation, its gambles don't always work – like Rome itself, this is also a world subject to eruptions of sensation and scandal. In its ungodly resolutions, in its unfolding Byzantine twists and turns, its study appeals immensely to the political animal in Father Michael. He is a man who has seen the heavenly mission carried out in the cut and thrust of the real world, and nowhere is the action more flamboyantly executed than here in Jerusalem.

I casually mention that I am planning a visit to the Russian Orthodox church which lies just a five-minute walk down the road – every time I pass it by, its high, golden onion-domes seem to me to be among the loveliest things in Jerusalem. I believe it is called, I say to Father Michael, the Church of Mary Magdalene.

'Ah, the White Church, you mean?' he replies. 'That's what old hands here call it.' He is referring not to its colour but its political allegiance. Immediately he launches into tales of its rivalry with the Red Church, the Orthodox establishment in the city's Russian Compound which, after the Russian revolution, chose to retain its links to Moscow. It was widely assumed for decades that both churches were acting as listening posts, harbouring robed and bearded spies attached to opposing intelligence services. The two are coming a bit closer together now, Father Michael acknowledges, but for decades their priests and prelates wouldn't even speak to each other. He moves on to more recent scuttlebutt – the exposure of a Jerusalem archbishop's private secretary in his covert role as middleman in the illegal sale of Church property to Israeli businessmen. When it comes to human ambition Father Michael sees duplicity and imperfection everywhere. And in the more obscure corridors of Jerusalem's public life – a murky labyrinth where the darker sides of religion and politics meet and often fuse – he is probably right to do so.

This seems the moment to ask Father Michael for some advice about finding a way through a labyrinth of my own. I am not seeking to untangle the complexities of international espionage in Jerusalem or the deceptions of Church financial scandals – these arcane matters are the studies of a lifetime. I am not a theologian or a political scientist, an Arabist or a diplomat, an anti-globalisation activist or a specialist in superpower geostrategic maneuvering. Those disciplines are complex enough anywhere, but in Jerusalem they fast become opaque, over-the-head quagmires. I am looking for something far simpler. Like the pilgrims who even now are waiting to hear a dinner-bell after a long day's visit to shrine or tomb or grotto, I too have come to Jerusalem on a kind of quest. What I want is a sense of place, a feeling for the spirit that inhabits this city.

It's something we all look for, pretty much subconsciously, wherever we go. It doesn't matter what the situation we find there – we like to know, quite literally, where we stand. And usually we figure it out. Every spot in every corner of the globe has its own specific nature, however hidden.

Listen quietly for the essential workings by which a city maintains its internal make-up through centuries of outward change, and you'll begin to get a feeling for its immutability. Cock your ears for a slight alteration of timbre or change of rhythm, and you'll learn how at the same time it adapts in order to survive. These are the subtle elements that make one city unlike another – each one has a signature note. Sometimes the mechanism fires on all cylinders with a loud staccato hammering; at others it hums, almost inaudibly, from deep inside. London is an unabashedly commercial city, Canberra is unmistakably a government town, and Rio de Janeiro is a place where human physicality sends most ideas of finance and administration flying straight out of the window. No one has much trouble understanding these things. A place like Lisbon, on the other hand, is an altogether more difficult place to figure out, and its gentle and nostalgic regrets for a grander past echo ever more softly across the centuries. No matter – that old sound hangs in the air there still, and it defines the way Lisbon sees itself and the world sees Lisbon.

But Jerusalem? Over the years I have passed through the city a good number of times, always on the way somewhere else. Wherever I have ended up, though, Jerusalem has remained on my mind and left me always and entirely puzzled. There are many sounds coming out of Jerusalem, but none of them is clear – what floats out over the city instead is cacophony, a bottomless, incoherent rumbling of voices whose different strains I am incapable of separating or deciphering.

Is there any sense in it at all? What is one to make of a city which in the language of three faiths preaches the only message that really counts in religious belief – universal love – and which at the same time cannot love itself? A city which instead does its level best to cut its own throat?

It is this incomprehensible contradiction that has seized hold of my attention, and I want to find out why and how it exists. You don't have to be spiritually involved for such a thing to seem important – there are immediate, physical, flesh-and-blood consequences of this contradiction that threaten us all, right now, believer and unbeliever alike, from Afghanistan to New York.

Perhaps, too, a lifetime spent as a traveller in unfamiliar places has heightened my need to know these things. The search for the vital connections that hold things together in strange cities is not so very different from the same search at home. It's just a little more pressing – it's the only way of making a satisfactory mental map of an unknown world. Without it you are lost. Or at least I am – and in Jerusalem I have no sense of these connections at all.

It's all rather difficult to explain to Father Michael, for unlike most pilgrims at the Maison d'Abraham I cannot claim my quest goes much beyond the temporal. Jerusalem mystifies me in everything but my certainty that it is this world, and not the next, that needs worrying about. But I do my best and Father Michael takes it all in stride. Although I shall be staying in his pilgrim's household from October until Christmas, he doesn't bat an eye when I admit to him I'm profoundly skeptical of religion. In his time in Jerusalem, I suppose, he's met every possible kind of Grail-searcher. More important, he is a practical man, and not overly preoccupied with the Big Answers. It's the right questions that concern him. This side of the grave, his expression seems to tell me, they're about the best we can hope for.

Right away Father Michael is jotting down for me names and cell-phone numbers and addresses of people I might talk to. There's an obscure but brilliant Jesuit priest I must see; an eminent biblical scholar; a radical religious iconoclast; a controversial bishop; an interfaith conciliator; the head of Jerusalem's Status Quo Commission. And when the name of a certain liberation theologist active in Jerusalem comes up, I ask if there isn't a marked political element in his work.

'But it's all political, right from the very start.' Father Michael looks at me for a long moment without saying anything, then continues. 'There is no priest or imam or rabbi, no archbishop's council or mosque committee or synagogue *minyan* in all Jerusalem that is not deeply political in nature. Politics is the essence of religion here, and religion is the essence of politics. This is what makes the city.'

The priest fills me with qualms. Nothing, he appears to be saying, is quite as it might look at first. What ultimately counts here? Whatever I've come looking for, it's not going to be easy to find in such a place. I have more questions about the obscure mysteries of Jerusalem, but we are saved by the bell. Far away Soeur Marta is ringing for dinner. The Irish priest and I are both relieved, I think – no one can even think of asking such questions on an empty stomach. We are hungry, and make our way to the refectory with our heels echoing down the long, high corridor in double time.

The contingent of UN observers has already arrived, and thirty men are standing lined up at wooden tables set out between the refectory's high stone roof-pillars. They are in civilian clothing – the light slacks and short-sleeved sports shirts that suit this warm autumn weather – but from top to bottom there is nothing they could be but soldiers. They are large, wide of shoulder, thick of neck, and have the kind of biceps that only endless, bored hours of body-building in isolated military camps could give them. Their hair is shorn so close on back and sides that you can see every nick and scrape they have given their heads in the course of rambunctious boyhoods. Not that those boyhoods were so long ago – some of these soldiers are teenagers still, and the rest are in their early twenties. What unites them apart from their youth is their country. If today they are overseeing a desert peace between Israelis and Egyptians, only yesterday they were engaged in a jungle war. Trained for a life of combat with the rebels of the FARC, my fellow diners are Columbians.

Are the arid wastes of the Sinai any easier than the tropical forests they've left behind? There are no bullets flying about Suez these days, but these boys are lonely and a long way from home. What is it that pulls them to the Maison d'Abraham each two-day leave they earn? No doubt, like most Latin Americans, they're good Catholics. But God alone would not be enough to keep them from the bars, the discos and streetwalkers of Tel Aviv. Nor would the half-dozen French volunteers who help out at the Maision d'Abraham, women who even now are finishing the last touches to the table settings. What they've really come for are the motherly comforts provided by God's own helpers, who in the form of Soeurs Marta, Azucena and Ana, also happen to be Columbian. They have come to be with their own countrywomen.

The Dominican Sisters of the Presentation of Tours are an old order of nuns, and they still keep their mother-house in the south of France. But despite their 17th century origins there, the order draws most of its womanpower these days from Columbia, Venezuela and Cuba. I used to think of nuns, wherever they came from, as vulnerable, cloistered, passive creatures. If they were not unaware of the real world outside, then they were uniquely unequipped to deal effectively with it. But I hadn't reckoned on Marta, Azucena, Ana, or their colleague from south India, Soeur Nirmala. Forget the pious Albanian, Mother Teresa. Nuns from the tropics, I now know, not only perform the most mundane and humble of tasks with Christian fortitude – they put a zippy spark of Latin *joie de vivre* into it too. Meals at the Maison d'Abraham may not be the 11 p.m. dinner show at the Copacabana, but they do hum right along.

The Dominicans move efficiently about the refectory carrying tureens of soup, refilling water pitchers, removing used bowls and empty platters. Even if they weren't dressed in their nuns' stark habits of black and white you would see these are no ordinary waitresses. Everything they do they take on with a special sense of duty, energy and, dare I say it, something approaching joy. They not only wait on tables with competence and grace – these women are also well-travelled, speak three or four languages apiece, have multiple degrees, read voraciously, and are professionally specialised in a number of demanding fields. They are in fact the indispensable backbone to the entire operation at the Maison d'Abraham.

Soeur Marta, the senior nun, for example, is a dab hand with a computer spreadsheet, which helps her as the Maison d'Abraham's administrative coordinator. But she has just recently come to Jerusalem from an orphanage in Korea, where she spent eleven years as a child development specialist. Soeur Azucena, the youngest nun, on the other hand, spends her days not far away in the Maison d'Abraham's neighbourhood medical dispensary, advising on free treatment and drugs for some of the city's poorest Palestinians. To my mind there's no need for medication; I feel all the better just for looking at Soeur Azucena. She has a brilliant smile and bright, dark eyes. She is a bit of a tease, and giggles sometimes. She is also something of a coquette, and tailors her own habits so they look form-fitting and stylish rather than like burlap sacks. As nuns go, she's a looker. Like a number of other pilgrims here, I suspect, I have to admit I have fallen for Soeur Azucena. Watching her, I sometimes find myself trying to remember the words to '*How do you solve a problem like Maria?*' Often I wonder if it is she, and not the food, that causes some of us to clatter down the stairway at dinnertime with such eagerness.

But there are plenty of other characters at dinner each evening to keep me busy and entertained. While pilgrim tour parties and larger groups sit with each other in unaltering company, singles like me are seated together in groups that are constantly changing and reforming. As we sit down to eat tonight, less than half of last night's group is present. The Swiss farming couple from Appenzell have flown back to their mountain fastness, the Calabrian woman who came to Jerusalem to study Hebrew has gone to Galilee for the week, and the Jewish boy who cannot make up his mind between Christianity and Zen Buddhism has returned to his parents' home on the far side of the city.

Tonight's group is more mixed still. Jacques I already know – he has been with us for several days, and each evening describes his encounters, in solid stone and mortar, with objects that until now have had only an allegorical existence. Jacques, spare and balding and cerebral, has been a Freemason, a member of the Grand Lodge of Lyon, all his adult life. A scholar of Masonic tradition, he has been fascinated for forty years by the

Temple of Solomon. It plays a central role in the Masons' symbolic cosmology, and now he is realising a long-held dream – the discovery of the site where the Temple is believed to have stood.

Jacques' Temple and the Temple which, according to Hebrew tradition, was destroyed by the Babylonians in the sixth century B.C., have little in common. For Freemasons, he tells me, Jerusalem's most celebrated construction represents wisdom and also, lying as it does in the East like the rising sun, the light of realisation. But that's just one level of symbolism; beneath that, the Temple stands for the individual, while the light is the work of self-realisation he has brought to his own life. There are still further, more complex layers of esoteric symbolism beneath that.

Why, I ask Jacques as he ladles a bowl of soup for me, must one thing symbolically represent another thing, and that thing represent yet something else? Surely in the realm of human understanding matters are obscure enough already. There is creative complexity aplenty in the world – why purposely add further layers of mystification for the sheer complicated joy of it? I don't say it to Jacques, but it's like those silly Masonic handshakes. Simply grasping the other person's hand is not enough – you've got to lock thumbs, wiggle pinkies and bump elbows three times before Masons are satisfied. But Jacques, seeing as much of biblical Jerusalem as he can in a week, is wholly thrilled by the experience – he can only marvel at the way substantial fact continually transforms itself metaphysical thought. Besides, at our dinners the Temple for Jacques is a mere jumping-off spot for broader discussion on any number of subjects. In between spoonfuls of soup he starts telling me about Rudyard Kipling's early Masonic days at Lodge 782 in Lahore in colonial India.

It is just as well, then, that the two men on the other side of me sit broodily eating their dinner in almost complete silence. They are bears, towering men with long greasy hair tied back in pony-tails. Luxurious, unkempt beards tumble down their barrel chests. Their fingernails are less than impeccably manicured. They are dressed, despite the summer-like heat, in coarse brown woollen robes that fall to their sandalled feet. Around their necks they wear necklaces of wooden beads and metallic crosses so large and heavy they might cause lesser men severe back-strain. They look like twins spawned by Rasputin.

The only possession that places them in this century rather than in an earlier one is the large video camera they tote about wherever they go. They are, it turns out, Catholic Croats sent to Jerusalem at great expense by their poor and isolated fellow congregationalists. They will be returning home with a record of Christian rites and rituals as they are currently practised by different churches from around the world – Jerusalem, they tell me, is a perfect place to see as many churches in action as possible.

This is not, as I at first imagine, so that Croats, separated from the rest of the Christian community for half a century by communist iniquity, can update and bring their church into the modern world. On the contrary, my monkish fellow diners have set out from deepest Croatia to document the deviant, non-conventional behaviour that has crept into church practice worldwide in the last fifty years. Their congregation, whichever obscure Balkan valley it remains hidden in, sees itself as the last true guardian of authentic ritual.

'You look,' growls one of the bears. He has finished scraping the pattern off the bottom of his soup bowl and turns his attention to the video camera on the table beside him. 'We make new movie today. Spanish cult.' He looks upset. He turns the camera so I can see the action on its tiny LCD screen. I cannot be sure, but I see what appears to be an outdoor communion celebrated by worshippers in white robes. They are sitting on chairs in a sunny garden as a priest moves among them transferring wafers to their open mouths from a silver chalice. It all looks ordinary enough.

'What's wrong with that?' I ask, not overly familiar with the practicalities of turning bread and wine into the body and blood of Christ.

'Heretics!' thunders one of the Rasputin twins, loud enough to momentarily stop the happy buzz of conversation around us. His face has turned dark and angry. 'Again you look,' he says. 'Congregation is sitting. Host is falling to ground sometimes. Where is respect? God is big. Man is small. We must go on knees, not sit.' Together, heads close and bent over the screen, the Rasputin Brothers make low Croatian mutterings at other

27

improprieties they have noticed. Dinner seems entirely forgotten. It's hard to imagine generalised outrage in the Croatian provinces when these two return home. But of such things is sanctimonious wrath, if not holy war itself, sometimes made.

Opposite me, on the far side of the table, sit another couple of men. In every respect they are the complete opposite of the Croats. They are small in size and getting on in years. They are compact, pink, bright, and energetic. They wear no sign of religious affiliation and display no sense of religious decorum. On the contrary, they're in irrepressible high spirits. They talk to each other with great energy, endlessly chuckling, chortling and digging each other in the ribs when any riposte seems particularly humorous. As the meal progresses, the humour rises a notch or two – they are in a continuous state of merriment. They're like gnomes on laughing gas. I have seen them before in the Maison d'Abraham's multilingual library, a room well stocked with works of theology, history, the natural sciences and serious fiction. What they enjoy poring over together, though, are the illustrated comic-book adventures of those famous first-century Gauls, Asterix and Obelix.

They seem to genuinely admire the patriotic, mismatched pair who've managed to keep their small corner of Brittany free from the legions of Rome. But they like laughing with them even more. There is nothing funnier in the world, apparently, than seeing large numbers of centurions hurled into the tree-tops by the little Asterix fuelled on magical druidic potion.

'Hee, hee!' one of the little gnomes often snickers. '*Scrotch scrotch scrotch!*' the other occasionally says, imitating the sound Obelix makes as he gnaws an entire haunch of wild boar to bare bone. Sometimes it's all too much for the elderly pair, and ignoring the library law of silence, they fall apart with helpless laughter.

What they are laughing over at the dinner-table now I cannot tell, for they are using a language the likes of which I have never heard. It sounds barbaric, outlandish, antiquated. As Soeur Nirmala removes our bowls, I can no longer resist asking them what it is they are speaking.

They look at each other for a quick moment, then one of them, in a serious tone, replies in French, 'Aramaic, of course, the ancient language of the Holy Land. Isn't that so, Frère Jean?'

'What else, Frère Paul?' replies the other. 'Is there any other language to speak when one is visiting Jerusalem? We are surprised you are not speaking it yourselves.' They look at each other for another moment, then burst into uncontrollable hoots of laughter

They're real cards, these two. In fact Frère Jean and Frère Paul are both priests from a small village – not unlike the village of Asterix and Obelix – deep in the rural hinterland of Brittany. And it is their pleasure, when they're together or in the company of their older parishioners, to speak Breton, the tongue they were raised in. Their French is perfect, they assure me. But not only are they more comfortable in the language of their childhood; they are Breton nationalists and enjoy the political gesture of linguistically thumbing their noses, not at Rome, but at Paris. They have made several trips together to Jerusalem and, despite their manner, are in fact serious students of biblical language. In the next few days, they say, they shall be making a tour of the *Ecole Biblique* of Jerusalem, the prestigious institution where both the Dead Sea Scrolls and the Bible currently in use in France were translated. Today the school and its renowned library is reserved to world-class scholars and difficult to visit. Frère Jean and Frère Paul must be as good at projecting gravitas as hilarity, for they have obtained the required permission. Now they promise to see if they can't get me in as well.

That leaves the last two people sitting at our table, a middle-aged couple who cross themselves before starting to eat and say little through the first half of the meal. They are more formal and less engaging than the rest of the pilgrims. The man wears a jacket and tie. The woman concentrates on the food before her, barely lifting her face. And although her husband shows no desire to communicate verbally, he appears for some unknown purpose to be studiously winking at me. Then I realise he has a facial tic, a sharp, irregular blink of the left eye.

He speaks up only when Jacques the Freemason, who in professional life is a civil engineer, begins enthusing over the structural complexity he finds in even the simplest objects in nature; evolution, he says, is astounding in the variety of ingenious solutions it finds to complex building challenges.

It's not something the man in the tie can let pass without comment. That, he says, is an impossibility. It is not evolution that comes up with adaptive solutions; it is God who has built such elegant conceptions of form and function into His creations in the first place.

Shouldn't he know? he adds conclusively, forestalling any argument. He has spent a lifetime working for a French aeronautics manufacturer. He designs executive jets. And as a result it has long been perfectly obvious to him that every complex object has to have an intelligent designer behind it. How else could executive jets come into existence? How else, he demands – perhaps not entirely aware of the personal irony of his question – could something as perfect and irreducibly complex as the human eye be created? God's hand is everywhere and Darwin's theory, along with Marx's, is the greatest red herring of modern history.

'That's right,' his wife chimes in for the first time. 'I always say that God knows exactly what we...'

'Shut up, Louise,' the intelligent designer interjects in a patient, long-suffering voice. 'You always say the silliest things.'

Louise shuts up and lowers her head again. But her husband can hardly tell Jacques to shut up, too, and after a minute or so it appears that a pitched battle is shaping up. Jacques is not one to be brow-beaten in argument, especially not by a luxury private jet designer. Not even the appearance of the main course and accompanying salad stops the tone escalating, and I can see Soeur Ana casting worried glances in our direction. The tables of Columbian soldiers, less concerned with the origins of life than with living it, have moved on to dessert.

The atmosphere of tension abruptly evaporates with the appearance of a man who is welcomed by the nuns with relieved greetings. He is one of their favourite characters. They make sure a place is set for him each evening, but more often than not since his recent arrival at the Maison d'Abraham he has arrived too late to eat with us. This is the first time I have seen him.

He is hardly striking, yet you would single him out in a crowd. He certainly doesn't look like one of the old monastery's regular seven-day visitors to Jerusalem. In his early fifties, perhaps, he wears a tweed jacket of grey herringbone that is old and has seen much use. His trousers are baggier than fashion calls for. The black leather case he carries, bulky, deep and oblong, is old – it's the sort of thing that European artisans used to carry their tools in a century ago. The man himself is not of any usual physical cut, either. He's not tall, but solid and compact, and his face is unusually round in shape – somewhat pale, its regular features set neatly within it, it is positively moon-like. The orotund effect is emphasised by grey hair cropped close to the skull.

There is something in this man's bearing as well, a certain collected poise, that sets him apart. It is not conscious or intended to create an impression, but in a quiet way, it does so nonetheless. There is no super-fluous gesture, no wasted energy in his movements. His voice, too, when he apologises to the table's diners for his late arrival, has the same modest, unhurried calm – he speaks softly, and low enough that you have to make some small effort to hear. Everything about him indicates reserves of energy and resource, quietly banked away for private use rather than set out on display for sale, but present all the same.

The new arrival doesn't bring the growing dispute over evolution and intelligent design to any conclusive halt. It simply fades away. This is some-thing which since that evening I have seen time and again: without impos-ing itself, Ashraf Noor's presence alone sets the talk going on around him on a different footing, or sends it off on another track altogether.

Perhaps it's because Ashraf, without calculation, sees and acts sponta-neously on the best qualities he sees in the people around him. They, intu-itively recognising this, only wish to respond in kind. It's not some kind of showy trick. Often it involves no word or action at all, but simply patience and silence. Sometimes in Ashraf the merest raising of an eyebrow in an otherwise impassive face is enough of an opening to invite some unantici-pated confidence. By such behaviour a curtain is unexpectedly lifted with small, sudden drama, and a view into an individual's existence revealed.

It doesn't always happen, but in that round moon countenance there is always a sign of willing readiness to accept the other.

I am getting ahead of myself, though, for Ashraf Noor makes no effort at first meeting to play up his talents for human exchange. Perhaps in his role as Professor Noor, specialist in 19th-century German-Jewish philosophy at the Hebrew University of Jerusalem, he makes more of his authority. But we are not his students, this is not a lecture hall, and the man in front of us is by his deepest nature unaggressive and non-didactic. At the Maison d'Abraham he is told the most awful rubbish about subjects he knows inside out, but he never tries to show his own knowledge unless specifically asked. When he does so he speaks simply and quietly. But he spends more time actively seeking out other people's thoughts and emotions, and listens carefully. And from opinion, prejudice and half-baked truths he tries to encourage the emergence of some larger truth. None of this, though, is apparent on the evening I meet Ashraf Noor – it only slowly reveals itself to me in the days to come.

For the moment I am interested simply in the material practicalities of such an existence. How, I wonder when Ashraf explains he has once again been working late at the university, does an academic end up in a hospice for transient pilgrims?

Ashraf is not just the short-term visiting professor I imagined. He has pursued research in Jerusalem each year for the last fourteen years. Most years he's rented apartments in Jewish West Jerusalem. Sometimes he's stayed in the crowded Christian quarter of the Old City. But this year he wanted a change, and came to the eastern, Arab part of the city. Not only is the Maison d'Abraham closer to the Hebrew University on Mount Scopus – he also finds the meals, the nuns and the pilgrims' company entertaining and congenial.

With such a man one question, of course, only leads to a dozen others. But by the time we have finished dessert I have the bare bones of a life. Ashraf Noor is a perfect salad of genes. Born to a Welsh-Irish mother, his father was a Bengali banker, his grandfather a Postmaster General of Calcutta. He was born in London and grew up in London, Zurich,

Karachi and Dacca. In Zurich, Ashraf had no interest in money. Nor did he pursue the Islamic or Christian cultural heritage bequeathed to him by his parents. Instead, he took up philosophy and gravitated towards modern Jewish thought. He went on to study in Freiburg, Sussex, Paris and Jerusalem. Once the habits of a peripatetic life are established they are difficult to break – Ashraf has a family life in Leipzig, lectures in Europe and the US, escapes to a refuge in the Tuscan countryside when he can, and continues to research and teach. Despite his learning, he's a man of simple tastes. He's entirely willing to debate the German-Jewish phenomenological tradition if you wish, but at the end of a long day he's just as happy discussing another great passion, Italian league football.

Why do I bother to recount this wandering itinerary in some detail? Because immediately I find the man fascinating. This is an individual of cosmopolitan background, multilingual and multicultural, who could choose to work anywhere in the world. Yet here he is, an impermanent, unrooted figure, living from a suitcase among the even more impermanent figures that pilgrims temporarily become. It can't be easy.

And why Jerusalem? I have to ask myself. Is it because he himself, like the city at the centre of the world, is of a composite and indeterminate nature? Is it because in his fragmented life, Muslim and Christian and Jewish in equal parts, he can attempt some sort of synthesis here?

Ashraf Noor, I reflect as I climb the stairs to my room after dinner, fits into no category I can think of. Jerusalem is a city that attracts all sorts of seekers for all sorts of reasons. Some are sensible and clear-sighted, wafted here on a gentle breeze of genuine spiritual inspiration. Others are outright cranks, carried irresistibly along on violent gusts of religious compulsion they do not control or understand. Most fit somewhere in between. But there is something about this quiet man that makes me feel he stands somewhere not far from the heart of the conundrum that has brought me to Jerusalem.

It is almost midnight and cold when I step out into the inky black of the flat rooftop that lies beyond the door of my room. The Mediterranean may lie less than an hour's drive away, but Jerusalem sits in hills on the edge of the Judean desert, and at night temperatures drop steeply. I am new enough to the city, though, and so completely intrigued, that I want one more chilly look at it before I sleep.

This rooftop room, as far as I'm concerned, is the best accommodation in the whole of the Maison d'Abraham. Other rooms, lower and more cramped, are preferred because of the four long flights of stairs needed to get to the roof. But not only can I pop out of my door for one of the best views of the city; the room itself is a pleasure. It's more like a small split-level suite than simple pilgrim's accommodation. There's a sort of day-room with a desk and armchairs and bookshelves, an attached bathroom next door, and a bedroom up a short set of steps. The windows are high and narrow, with shutters that throw zebra stripes on bright sunlit walls, and between the windows are a carved wooden cross and a framed Renaissance Virgin and Child. As a monk's cell it is opulent, and as Jerusalem tourist lodging it's a steal – the price of the room, with breakfast and dinner thrown in, wouldn't rent you a basement broom-closet in a regular Jerusalem hotel.

When makers of documentary films and postcards want wide-angle pictures of Jerusalem this is the rooftop they come to. While the Maison d'Abraham doesn't have great height, the little promontory it's sited on juts out over the Kidron Valley at the southern end of the Mount of Olives; it brings the Old City so close that it lends the scene both broad sweep and an intimate sort of privacy. Viewed from here the gilded cupola of the Dome of the Rock, the most iconic of all of Jerusalem's symbols, protrudes above the high screen of surrounding city walls – alluring and seductive, glinting in sunlight by day and moonlight by night, it seems so close you might reach out and touch it.

From the edge of the roof I can also look down into the surrounding grounds. There are beat-up old cars and piles of garbage burning in the streets outside, and in the day tough Arab kids bang footballs against the old seminary gates. But inside lies a much gentler place, two acres of tall, shady pine trees cut off from the rest of the world. At sunset the trees fill with noisy, nesting rooks, but all is peaceful now, and in the dim light of a quarter-moon I can make out sleeping flower gardens, well-tended green lawns, a tinkling fountain, stands of feathery palms, and wooden benches strategically placed for quiet contemplation of the city. In the middle of it all rises the old seminary itself, a solid, foursquare construction made of roughly hewn blocks of Jerusalem limestone. For the moment the night is so quiet one might think it sits in some distant, imagined place where conflict is unknown.

It's not always silent here. The Maison d'Abraham sits just off the Jericho Road in the Arab neighbourhood of Ras al Ahmoud, and is surrounded by any number of mosques. Just how many I'm not sure, for it is impossible to disentangle their various calls to prayer. Five times a day, beginning in darkness and ending in darkness, there is a great rallying of voices. The *muzzein* begins at one minaret, with a single voice on a loudspeaker rising and falling in lonely solitude. It is progressively taken up by others, the voices twining around the old Benedictine monastery like the tendrils of a vine or the weaving arms of an octopus. Growing stronger all the time, eventually the cacophony announcing that God is great fills the entire sky in all directions. It is a paroxysm that lasts a few minutes and then the voices, one after another, slowly die away. Finally there is just one left, and it, too fades, until all is as it was before. When the call to prayer steals in on me in the pitch black of pre-dawn I always find it a bit spooky. I'm never sure if I'm dreaming or not.

There is not just a Muslim, but a Jewish element to the scene as well. A decade ago the Israeli settlement of Ma'ale Hazeitim was built on land directly behind the Maison d'Abraham – they are effectively joined back to back. It is just one of numerous Israeli settlements that have been constructed in East Jerusalem in recent years. They are strategically sited, Palestinians protest, in order to render impossible the future integration of the eastern part of the city as the capital of a Palestinian state. No one, least of all its residents, could persuade you that Ma'ale Hazeitim fits happily into its surroundings. It sits surrounded by coils of razor-wire, closed-circuit television cameras and thirty-foot high security fences. Settlers don't walk there, they drive. There are no open entrances to the settlement, and no windows on the ground floor of Ma'ale Hazetim's 130 housing units. A large black SUV manned by Israeli security agents patrols the settlement perimeter up to the entrance of the Maison d'Abraham at irregular intervals. But if you stop there too long, or begin taking pictures, you can count on them being there in just a minute or so.

Above me, as I stand on the roof, a French flag on a tall standard flutters almost invisibly on the night breeze. Why, I've already asked Father Michael, does the tricolour fly here, so far from France? The answer, in the disturbed logic of Jerusalem geopolitics, is simple enough. When Jewish settlers began building next door, Father Michael's predecessor, a Lebanese Christian, was outraged. He grew especially irate when they raised an Israeli flag over the settlement that now lay sprawled in the middle of an Arab community. It seemed such deliberate provocation. The city belongs to everyone, he protested; it has no single nationality and needs no flags. His protests went unacknowledged. He could hardly raise an Arab flag over Jerusalem in riposte, but any answer, he finally decided, was better than none. As a French-educated Beirut sophisticate and *plus Français que les Français*, he hauled up a French flag instead. It has been flying there ever since.

As I stand looking out over the city I hear a siren and trace its noise to a racing Israeli Defense Force jeep. It hasn't taken many days before sirens have become for me the emblematic sound of the city, more evocative of Jerusalem's spiritual existence than any *muzzein*, church bell, or Jewish lament. Police car, ambulance, olive-drab army jeep… these are the true vehicles of Jerusalem's lamentations. This one is moving along beneath the city walls with a blue light flashing on its roof. Where is it headed, I wonder? What night-time drama lies ahead for its soldier occupants, or for those they are hurrying to confront? Who, in the never-ending cycle, has this time done what to whom?

The jeep disappears, the city goes quiet once again. The flag above me snaps in a small, cold puff of wind. I feel like a *légionnaire* surveying his objective from some encircled outpost, surrounded but safe. At last I am ready for sleep.

Three

The time comes, sooner rather than later, when I admit to Ashraf Noor that I don't know what the hell I'm doing. I bump into him in the refectory as he is finishing his breakfast of baguette and café au lait. He is up early to teach. I am up early because already I am growing panicky with another day's indecision. Shouldn't I be out there, pursing politicians, interviewing academics, questioning clerics? I could be on the telephone even now, I tell Ashraf, lining up meetings with Arabs and Jews, with hard men and reconcilers alike. Or what about trying for a more neutral view? Father Michael's list of Christian church notables remains in my pocket unconsulted.

Ashraf adds a last knife-wedge of butter and spoonful of cherry jam to his slice of baguette. The nuns have noted his fondness of eating, and tease him that by the time he leaves the Maison d'Abraham they will have added significantly to the little bulge that is beginning to appear at his midriff. Any more and he will begin to look like a plump Buddha.

'The trouble in Jerusalem,' he says, chewing, 'is that there is no objective view. Not of anything. This year I am working on the loss of Jewish identity, the effects of the Holocaust on contemporary Jewish thought, and the influence of Hebrew on western language formation.

'Do you think for a moment that even these topics will remain subject to the rigours of academic objectivity?' he asks. 'Despite their best efforts, things have a habit of getting away on people here.' He screws the jam-jar lid back on. '*When* they make their best effort, that is,' he adds. 'And that's never a sure thing.'

He hesitates for a moment, and a little frown of concentration appears on his smooth, round forehead. 'If I were you, I might be a little wary of politicians and religious figures. They grab more than enough of the lime-light as it is already. All things considered, I'd avoid politics and religion altogether if I could. You might as well throw away notions of history while you're at it. Throw away all the books, in fact. Why not keep things honest?'

I blink at Ashraf. Avoid politics and religion in Jerusalem? Surely the man is having me on? Take them away, ignore the history, and there's nothing left of the city, I protest. Without them Jerusalem is an empty shell. What's left to understand?

But Ashraf knows three things. He knows that sometimes the best teaching involves helping to unlearn the things that have already been learnt. He knows that the best lessons do not always take the most direct or simplest route. And he knows that students often do their best learn-ing when they begin discovering things by themselves. So he doesn't say a great deal more; he concentrates instead on clearing up the boiled-egg shells and Vache Qui Rit silver wrapping that litter the table in front of him. But just before he picks up his black leather plumber's case and heads off for Mount Scopus, he makes a suggestion.

'There is not a single ethnic or religious group in Jerusalem which will give you the same version of the city, tell you the same story as the next group. Common themes are rather scarce on the ground here. But there are some things that no one in Jerusalem can avoid. The simpler and more basic the activity, the more people are obliged to share in it.'

Abruptly, surprisingly, he begins sniffing the air. 'There...smell that. Maybe that's a good place to begin.'

I take a sniff. All I can smell is a faint odour of smoke. It's aubergines. The cook has come in with a crate of aubergines, and now he's scorching their skins off.

'Vegetables,' I say to Ashraf. 'I can smell vegetables in the oven. The cook's been to the market.'

'Quite so,' Ashraf replies. 'At least everyone in Jerusalem eats. Everyone buys vegetables. Why not try a market or two?' He has nothing else to add. It seems an odd angle from which to approach one of the more complex cities in the world. But I'm at a loss for any other way to proceed. So when breakfast is over and we take our leave, I take a bus to the market.

Like the citizens of West Jerusalem themselves, municipal city buses do not venture onto the east side of town – not even a taxi will ferry you between the Jewish and Arab parts of the city. But there are plenty of Arab buses that circle the busy Ras al Ahmoud roundabout near the Maison d'Abraham. After a few days of hopping onto the Number 36, I know my chances of finding a place to sit are few. Early mornings are especially difficult. The bus is jam-packed with students and old men with canes and headscarved housewives, all on their way to the Damascus Gate.

When I step down, the sidewalk outside is hardly less crowded. For not only is the Damascus Gate the principal entrance to the Old City from Arab Jerusalem, it is also the site of a vast and teeming bazaar. Inside the walls, tightly packed in a warren of covered alleys and passageways, are hundreds of merchant's stalls. Outside the walls, the streets that lead to the Gate are the drop-off point for countless wholesale delivery trucks – every morning, tons of fresh produce from all over Israel are unloaded onto the tarmac here. What the sidewalk lacks in *pittoresque* it makes up for in smells, noise, crush and a gray pall of diesel exhaust.

As I make my way towards the Gate, I pass outdoor tables shared by busy, hungry people – it's chicken dinner for all-night taxi drivers at the end of their shifts, breakfasts of hummus and flat-bread and onions for market traders at the start of their day. Blocked by stacked boxes of peppers and avocados, I dodge young Arabs shouting warnings and trundling produce on wheeled dollies from the back of trucks. So overused is the sidewalk, so stained by leaking strawberries, bruised mangoes and the juices of other assorted fruits, that its surface is dark and gummy. Only when I cross the street and head down the stone steps leading to the Gate do I leave the world of wholesale produce behind. Even today when I hear that expression, 'the Arab Street', I don't think of popular opinion and its political consequences in the Middle East; I think of over-ripe lettuce and bananas and the sticky black mess they make on Jerusalem sidewalks.

When I first arrived in Jerusalem at five o'clock one morning from Ben Gurion airport this is where I waited for the city to wake up. Then the Damascus Gate was still and deserted. The sole opening in a long, high stretch of tightly-mortised stone blocks and crenelated battlements, the gate's arched entranceway was occupied by just two men – a pair of Israeli soldiers on foot patrol.

They were sitting on the low parapet of the bridge leading to the gate, their torsos bulked out in body-armour, two-way radios, billy-sticks, chest-slung automatic weapons and webbed belts hung with crowd-control devices. At the end of long hours of night-patrolling they were chilly and bored witless – both were fooling around with the keyboards of their mobile telephones. But now the sun is up, the crowds are out and the Damascus Gate is so packed you couldn't text-message your girlfriend from here if your next heavy date depended on it. There are so many bodies pressed rib to rib and surging in opposite directions it's the best anyone can do simply to stay on course and keep moving.

Things are tightest in the covered interior of the gate itself. At a place where you have to make a little dog-leg before straightening out and descending a long, stepped passage to the bazaar below, money-changers and vendors of Palestinian music have little kiosks built right into the old Turkish Ottoman walls. Catching business on the fly, they gum up the air with music and the passage with customers. Matters don't get any easier on the steps that follow.

It's not enough that shoppers stand three deep on either side of the steps, that the purchase of vegetables is a long and complex affair of negotiation, or that the noise here approaches the construction-site level. There are a dozen elderly Bedouin women, small, fragile, but very determined, selling fresh herbs in the middle of the steps themselves. One misplaced step could crush an ankle as easily as a bunch of mint. But the only thing that manages to move these women is one of the miniature green tractors which hauls rubbish out of the Old City. It comes charging up the stairs determined and unstoppable, and even then it's a contest of wills. As for biblical rulers of old, so for vegetable ladies today – in Jerusalem you defend your corner against all comers, or you are swept away.

At the bottom of the descent begins the souk proper, a long, crowded passageway leading on to other long and equally crowded passageways. Some stretches lie open to the sky. Others, shadowy and covered over by solid galleries of vaulted stone, are theatrically lit by thin, bright shafts of sunlight angling down from apertures above. In some ways the souk really is theatrical – it is given over entirely to that intimate and essential artform of the Middle East, buying and selling.

But it's hardly an Ali Baba's cave of perfumed and gilded eastern exotica – it's where you go when you want jeans, tripe, handbags, electric orange-juicers, bird-seed, running shoes, olives, elasticised foundation garments, toothbrushes, tea-bags or toys for your children. Here you can buy them a kitten, or you can procure for them that even more alluring item on display in numerous stalls – a plastic, kid-sized kit of soldier's gear. The miniature assault rifle contained in it, the Rambo-style combat knife, baton, handcuffs, grenade and whistle are small boys' fantasies, wishes inspired by the bigger boys patrolling never far away.

If the souk isn't quite a thousand-and-one-nights romance, it so cunningly packs a thousand things into a thousand tiny spaces that you have to wonder at it anyway. It is a place of hole-in-the-wall business, of tiny shops endlessly reproduced down both sides of alleys that grow ever narrower. Not a square inch of private or public space is wasted – in a market where pull-down metal blinds replace front walls and doors and windows, such spaces merge and became one. The passages are lined with materials and fabrics. Outer stone walls are festooned with goods on hooks and hangers. Dresses and trousers hang suspended from cords strung overhead. Not even the ground below is left unadorned – the flagstone paving there is buffed bright and glossy by the continuous passage of feet. Heavily freighted with music, chatter and long centuries of hard-driven haggling, the very air is saturated and used to capacity here.

Not only are the markets of the Old City among the most congested in the world, they are among the most confusing. Even in sticking to main thoroughfares, the further I move into the Muslim Quarter the more directionless and disoriented I become. As functioning medieval cities go, old Jerusalem is as tough as Fez or Venice to find your way around.

The tourist map I buy is useless – not even the best of them can show the complex skein of passages, lanes and alleyways that channel circulation through these tightly-packed buildings. Enclosed by high walls, roughly rectangular and barely a kilometre on its longest side, the Old City has all the internal complexity of a human body. Like arteries branching off into veins and veins feeding into smaller and more delicate systems of capillaries, it is a place reduced and categorised through ever finer magnitudes of gradation. At one end of the scale is the city's roughly equal division into its four main quarters – Muslim, Christian, Jewish and Armenian. It's a partition that even strangers like me are aware of. At the other end, not even the single, low door in the narrowest cul-de-sac is the end of compartmentalisation in Jerusalem. Near the vast Franciscan complex of the Terra Sancta in the Christian Quarter – I am wandering indiscriminately across invisible borders – I open one of these doors. Beyond lies a small open courtyard and on the far side of it a number of yet narrower passageways, more private and particular still, leading off it to heaven knows where. Who would dare continue? Not I.

Futile, too, are my attempts to navigate by asking shopkeepers or passers-by for street names. The lane that goes by one name for Arabs is often known under a second name by Jews and a third by Christians. And if I think the street-signs posted on the walls and at intersections are going to save me, I'm in for another disappointment. Throughout the city's quarters such signs start out trilingually, in Hebrew, Arabic and Roman characters. They rarely stay that way, though – which two scripts end up being defaced and illegible depends on which quarter you're wandering through.

'Hello, shopping?!'

They were the first words addressed to me in Jerusalem, and now I hear them in a hundred variants through the course of the morning.

Given its otherwise strangled economy, small-time trade is the life-blood of the Old City, and the souvenir stalls that line the city's streets and cluster around its holy places keep the whole area going. My Jerusalem Cross is just one of countless keepsakes. In Bethlehem and other Christian Arab West Bank towns there are entire streets of dusty little workshops full of lathes and fretsaws knocking out olive-wood knick-knacks by the thousands. Each year astounding quantities of these cruci-fixes and mangers and rosaries and baby Jesuses in swaddling clothes are sold in Old City markets. It's not just a Christmas trade – the Three Wise Men on their desert camels are as popular in July as they are in December.

The market in tourist gew-gaws may be all very necessary to local arti-sans. But does the world at large really need the handsome gift-boxes I see piled on the Via Dolorosa? Each, accompanied by an official 'Certifi-cate of Origin' and sanctified in the Church of the Holy Sepulcher itself, contains an authentic Crown of Thorns suitable for proud home display. Things only get tackier from there. What about the giant, phosphorescent glow-in-the-dark rosary, each bead as big as a hen's egg, I see hanging near the Seventh Station of the Cross? Or the plug-in Virgin Mary that flashes blue and green and red? The outsized postcard of Jesus in crucified agony, his eyes blinking alternately open and shut, open and shut, as I pass by?

Jewish kitsch in Jerusalem is no less gaudy than Christian kitsch, and aimed at the crowds of foreign Jews, mostly American, who pass through the city on their Israel holidays. There are Star of David ceramic tiles reading 'Shalom Y'all'. There are 'Super-Jew' T-shirts with the familiar 'S' symbol of Superman topped by a Hasidic black hat and side-curls. Another, an 'Israeli Intelligence' T-shirt, announces 'My job is so secret I don't even know what I'm doing!' A third, presumably appealing to jokey

Jewish pot-smokers, reads 'I got stoned in Gaza'. The most encouraging thing to be said about all this awful dreck, I suppose, is that it is sold indiscriminately – the higher faith of Jerusalem shopkeepers lies not in religion, but in the dollar that religion attracts. On the T-shirt stand kept by one and the same merchant you can find a beaming Yassir Arafat right beside such cheerful swagger as 'Don't Worry America, Israel Is Behind You' As long as it pleases someone – anyone, really – well then, it's for sale.

In the end the stalls and come-ons of tourist Jerusalem pall rather quickly, and I'm just as happy to make my way back to the vegetable market at the Damascus Gate. There is even less room at noon than there was earlier on – crates of marrows, melons and mangoes do not now pass through the massed throngs, but over their heads.

Here at the bottom of the steps, parting the crowds where the narrow thoroughfare forks into the bazaar streets of al-Wad and Khan-as-Zeit, sits what is perhaps the best falafel shop in Jersualem. At least, it's the falafel shop I like best because it commands a front-row view of the market and of the comings and goings through the Gate. In time it will become for me a kind of forward observation post, the place I like to come when I want the full blast – the whole nervy, jangled, disruptive energy, enervating and stimulating at the same time, that is peculiar to this city. It will also become a place where in the heaving chaos of it all I feel more or less comfortable, and on joking terms with the extended Palestinian family who run this shop. Like everything about the Damascus Gate, the falafel shop is hectic and pressured. Hungry market-shoppers swarm the stand, orders are shouted over a perpetual din, and the exchange over the counter – falafels heading one way and shekels the other – is rapid and unflagging. Somehow there's always enough time, though, for a laugh and a few words.

But for now I am happy to grab a plastic chair and sit with my own falafel in hand. Behind me brothers and cousins repeat the same frantic routine – chopping, slicing, scooping, dicing – they practice a thousand times a day. In front of me the entire market presses ahead with a routine of its own it has practiced for a thousand years. The elderly Bedouin women, I notice, ever obstinate, ever underfoot, have returned to their places with mint and coriander. Jerusalem endures, and they with it. I eat, sniff the scented air, and watch the energy and persistence of the world around me unfold.

If the Damascus Gate is all purposeful energy devoted to the Arab buying and selling of food in Jerusalem, Mahane Yehuda is its Jewish equivalent. The market lies up the Jaffa Road, well away from the Old City. A forty-minute walk there takes me past shops and premises that have been here since British Mandate times. Like Mahane Yehuda itself, they are some-what run-down and shabby these days. They are not alone. The shoppers who crowd the market's open streets and covered aisles may wear Jewish *kippahs* rather than Arab *keffiyehs* on their heads, but they, too, are often from the less affluent strata of Israeli society. Not surprisingly, they are a little tattered around the edges as well.

But Mahane Yehuda surprises me for other reasons. Around the world, daily markets tend to wind down some time after noon. But this market is visibly gearing up as the day progresses – by two o'clock, you can feel the energy rising by the minute. Geared up, too, is the security. If I've bumped into the occasional armed patrol in the Muslim Quarter, here uniforms and guns are inescapable and everywhere.

For most Westerners such displays are an offence to the background rhythms, however aggressive they may be, of everyday city life – they immediately indicate some sort of crisis. In Jerusalem, where over the decades crisis has become an ingrained mental constant, these *are* the background rhythms of everyday city life. Rather than alarm the popu-lace, they reassure.

Everything is normal at the Mahane Yehuda market – there are armoured police vehicles parked on the sidewalks outside and metal bar-riers at the market entrances. Shoppers are filtered through them, bags are checked; it's all as ordinary as buying cheese, and the defenders are as blasé about it as the defended. In a place like this it's not hard to spot the foreign visitors and newcomers like me.

Distracted, their eyes linger a little longer over the armed soldiers at the barriers than over the shoppers passing through them. Perhaps the worry is even greater, and the glances persist, because these khaki-clad soldiers are barely eighteen years old, and girls.

Anywhere else they might be picking up groceries for their mothers on their way home from school. But in Jerusalem's biggest market it's not baskets of shopping they cradle in their arms with nonchalant aplomb, but snub-barreled automatic weapons. It seems to me there is also a certain fascination, perhaps even attraction, in the looks these self-confident young women draw. Is there admiration in the stare of the two French women buying oranges near the market entrance? Could it be a certain regard for the way these conscripts wield their weapons – and their power over the men in front of them – with such cool, aloof indifference? There is definitely some yearning in the perusal of the young Australian backpacker standing beside me at a sidewalk delicatessen counter – his gaze is firmly fixed on a blue-eyed soldier whose long pony-tail spills uninhibited down her uniformed back. There is something about armed babes in boots that cannot help but catch a certain male eye.

I'm hungry. I fill a small plastic tub at the counter with stuffed vine-leaves and chicken cooked in sesame-seed batter. Eating contentedly, I stroll on from stall to stall. For the second time in a day I am assailed by all the colours and smells of a cuisine belonging to a complex people and a complex past. There are things here you couldn't get in the Damascus Gate market – gifilte fish, sour cream, knishes, bagels, blintzes, blinis, latkes, lox. There is kosher food only licensed Orthodox Jews can prepare. There is wine Muslims are prohibited from touching. There is Jewish Ashkenazi cooking from eastern Europe, familiar in American delicatessens perhaps, but that few Arabs have even heard about, much less seen or eaten.

But I am surprised nonetheless at how similar the two markets feel. Instead of watching little old Arab ladies in Bedouin headscarves dealing out herbs, I watch little old Jewish ladies in Russian headscarves doing the same thing. Among the mountains of produce at Mahane Yehhuda – meat and fish, poultry and dairy, fruit and veg and a hundred delicatessen foods – there are things eaten and loved by both peoples. Sometimes it is only a question of names – Sephardic shishlik is in substance little different from Palestinian shawarma. If Israelis adore hummus and chick-peas, sesame-seed tehina, baba ghanoush and those fabulous oriental stuffed vegetables I see tempting me from behind glass counters, it is because many Israelis are by origin oriental themselves – in the last half-century their Jewish families have immigrated to Israel from Cairo or Baghdad, Casablanca or Teheran. And if they are not eastern by blood they are eastern by accul-turation; inevitably, they have rapidly adapted to the ways of the place they have settled. The falafel is fast food in more ways than one. I would adapt rapidly, too – the Mediterranean and Middle Eastern cooking of the Sepharads is simply too good to miss out on.

But it isn't just the food itself at Mahane Yehuda that makes me think that Muslim Arabs and Jewish Israelis are in fact very much alike. It is their entire attitude, their passionate engagement with what they eat. As I watch a bristly-chinned, skull-capped Israeli poring over a display of dried fruit and nuts, I realize I am watching the same avid involvement I've already seen this morning.

There wouldn't be much fuss if it were I doing the shopping. I'd ask for a small bag of these and half a dozen of those, and that would be it – end of transaction. But that's not the way things work in Jerusalem, on either side of the city.

It's talk, talk, and then more talk. As half-a-dozen small paper packets are filled with different items there is the same drawn-out, back-and-forth, point-scoring exchange you'd hear at the Damascus Gate. When it comes to contention, Arabs and Israelis are both in their element. They love – no, more than that, they live – to disagree. It hardly matters with whom. Anyone will do in a pinch. Nor does it matter all that much what they disagree about. It's the reciprocation that counts, not the subject itself. The city's shoppers and stall-keepers are masters of bickering and barter-ing, huckstering and wrangling, feints of sharp invective and sallies of honey-tongued persuasion. I watch similar critical examinations of hazelnuts and almonds, identical keen debates over the price of dried apricots that I've watched in the Muslim Quarter. I see the same deft practice of negotiation and compromise, observe the same meticulous measuring and weighing of each purchase, gauge the same sense of common accord over a deal finally done. Why, you have to ask yourself, can't the same deals be done on a stage larger than a market-stall counter and with objects larger than pistachios? What about nation states, for example?

Market shopping in Jerusalem is a visceral activity, sensual, tactile, noisy and, in its own strange way, intensely sociable. Passionate about many things, Arabs and Israelis are passionate about how they buy and sell. Such contests are a vital part of the daily exchanges of existence. For some they are life itself. Perhaps comparing walnuts and warplanes sounds a little overwrought, and the difference between Arab-Israeli shopping and our own shopping over-exaggerated. If it does, I propose a test – try to find the same liveliness, the same loud and contentious vitality, the next time you're pushing a cart through the aisles of your local Sainsburys.

At around four-thirty Mahane Yahuda grinds to a reluctant, screeching halt. Culmination comes in the form of a man in a beard, side-curls and a long satin coat. Why, in Jerusalem, do men of pronounced religious views always turn up in outlandish hats? This man's hat is the shape and colour of a large chocolate cake – circular, wider than it is high, it's made of luxurious brown fur that's been brushed to a high gloss. The man beneath all this extravagance has a hard, determined look on his face and a brass horn in his hand. As he strides rapidly about the market he stops every few yards and raises it to his lips, producing a sustained note, harsh and loud and ugly. He is not playing music. He is issuing admonishment.

'Shabbat! Shabbat!' he cries, moving down one side of the market and up the other. He seems to grow angrier as he goes, calling on busy shopkeepers and stall-holders to bring trading to an end. Few merchants stop work immediately. Most redouble their efforts, moving faster and faster to satisfy the demands of customers still crowded around them and waiting to be served.

But most also grudgingly acknowledge the horn-blower's authority. 'All right, already!' I hear one Jewish-American shopper in a *kippah* say. 'We'll call it a day.' Any argument is met with sharp rebuke. Purchases are made more urgently, watches are glanced at more frequently, and out on the Jaffa Road waiting bus-queues grow longer and longer.

'What's going on?' I ask the American shopper as he packs sticky, fragrant *rugelach* pastries into his shopping bag.

He's a New Yorker. 'This doesn't happen in Borough Park,' he says with a grin, watching the horn-blower become more insistent by the minute. 'But here it happens every week. Tomorrow's Shabbat, the holy day. In fact Shabbat really begins at sunset on Friday, and goes for 24 hours until the next sunset. It's God's day, a day of rest.' He shrugs. 'You can't do anything.'

And like the man in the hat, there are a good number of Jerusalemites determined that it's going to stay that way. Nothing and nobody is supposed to do any work at all. But in Judaism's holiest city it all depends how you interpret work. Even in Borough Park, my American acquaintance tells me, there are many ultra-Orthodox Jews who insist that turning on a light-switch, striking a match or pushing an elevator button is making things work. For such people, shopping on the eve of Shabbat is quite evidently out of the question.

I watch the horn-blower, angry and gesturing at a rebellious cheese-monger setting out a couple of more cheeses.

'But it's an hour until sunset,' I object. 'Maybe more.'

'Sure,' the New Yorker shrugs. 'But cars and public transport are also no-nos. That's work, too. Do you realise how big Jerusalem has become? How crowded the buses get? How bad traffic can be? It can take an hour, two hours, to get home from here.'

Everyone's shopping, I learn, because Shabbat eve is the most important meal of the week – people want to prepare dinners for family and friends. But they also have to get home before dark. And the best way to get them home is to shut everything down.

The pressure only increases when reinforcements show up a few minutes later. There are now six or seven fur-hatted Hasidic Jews haranguing shopkeepers and customers. Tempers are fraying. One side-curled boy no more than fourteen years old is yelling 'Shabbat! Shabbat!' so loudly and so insistently outside a dry-goods store that its owner rushes out in a rage, shouting and red-faced. Obdurate, his features set and stony, the boy simply stands there weathering the outburst just inches from his face. Then he begins again.

By four-thirty the horn-blowing and the unremitting pestering succeed. The crowds melt away. One after another, counters are wiped down, shop-fronts swept, keys turned in locks. No shoppers remain but a small knot of poor migrant workers. Christian Filipino women, they are waiting for florists to close and throw the last bouquets of the day into the gutter. Finally they, too, depart with bruised and wilting flowers. In the end nothing and no one is left but Arab municipal labourers sweeping up piles of market refuse.

In the evening twilight I walk back to the Old City down vacant and still thoroughfares. Once or twice I see a lone pedestrian, probably a foreigner like me. Once or twice a taxi ghosts by. Otherwise I am alone in the streets of Jerusalem. Far down the Jaffa Road I watch sets of traffic lights at empty intersections turn green, then red, then green again, without a car ever travelling through them. I'd never seen the streets of a major city wholly abandoned at six o'clock on a weekday evening. Even the silence is eerie. It's like being the sole survivor of a neutron bomb, those atomic devices which destroy people but leave places standing intact and undamaged.

I'm glad when I finally reach the narrow lanes of the Old City. They are still noisy and bustling with humanity. Without religion Jerusalem might well be an empty shell. But with it, it can sometimes seem emptier still.

Four

Sometimes, if I get going just after breakfast, I enjoy walking to the Old City from the Maison d'Abraham – the Lion's Gate lies fifteen minutes away. At that time of day, the air is fresh and alive and the lower flanks of the Mount of Olives are at their best. The cypress trees in the Garden of Gethsemene rise upwards like cool green flames and the sun glints seductively off the Mary Magdalene's onion domes. Beneath the glittering mosaic tympanum of the Church of all Nations the roadside is tout- and trinket-seller free. Walk the same route later in the day and it can all get a little nasty. The sun grows fiercer, the air-pollution thicker, and the Jerusalem holy site tour-buses – up to three dozen of them at a time – park nose to tail across the hillside. Not only that; as they wait hour after hour the bus-drivers start peeing between the buses. By noon the road has become an obstacle course of half-melted tarmac, whiffy in the heat and stained with little rivulets coursing down the hill.

But on this particular morning I'm more upset by a run-in with a gunman. That's a dramatic way of putting it. Really I just collide with a man holding a gun. He doesn't level it at me and it's all over in a moment. But still, the split-second of fear that rushes up my spine seems to tip something inside. For the rest of the morning I am anxious and looking everywhere for weaponry, and if I don't find the guns themselves I find the people that go with them.

It happens on the Via Dolorosa, a couple of hundred yards inside the Lion's Gate. In Christian belief this is the route Jesus followed on his last day of his life. Followed by pilgrims for centuries, it stretches from the one-time palace where Pontius Pilate condemned him to death, to the hill of Calvary where he was crucified. This first part of the Via Dolorosa may lie inside the Muslim Quarter, but it's always crowded with Christian tour groups. From one site to the next guides push ahead on a bow-wave of high-speed recital, while knots of chatty holiday makers straggle behind.

'OK folks, stick together, we're not shopping now!' It's is the kind of thing you hear outside the Second Station of the Cross, where the arched cloisters of the Chapel of the Flagellation now stand in commemoration. It's an odd place, serene in its shady palms and carefully tended garden, troubled in its stained-glass depictions of Roman whips and torn flesh. It's here, tradition has it, that Jesus was stripped, beaten, and forced to take up the cross which he dragged through the streets of Jerusalem to the site of his death.

But today it's not distracted shoppers who stand clustered inside the chapel doorway. As I approach I can hear the slow, measured rhythms of a Latin hymn. The voices belong to devout Italian monks and nuns, and before starting out in procession they are hoisting wooden crosses of their own to their shoulders. Chanting and praying, they will carry them across the city, past all fourteen Stations, to the place of the crucifixion inside the Church of the Holy Sepulcher. It's an arresting site, and as I walk past the door I have my head turned towards these elderly, devoted pilgrims. Without seeing him, I walk hard into a man facing up the road, his back and shoulders towards me.

He's not a soldier. Like the three men with him he's wearing a light, Lacoste-style tennis shirt and beige trousers. But as he whirls around I see a gun in his hand. It's an odd-looking thing, a pistol whose finish appears plastic rather than metallic and whose barrel-sight is bright orange. Attached to its butt is a light frame, a sort of extended skeletal stock intended, I suppose, to fit against the shooter's shoulder. Somehow it looks toy-like and at the same time more ugly and lethal than an ordinary pistol. But that's not what really frightens me. It's the man's face. For an instant he's as startled and scared as I am, but aggressive and angry also. Whatever it is he's holding in his hand, he's ready to use it.

It's over as soon as it begins. The man raises the gun only an inch or two before he sees I'm just another dumb tourist and lowers it again. Right away I'm excusing myself profusely and he's swearing softly in Russian. The other men, too, are speaking Russian among each other and over two-way radios. I move off and the men regroup outside a recessed door in the stone wall opposite the Church of the Flagellation.

It doesn't matter whether Israelis live in Sderot under the threat of Kassam rocket-fire from Gaza or in the quietest of Tel Aviv suburbs. At the back of the mind of them all lurks the fear of sudden, unforeseen attack. The question of whether the violence itself is inevitable is, of course, an entirely different one. But given the events of the last six decades the fear of that violence, like a constant, low-moaning siren in the distant background, can hardly be escaped. Somewhere very close at hand, it whispers daily into Israeli ears, are people who would, if they could, do them harm. In Jerusalem those inner voices speak somewhat louder – no Jew here has forgotten that between 2001 and 2004 six suicide bus-bombings killed 77 people and wounded many more. And more recently, Jerusalemites add to the litany as proof of the utter unpredictability of it all, terror seems to have outgrown the need for explosives – it takes no more than an Arab and a ten-ton Caterpillar tractor to spill mayhem and blood out onto the streets.

Walking away, I am thinking of Father Michael and his tales of cloak-and-dagger intrigue in the Old City. But, of course, these men are not White Russians or Red Russians – they are simply Jewish Russians, part of the last wave of the hundreds of thousands of Russian immigrants to arrive in Israel. These particular ones, nonetheless, are part of a dangerous game. As I soon discover, they are private security guards employed by the Western Wall Heritage Foundation, a state-supported religious and cultural organisation. Founded to enhance the image of the Wall as the supreme symbol of Jewish identity, it offers, among other activities, Tunnel Tours to foreign visitors. And if these young men are the slightest bit keyed-up, perhaps it is because such an outfit serves as more than a mere provider of subterranean tourist entertainment. In the end these tours aim to provide justification for the Israeli claim to the eternal ownership of all Jerusalem.

It doesn't take much asking around to find out why four armed Israelis spend their day hanging around outside the Church of the Flagellation in the city's Muslim Quarter. The discreet, recessed door on the opposite side of the Via Dolorosa, it turns out, is the exit of the Tunnel Tour – the end of a half-kilometre-long tunnel running beneath what was once the western facade of the Jewish Temple Mount. It is, in effect, an annex of the Jewish Quarter extended far into the Old City's Muslim area.

Tourists enter the tunnel at the Western, or Wailing, Wall, the last exposed remains of the great stone retaining wall built by Herod the Great in 20 BC. With the Temple's destruction by Rome and the centuries-old Muslim control of the Temple Mount it once sat on, the base of the Western Wall remains the place where today Jews from around the world come to pray and commune directly with their past. But the site they pray at is only one section of the original western side of the Herodian wall – the rest, buried over centuries by the growth of medieval Arab Jerusalem, lies underground. By the time they have exited the tunnel in the Muslim Quarter tourists have walked the entire length of the Temple Mount underground. Far above them imams preach in the Al Aqsa mosque and the Muslim faithful prostrate themselves before the Dome of the Rock, third holiest place in Islam. And if the deepest desires of the Heritage Foundation have been fulfilled, the tourists, *goy* as well as Jewish, are in the end convinced that the Muslims overhead have no right to be there.

For the tunnel, whose digging was completed only in the last decade, is filled with remains more than two millennia old. As visitors wind their way through the foundations of the Temple Mount, they are shown ancient sites excavated by Israeli archaeologists. There are hallways and vaults, cisterns and roadbeds, quarries and water conduits, moats, pools and dams. And in the middle of it all is a place known as 'Opposite the

Foundation Stone'. If the sacred rock on which Abraham prepared to sacrifice his son Issac lies on the surface above the tourist's heads, here they find themselves in the oldest place in existence, the first place in existence – the heart of Mount Moriah. This, Jewish tradition has it, is the site from which the earth itself was created by God and took physical form. It is the spot Jews revere as the very centre of the world.

Metaphysics aside, these stone vestiges are for Israelis part of a search for vital archaeological evidence. They are an effort to prove through solid material remains what Jews have always maintained through faith – that this is the site of Solomon's First Jewish Temple. A stone's throw from Jerusalem's southern walls a similar search continues, an ongoing probe through the deepest, earliest layers of urban habitation here, into the biblical City of David. All over Israel, in middens, foundation-works and ancient passages Israeli archaeologists are scratching the soil down to original bedrock. It is all directed to bringing to the light of day proof of that most crucial assertion – that the Jewish people were here first.

You can't help reflecting on the complete abstraction, the unanswerable nature of it all. At least I can't as I continue walking up the Via Dolorosa. The question – who was first? – lies somewhere close to the bottom of all Jerusalem's troubles, and persists as an enduring *leitmotif* of relations between Jews and Arabs. Many leading Muslim religious authorities refuse to this day to concede that a Jewish temple ever existed at all on this site. With neither side willing to grant even part-time spiritual ownership of the place to the other, none of this limestone spelunking in the centre of Jerusalem has much to do with the cold objectives of scientific enquiry. It has everything to do instead with the heat and emotion of politics. In Israel archaeology has been pressed firmly into the service of state ideology; the Heritage Commission would like to strike the living Jerusalem rock with a staff and have a spate of clear and unambiguous proof spring forth. The best efforts of the archaeologists notwithstanding, though, the 'who first' question remains without answer. No material evidence of a First Temple, home to the lost Ark of the Covenant before a Babylonian exile, has ever surfaced. And if it did, the even more distant human past is too remote, too obscure, too genetically confused for any meaningful response to the question of the land's original inhabitants.

For both parties it is a recurring exercise in futility – Palestinians, too, have their own unprovable order of events. And how could Jerusalemites hope to resolve abstractions lying deep inside the earth if they cannot even agree on a much more recent, surface-layer enquiry – the path of Jesus on the way to crucifixion? Past the Third and Fourth Stations of the Cross, the road I continue following after my run-in with the Russians is simply a latter-day convenience. Over the centuries medieval pilgrims have altered the route of the Via Dolorosa numerous times. They've added and removed stations of the cross at will. Long before Catholics and Protestants went their different ways and decided on two completely different sites for the crucifixion, Latin and Byzantine Christians each had their own different Via Dolorosas and followed them simultaneously. They did what we all, Jews, Christians and Muslims, do – huddle together in our respective beliefs and agree on a collectively created narrative that suits us. Each act and artifact of faith in Jerusalem has its own Genesis, its own imagined history, its own myth.

I walk on, crossing from the Muslim Quarter, over a corner of the Christian Quarter, into the Jewish Quarter. One small city can only handle so many contradictory myths squeezed so tightly together. In a climate like Jerusalem's, myths become the foundation stones of separation, separation of fear, and fear of aggression. In this way the story circulates among Arabs that the Israelis are digging beneath Al Aqsa in order to cause its collapse, and the rumour develops a certain following. In this way, too, the story circulates among Israelis that the Arabs, incensed by this underground threat to their spiritual lives, are preparing to retaliate with violence. This rumour also gathers its followers. So for both Arabs and Israelis, digging in the Old City becomes a highly sensitive and controversial act – in the end it is as likely as not to generate genuine physical violence. Playing with the past is playing with fire, and at the very least leads to nervous men standing around in the streets with guns in their hands. Scarcely hidden beneath the ordinary events of daily life, the record of fear and aggression is there for all to read – for me it becomes instantly legible on a Russian face in a moment of simple carelessness.

Excavating the subterranean past, though, is the least, the most discreet of acts in this continuous exchange of antipathy. In the same way that Israelis are looking for a symbolic victory in archaeology, they have claimed it already through architecture.

I don't do much strolling, much street-interacting at all, in the Jewish Quarter of Jerusalem, because there isn't a great deal to interact with. No doubt just as much is happening here as is happening in the other quarters of Jerusalem, but it mostly takes place behind sealed security barriers, wire-topped walls and high, blind façades. After an hour's wandering through streets visibly emptier than other streets in the Old City, I begin to feel, like the quarter itself, just a little desolate – the Jewish Quarter of Jerusalem is built like a concrete bunker.

When Israel took the Old City in the Six Day War, almost two decades after losing it to Jordanian forces in their War of Independence, they found the quarter decimated. Run-down and overcrowded during Mandate days, many of its once 20,000 residents had even then removed themselves outside city walls. But, continuing the work accomplished by ten days of fierce battle in 1948, the Arab occupiers actively disfigured it. Synagogues were destroyed, schools of religious learning knocked down, headstones from Jewish burial sites broken off and sold for use as rough construction material. What the soldiers found to reclaim for Israel in 1967 – old Jewish Jerusalem's heritage – was a ruin.

Even now the rebuilding work is not entirely finished, and as I wander about the quarter the construction site of the Hurva Synagogue seems the busiest place around. Razed by the Old City's Arab conquerors in 1948, the Hurva was the centre of Jerusalem's eastern-European Ashkenazi community for 500 years. Early efforts at restoration amounted only to the rebuilding of the synagogue's central arch, but now I watch cranes swivelling and cement-mixers churning as workers near the end of the quarter's last major rebuilding project.

I hope very much the old synagogue will be faithfully completed as it once existed – an old synagogue – because nothing I've seen in the new Jewish Quarter owes much to the past anymore. After years of intense effort the parastatal Company for the Reconstruction and Development of the Jewish Quarter has hailed its work a triumph. Of course new building can never have the character of old, but of genuine reconstruction – the recreation of once-standing structures – there is scant evidence at all. And the remainder, the new development portion of the project, is not pretty at all.

Why constructions so reminiscent of the blockhouse, why these massive façades unrelieved by the slightest variety or ornamentation? The quarter's public buildings loom grim and blind. Private residences, barricaded behind thick walls, are even less visible. Although the revived Jewish Quarter was born of an overwhelming Israeli victory and their physical reunification of the city, nowhere do I find an atmosphere you could call joyful or self-confident. It is instead one of guarded and watchful defiance. The mood, above all, is defensive. Evicted twice from this city in ancient times, evicted yet once again in the middle of the last century, the Jewish determination to avoid risking the same fate still one more time is absolute. The Quarter is not meant to be pretty. It was rebuilt to make a formal and unambiguous declaration of intent.

And that intent, that bristly, siege-like, here-to-stay determination, has been transmuted not just into architectural style. It is the essence of the neighbourhood's official, symbolic function, too. The quarter is a repository of a Jewishness that is itself official and symbolic. Visible from all over the city, a vast menorah – the seven-stemmed candelabra of Judaism – tops the highest building in the quarter. Almost every corner I turn reveals yet another cultural foundation or institute of traditional learning. The quarter contains more than forty yeshivas – Orthodox religious schools for men – and dozens of midrashas – similar institutions for women. For practicing Jewish visitors there are synagogues and religious hostels. For secular tourists like me there are visitors' centres, museums, memorials, exhibition sites and archaeological displays. All have the same objective – to show that Jews have always been in Jerusalem, and that they always will be in Jerusalem.

The residents of such a quarter are necessarily made of the same determined stuff. Although Jews make up less than ten percent of the Old City's 35,000 inhabitants, what they lack in numbers they make up for in dedication. The Western Wall lies only yards away. To live at the very centre of the Jewish world, in a place only dreamed of by the Jewish diaspora for centuries, is a rare thing. Such residents are invariably here through political choice, establishing a presence that reflects the will of the entire country. They also represent Judaic belief in its many forms throughout the world.

There aren't many shops or businesses in the Jewish Quarter, but at one, a boutique selling gifts and jewelry, I stop to watch a video playing on a wall-mounted television just inside the door. It shows a black-suited, fedora-hatted man talking to a crowd who obviously adore him. He looks familiar. I've seen the white-bearded face before.

'Who is it?' I ask the boutique owner, a middle-aged blonde named Nicole.

'He's very special,' she answers with a smile. She gazes up at the screen, her face brightening. 'He lives in Crown Heights, Brooklyn, but he's here with us too. It's the Rebbe, Menachem Mendel Schneerson.'

Of course. Even I have heard of the Rebbe Schneerson. In Jerusalem he's hard to avoid – his face is plastered on walls everywhere. He was the last in a family line of leaders of the Chabad Lubavitch movement. Founded in 18th-century Poland, it is one of the most notable schools of Hasidic Judaism, which is itself one of the most prominent branches of Jewish Ultra-Orthodox belief. Schneerson took the Lubavitcher's fundamentalist beliefs to the New World, where they found enthusiastic support among the religious bedrock of Jewish American immigrants. Schneerson is famous for his unflagging efforts to bring secular Jews back to their faith – today there are hundreds of Lubavitch centres around the world. The Rebbe is also famous among his followers not as a man, but as a divine being whose emergence as the Jewish Messiah is imminent.

'But isn't he dead?' I ask. Schneerson passed away in 1994.

'No, he's not dead,' Nicole says firmly. 'You just can't see him.'

I frown.

'Look,' she says. These matters are too serious, too spiritual I can't talk about them here, like this. If you like, there is a Chabad outreach centre just down the street.' She hands me a card with a photo of the Rebbe Schneerson and a caption reading "Long Live the Rebbe King Messiah Forever". 'But believe me,' she says, 'the Rebbe is here with us at this moment. Today, tomorrow, who knows? – it could be the next minute – he will appear to us all.'

I cannot vouch for the presence of the Rebbe in the Jewish Quarter of the Old City. But what I can attest to as I continue walking is an equally invisible but none-the-less palpable feeling of tension that pervades the atmosphere. While some kind of surface tension is always present in Jerusalem, it rises and falls along with the ebb and flow of events. This particular unease in this particular quarter is more diffuse and non-specific. It's constant. Like the second coming of the invisible Rebbe himself, it's the apprehension of an event forever and eternally imminent.

What is it in the surroundings that generates this feeling? You could do worse than to look at the Quarter's windows for an answer. Is it the schools whose open windows are never really open, but instead grilled over with heavy protective wire mesh? Is it the shape of the few openings that exist at ground-floor level, almost all of them built as narrow slits or loopholes? Or is it the frequent lack of any windows at all, street after blind street where there are no openings whatsoever?

But there's little point in looking at such clues when there are blunt answers staring you in the face. What hangs immanent over the Old City is a heightened apprehension of physical threat and the immediate violent response that will accompany it. Three times in my little stroll I come across a community's casual and intimate co-existence with weaponry.

Once I run into a group of small children kicking a ball in a square.

They are accompanied by a kindly-looking man I take to be a kindergarten supervisor until I see the pistol in an unbuckled holster at his waist. Once I stand looking out from a high terrace with a good view of the Western Wall – the man beside me appears to be another tourist, dressed in civilian clothes and keenly surveying the panorama below, until I see the long-barreled sniper's rifle held between his knees against the parapet. On a third occasion I sit in a plastic chair on the Western Wall Plaza, the large, often crowded open space that leads to the Wall itself; the boy sitting beside me in jeans and T-shirt looks about sixteen years old, but he, too, is watchful, and cradles a semi-automatic in his lap.

It might sound reasonable enough: civilian members of a community organizing themselves in neighbourhood watches in order to protect their homes and families. It happens in all sorts of cities all over the world. But in Jerusalem I find such men far more disturbing than the entire platoons of uniformed troops I run across soon after, trudging through the Jewish Quarter on their way to pray at the Wall.

As I stroll back through the Christian and Muslim Quarters, down the Via Dolorosa and out of the Lion's Gate, such casual preparedness for violence begins to appear more than just disturbing. What I've been watching is not just individuals carrying guns. In a city where symbol is supreme, the firepower is a physical sign of a deeper defensiveness of the spirit. What I am seeing are whole communities, Jewish, Christian and Muslim, equipped with the emotional armament they need to inure themselves to a permanently fractured existence. The hardening of feeling, the withdrawal of compassion, the refusal of empathy – these are the weapons that have brought separation and malaise to a city that is holy, perhaps, but not whole. Paranoia is now the only element common to the entire place.

Jerusalem, the Six Day War notwithstanding, has never been reunified at all.

Five

Father Michael is right. There's too much politics in Jerusalem, I tell Ashraf Noor at dinner after a particularly trying day. There's too much religion fueled by too many motives having nothing to do with God. God, I complain, is a character a lot of people here like to hide behind. In Jerusalem there are so many people crowded around him, each hiding from the other, that for an atheist he's impossible to see at all. What I'd like is a closer peek.

We're sitting over the remains of our meal, the last diners in the refectory, and the nuns are clearing tables and trying to shoo us out. They have evening prayers to attend to in the Maison d'Abraham's little chapel on the far side of the hallway. Once again the contingent of Columbian soldiers, back from the Sinai frontier, is with us. Sometimes, feeling frazzled, I sit in the back of the chapel just for the calm of the service at the end of the day. And for the music, too. The Columbian army chaplain who leads his men in prayer also has a guitar and leads them in song. Usually these songs are about Galilee storms, fishing boats, shepherds, lost flocks and Jesus, son of a lowly carpenter. The soldiers follow in deep, melodic voice. They put sweetness and feeling into the simple Spanish words. They make Jesus' life sound as humble as their own lives in their poor villages and barrios. But above all the men come for something even more evocative of home – the company of the nuns, who sing and pray beside them.

We don't linger, therefore, and Ashraf is spared the full development of my theme. Nor, if I were to pursue it, would he launch into a philosophical treatise of his own to correct or counter it. Much as he enjoys talk and ideas, when it comes to Jerusalem Ashraf finds there is talk enough already. He prefers to help with concrete examples, with the briefest inclination of his head to show the direction of a possible way forward.

So when, rising from the table, I say to him, 'You know, what I'd really like to see is all or nothing – the full works, politics or religion, one way or the other,' he doesn't reply.

'Imagine it,' I continue. 'A full-blown theocracy, without political ideology, without the army, without material ambition, without the slightest concern for the state. A Jewish utopia in Jerusalem revolving solely around the ethics of personal salvation and the biblical law of Moses.'

Ashraf only nods politely.

'On the other hand,' I go on, 'imagine the opposite – the wholesale dumping of Judaic religious tradition. No more synagogues, no more beards and funny hats, no more domineering patriarchal morality. A brave new world – a Jewish Jerusalem based on Western technological certainty and secular material progress.'

Ashraf remains quiet and diffident in manner. Sometimes I think it's a deliberate tactic, calculated to draw his interlocutors far enough down the line of their own logic to see its contradictions. Now it provokes me to greater rhetoric.

I consider a half-emptied tureen of Boeuf Bourguignon sitting at the serving-hatch by the door out. 'I'm tired of the fixed menu,' I say. 'I'd like a buffet laid out so you can see exactly what's on offer. Surely two clear choices would be better than the mixed stew that's been swirling around Jerusalem all these years. You just don't know what you're getting.'

Ashraf smiles. 'But Jerusalem has been eating both the dishes you're describing for a long time now,' he says in his soft voice. 'Neither of them are secret recipes. If you like you can sample them yourself.'

We walk down the hallway. I am off to watch the television news with a gaggle of the Maison d'Abraham's lady volunteers. Ashraf is returning to work on a monograph on the Jewish phenomenologist Edmund Husserl. But before we part he gives me the direction I am looking for. 'Try a place not far outside the Old City – it's called Mea Shearim. If God's a meal they serve the full five courses there.' He halts for a moment, and adds 'Go easy, though. You might find it an acquired taste.' Then he's gone.

Ashraf is right. Mea Shearim is strong meat. Buried in the swirl and bustle of downtown West Jerusalem, the area is unconnected to the modern life of the city. There is no border surrounding it, but suddenly the next after-noon, stepping onto the far side of Ha-Neviim, the Street of the Prophets, I am in that fabled country I spoke so lightly of – a full-blown theocracy, without the slightest concern for the civil state, where the supreme law is the law of Moses. Immediately I am disoriented. You can accept that such things might exist – in the tribal zone of south Waziristan, say – but to find a mini-kingdom of militant divine rule surrounded by rush-hour traffic and fast-food outlets is disconcerting.

Mea Shearim is not without some kind of frontier. If there are no fences demarcating the neighbourhood's boundary lines, there is instead a sort of moral-practices customs control. There are certain things, like loose behaviour and tight trousers, you cannot import into Mea Shearim. I haven't gotten past the first block of streets when I am confronted by a large signboard. It's a bizarre thing, a sign-painter's nightmare of words variously printed large and small, in upper and lower case, in red and black. It seems to have been conceived according to the degree of emo-tional stress the individual words have provoked. It reads:

GROUPS passing through our neighborhoods
SEVERELY OFFEND THE RESIDENTS
PLEASE STOP THIS
TO WOMEN AND GIRLS who pass through our neighborhoods
WE BEG YOU WITH ALL OUR HEARTS
DO NOT PASS
through our neighborhood in

IMMODEST CLOTHES
Modest clothes include:
CLOSED BLOUSE, WITH LONG SLEEVES
LONG SKIRT. NO TROUSERS, NO TIGHT-FITTING CLOTHES
Please do not distress us by disturbing the sanctity of our neighborhood and our way of life as Jews committed to G-d and his Torah Neighborhood Rabbis – Torah and Welfare Institutions – Local Residents' Councils

I look down, giving myself a quick once-over. I am neither a group, nor am I wearing a tank-top, shorts or any other item of clothing that even on a male might be seen as offensive. Heaven knows what such Jerusalemites must think of the city's Gay Pride parade – it's hotly contested even outside Mea Shearim.

I read the notice again. Finally it's not the prohibitions imposed on outsiders that impress most. It's the prohibitions which neighbourhood insiders impose on themselves. It's that tiny hyphen in the three letter formation, G-d. Here's an observance that extends far past reverence for the word of God, to the word 'God' itself. What are they made of, these people whose god is so holy that his name cannot be uttered aloud?

I'll never know. This is a world hermetically sealed even to other Jews. It is alien not just to secular, non-observant Jews – it is foreign to most practicing believers as well, from Reform Jews, to Conservative Jews, to the more liberal of Modern Orthodox Jews. It is closed, in fact, to all those who fail to regulate their lives, through every waking moment, by the exact prescriptions detailed by *halacha* – the law given to the Israelites by God on Mount Sinai. Mea Shearim is the fief of the most conservative of all Jerusalem's Jews, it's Ultra-Orthodox community. Should the Ultra-Orthodox, who alone truly cleave to the faith, shun mobile telephones altogether? Outside the Sabbath, can they use them provided they disable their more frivolous functions? Are multiple ringtones allowed? These are the kinds of questions modern interpreters of *halacha* are faced with today. To outsiders like me the Ultra-Orthodox

Jews of Mea Shearim are creatures from a distant and incomprehensible planet.

But to the Ultra-Orthodox I'm no less an alien, and what's more, an alien voyeur.

Once, not long after the Steven Spielberg film 'Schindler's List' came out, I found myself in Krakow watching summertime tourists setting out on 'the Ghetto Tour'. It was popular, especially with Americans, who in large conducted groups were led through the dingy streets of the Krakow district of Kazimierz. It's an authentic old quarter, not much changed since the 1940s, and today the home of the city's tiny, regenerated Jewish community. It is not, though, the place where Oscar Schindler saved over a thousand Jewish residents from Nazi extermination camps – Kazimierz was chosen for filming because Podgorze, the real wartime Jewish ghetto of Krakow, has since been rebuilt and modernized. No Jews live there anymore. But that was of little concern to the tourists. The drama they sought was the drama of movie location. 'Where's the staircase Mrs Dresner hid under in the roundup scene?' I heard a woman asking the tour-guide, and when he showed her she was happy, and asked no more questions.

It seemed a little odd to me at the time, an enthusiasm not just geographically, but also emotionally, misplaced. How can the making of a film be more important than the events it portrays? I could only wonder what the residents of Kazimierz, a site entirely ignored by the world until 'Schindler's List' came out, made of it all. These were sad survivors of the Polish holocaust, the rare ones who hadn't ended up in the ovens and gas chambers. And here they were, suddenly overwhelmed by strangers lucky and prosperous in life, seeking out a nightmare past not as it really existed, but in its recreated cinematic form. Now it is I who am walking grim streets and gazing around, yet one more voyeur. And if I feel like a tourist on the set of a ghetto movie it's because Mea Shearim, too, is the recreation of a ghetto.

The place is poor – poorer, maybe, than most real Jewish ghettos of the cities of Central Europe were a century ago. There are certainly no fiddlers on the roof here, no Chagall winged angels or lovers floating dreamily over brightly-coloured houses. The quarter is insalubrious and shabby. This is an old-world place, a cramped quarter settled by Jews in the 1870s to escape an even more cramped and unhealthy life in the Old City. But they weren't much freer here than their fathers had been in their earlier homes in the cities of Europe. Afraid of depredations by Arab marauders ranging the countryside around Jerusalem, its inhabitants built a high wall and locked themselves in every night. Today the wall is gone, but they still hold off the life that encircles them, now the modern life of the prosperous country to which they belong.

From the street called Hevrat Shas I stroll through passages that are narrow and grimy. The multi-storied blocks of homes, built around open courtyards that once held vegetable plots and cow barns, are aged and dilapidated, stained and fragile. There's a good deal of corrugated iron roofing about. The narrow balconies on upper floors are cluttered homes to old furniture, hanging laundry and sundry recuperated junk.

But it is the inhabitants themselves who more than anything else contribute to the illusion that I am walking through the ghetto streets of pre-war central Europe. The *Haredim*, as the Ultra-Orthodox call themselves, are bearded and dressed, in summer as in winter, in heavy black suits and broad-brimmed black fedoras. Their women, too, are clothed in sombre tones, skirts swishing around their ankles and sleeves falling to their wrists. The younger women walk by in groups, pushing prams and talking not in Hebrew, but Yiddish. Modest, they wear scarves over their hair. Many, having rid themselves of the earthly vanity of real hair, cover their heads with wigs. A school lets out, and suddenly the street is crowded with small boys wearing knickerbocker-like pants and white leggings. Their heads are shaved, and covered in pointed *kippahs*. They, too, wear sidelocks. Instead of wearing them tightly curled and chin-length as their fathers do, they are long and straight and spill down over their shoulders and chests.

I'm far from the Visitor Center of the Jewish Quarter in the Old City. The idealized Jewish image of the native-born Israeli – all action and confidence, the kind of strong, athletic, sun-browned youth best embodied in the recruits of the Israeli Defense Force – might no longer exist. There are threadbare *Haredim* with broken shoes and aged *Haredim* shuffling along with canes. I pass by a *Haredi* sitting on the sidewalk with a matted beard and a tin begging cup. There's a tall, ascetic-looking *Haredi* striding down the street, furiously smoking a cigarette with slender, nervous fingers. His skin is pale, as if he spends all his time indoors, and behind his wire-rim glasses his eyes look tired and weak, as if he spends all day reading. It is quite possible he does both – he disappears into a building whose windows are curtained, and through whose door in dim light I can see long tables at which men sit bobbing and reading aloud. There is a plaque by the door, identifying the place as a yeshiva for the Hasidic Jews of Transylvania.

Transylvania – I turn the word over on my tongue a couple of times. Even said aloud it sounds improbable. Like so many other places of Judaic tradition buried deep in central Europe, it seems mythical, 19th-century, cob-webbed with age. Now here it is, recreated in Jerusalem.

The more time I walk the streets of Mea Shearim the more I feel I am trapped in the past, spliced into a grainy reel of old documentary film. In a country bursting with colour, Mea Shearim has achieved that rare thing – it is monochrome. Everything is in black and white: the men in their long coats and hats; the bare streets and buildings encased in the accumulated grime of decades; the small, dark shops selling Judaica and unadorned by the brightness of advertising or the glitter of consumer goods.

Covered in the posters known as *pashkeviln*, even the walls themselves are patterned black and white in Mea Shearim. The roughly-printed broadsheets line the streets, weathered and accumulated layers of Hebrew text that exhort the *Haredim* to lead just and righteous lives. They tell residents not to buy newspapers, not to watch films, not to read anything but religious books, not to use computers for anything but work. They also tell *Haredim* not to look at pictures of women. They are referring not just to brazenly naked women, nor even to inappropriately covered women – the prohibition applies to all women. I come across an old *pashkeviln*, a *Haredi* attack on government policy, which show a group-photo of the Israeli cabinet. It's not quite complete – the images of two female cabinet ministers have been crudely blacked out.

Pashkeviln are directed not only at those individuals who violate God's laws – some of the more virulent posters protest the sacrilegious behaviour of the entire Zionist state of Israel. So insistent are the most vocal of Mea Shearim's Ultra-Orthodox that they are not content to deliver their message in Hebrew only – they want their condemnation of the Zionist state to be heard by the whole world. Swinging high over a street I find another metal signboard. It reads, in English:

JEWS ARE NOT ZIONISTS

ZIONISTS ARE NOT JEWS

ONLY RACISTS

WE PRAY TO G-D

FOR AN IMMEDIATE END OF

ZIONISM

AND THEIR OCCUPATION

It's enough to make anyone sit up and blink. To me the idea of religious Jews scorning Zionism is a novel contradiction – it's like radical Islamists rejecting Jihad. Judaism is too complex a faith, I know, with systems of belief springing from too many disparate sources, to be contained by any one rationale. But it takes me some time and a lot of asking around before getting anything like an explanation – the citizens of the quarter either can't, or won't, talk to me.

Eventually, emerging from quiet residential blocks onto Mea Shearim's busy main thoroughfare, I come across an office where a French tricolour is painted by the door. It's the premises of a weekly French-language newspaper, a publication selling real-estate and right-wing religious ideology to Jewish emigrants from France. It is, to say the least, a niche market, and the paper is struggling. But that doesn't stop David, subscriptions manager and a French immigrant himself, from disseminating his views however he can. I decline a subscription, and we do some sidewalk walking and talking instead.

Like all the men here David is wearing a black suit, black hat and white shirt. By the standards of Mea Shearim he isn't hard-line Orthodox. But he says that like thousands of other European and American Jews, he has emigrated to Israel to reconnect with a purer Jewish way of life. It is only natural then, he tells me, that he's sympathetic to the community's conservative views.

'The Jews who live here don't like the term "Ultra-Orthodox,"' he says. 'They never use it themselves. They prefer *"Haredim"* – it means "those who tremble in awe of God" – because they don't consider themselves Ultra-anything in the first place. It's just the opposite; it is they who have kept the original faith as it was first given to the Jews. It's other Jews who have deviated.'

The list of offenders is long, and includes most modern Israelis. But among those who've failed Judaism in spectacular fashion are the political leaders who've been in charge of Israel since its founding. From the beginning secular Zionists have rejected religion as an encumbrance, David says; with their own ideas springing from 19th century European socialism, Zionists have always viewed religious Jews as primitives and obsolete. This, of course, the *Haredim* resent. And while Israel, with its special identity as 'the Jewish State' acts to accommodate state and religion to each other, that old antipathy remains. Most modern Israelis think of *Haredim* as cranks, bothersome and not entirely harmless. Most *Haredim* see secular Israelis as traitors who've abandoned the most valuable thing they've ever owned.

David isn't opposed to the Ultra-Orthodox Jews who are willing to play things out in the political arena – as powerful partners in government coalitions the national religious parties can act as brakes on secular policies. But as the sign over the street indicates, there are others who refuse political activity and reject Zionism outright.

'Who's going to bring the final realization of God's promise to the Jews?' asks David. 'Corrupt and self-seeking politicians? The *Haredim* know in the end it cannot come about through political Zionism – however long it takes, they are waiting for God's kingdom to come to earth. They are relying on divine action, not human action. And if anyone attempts to force destiny by other means it's a rebellion against true Judaism. It's bound to fail.

'So most people in Mea Shearim turn away from the state and politics and pursue a spiritual life,' David says. He indicates the street with a sweep of his arm. It's a lively scene. There are black-hatted men pouring from the door of a synagogue down the road and bearded shopkeepers standing twirling their sidelocks in doorways. From some entranceways Yiddish music pours, from others wafts the fragrant odour of Jewish breads and pastries. Headscarved, uniformed schoolgirls wait for buses with satchels in hand. Mothers push prams, men stand on the corner deep in conversation. 'Rabbi! Rabbi!' shouts one Ultra-Orthodox Jew from a knot of men gathered on the far side of the street. He has something to communicate. Perhaps it's nothing more vital than a detail of an upcoming bar'mitzvah, or perhaps it's a crucial realization on some question of Torah philosophy. No matter how irrelevant the rest of humanity might think it, this is Jewish life as it is played out in few other places in the world. We stick our heads into an electrical shop where younger black-suited *Haredim* are buying, against the disapproval of their elders, bluetooth computer components. 'And they're not quite as old-fashioned as they used to be,' David adds approvingly.

Maybe not, but *Haredim* remain quite unlike other Israelis. By arrangements worked out with the state decades ago they do not perform the military service that is compulsory for the rest of the population. They do not pay income tax. Sixty per cent of the men do not have jobs. Instead they pass their day in prayer, in the study of sacred texts, and in strict observance of religious law. *Haredi* family life adds to the demands of such a routine – while sexual pleasure alone is condemned, producing children is a religious duty, and many families have half a dozen or more. When you see the *Haredim* at prayer you cannot doubt their depth of religious conviction. But neither can you doubt the constraints their community's beliefs impose on individual freedom and choice. Their life-style is subsidised by public grants, but two thirds of Ultra-Orthodox Jews live below the poverty-line. Nor can you doubt the restraints of personal freedom they would like to impose upon others – when secular Jerusalemites attempt to keep public parking lots open on the Sabbath, the *Haredim* are willing to take on riot police in pitched street battles to stop it. Waiting for a divine kingdom to come to earth does not come without a price.

The afternoon is growing on, the lengthening shadows plunging Mea Shearim into even greater contrasts of light and dark. I walk back towards the Old City, and am soon caught up again in a life where God shares his role with earthly powers. It's a relief, really. Jewish fundamentalism feels just as alien as any other fundamentalism. What does it mean to burn with an inner flame, all day, every day, to hold God to a promise of redemption for three thousand years? I have no idea – I've never felt that fire. The *Haredim* of Mea Shearim may be satisfied to live in heavenly expectation for as long as it takes. I, personally, wouldn't mind seeing a few earthly promises being made good on right now.

'Is this your idea of a godless Jerusalem?'

Ashraf Noor and I are standing outside the Rosenzweig Center on the Mount Scopus campus of the Hebrew University of Jerusalem. Ashraf is wearing his usual well-worn tweed jacket, carrying his usual plumber's tool-case, and to me he's the same person he always is. Waiting for a connecting bus at the Damascus Gate, I'm not surprised to see him jump in between two small Arab boys kicking a ball on the sidewalk, make a deft interception, and then show them a few star turns. But to the outside world Ashraf is here on Mount Scopus in a more formal guise, that of Doktor Noor, resident research and teaching fellow, come to the university today to deliver a talk on linguistic *Sprache und Rekognition*.

'Godless? Not quite,' smiles Ashraf, 'though you'll find it a little more worldly than Mea Shearim.'

In inviting me here I'd imagined Ashraf might have wanted to show me a second, alternate version of Jerusalem, that vision of secular progress I'd imagined at dinner. I can't really see, though, how the Hebrew University fits the bill. There's not a yeshiva student, not a beard or outlandish hat in sight. But the building we are standing in front of is named after Franz Rosenzweig, philosopher and pre-eminent representative of twentieth-century Jewish-German culture. It's hardly a place where God can be refused entry at the front door.

Looking at it more carefully it is, I realise, a very grand front door, and not one that any deity would lightly sneeze at. The entrance is, in fact, over-the-top opulent, designed in polished stone and marble. Immediately inside I can see a multi-storied, atrium-like central space filled with light. More reminiscent of prestigious public buildings like opera houses or museums than an academic study centre, it is built to dazzle, and it does. Nothing could be further from the Transylvanian Yeshiva for Hasidic Jews or any other of the low, dim study-halls of Mea Shearim.

And for good reason. The Rosenzwieg Center is funded by the foreign ministry of the German federal government. Since accords worked out between Konrad Adenauer and David Ben Gurion, Israel's first prime minister, Germany has been a major source of public grants to Israeli culture and education. Going farther than any official reparations ever could, this is one aspect of the 'special relationship' in which Germany seeks to atone for the past. Nor is Germany the only benefactor. Throughout the Hebrew University of Jerusalem, prominent on the walls of faculties, libraries and research facilities, are plaques acknowledging extensive financial endowment. They have been made by governments and private individuals, Jewish and non-Jewish, from around the world. Like many another public institution in Jerusalem, the university depends upon the world's support for its existence.

Sitting on the north-east edge of Jerusalem, Mount Scopus has always played a strategic and symbolic role in Jerusalem's life. Biblical history has it that from this hill, with its commanding position over the city spread out below, King David wrested Jerusalem from the Jesubites and made it the capital of the Israelites. The legions of Rome subdued the 1st-century Jewish revolt from here. Under British Mandate the hill was a major military base. In Israel's War of Independence troops took heavy losses in order to retain Mount Scopus as an Israeli enclave inside Arab territory. And today Mount Scopus remains a strategic site – public access is limited and the university's groomed lawns and well-appointed faculty buildings share the top of the hill with discreetly placed military and communications facilities.

Ashraf leads me into the bowels of the building, down stairways and along corridors, to his office. As modern offices go it's nothing out of the ordinary, but the view from the window stops me in my tracks. No longer am I looking towards the Old City. Now on the rear side of Mount Scopus, I am looking out into emptiness. Below us the flanks of the hill fall sharply away, and beneath the cloudless sky beyond lies a dun-coloured void that stretches away forever.

'What is it?' I ask Ashraf, who is standing beside me. I seem to have lost my sense of depth.

'The Judean desert,' he replies. 'The Dead Sea lies just forty kilometres away.' He points to fold after fold of naked, sandy ridge lying below. 'Look, you can see a corner of it from here. And there, on the horizon, are the Hills of Moab, in Jordan. We are on the edge of Israel here – the border runs just a few hundred metres below. Everything after that is Occupied Territories.'

We are interrupted in our gazing by the arrival of a colleague, her arms full of yellowed papers and faded black-and-white photographs. Her auburn hair cut in short, no-nonsense fashion, her glasses perched professorially on the end of her nose, Dr Julia Matveev teaches German literature at the Hebrew University. But this morning she has sought Ashraf out with research material for an article they are collaborating on, a centenary commemoration of a forgotten German-Jewish poet who perished in the Holocaust.

Julia is not German, but comes from St Petersburg. Over a cup of coffee she describes for me the great event of her life, the trip that transformed her from a Russian Jew into an Israeli. To me it sounds like a trip out of hell. But it was no worse a journey, she insists, than many Russians made at the time.

The first Gulf War was in full swing and the collapsing Soviet Union had not yet fully opened the doors to an outgoing rush of Jewish emigration. 'We had no documents when I left Russia in 1991 with my husband and child – we had no money either,' Julia says, gazing into the deep blue bowl of the sky in recollection. 'What I did have was acute tonsillitis and a high fever. I was ill. I couldn't talk. I couldn't even think.

'We took a train to Budapest, spent a dreadful night in a refugee centre, then flew into a Middle East war. We couldn't get out of Tel Aviv airport, and had to wear gas masks for sixteen hours. I was delirious.' Julia is laughing now. 'The ground kept rumbling and trembling underfoot – I was convinced it was Scud missiles landing nearby one after the other. I was terrified. But it was Patriot missiles fired from the base next door, heading the other way.'

There's a big smile on her face. 'Very pathetic!' she says, making fun of herself.

It's got to be one of the stranger ways, I say, of being welcomed to a new home, and Julia has to admit she had her doubts at first. But there are no regrets now. Jerusalem, she says, became a far more reassuring place for a Jew than St Petersburg ever was. She has security, a good life with her family, and the prospect of a new teaching post in Haifa. All she really misses in Israel is the snow that used to pile up in the streets around her home in St Petersburg.

And where, I enquire, is home now?

Julia points through the window. 'There.'

'Where?' I say, following her gaze. I can't see anything but sand and sky.

'Look further down. On the lower ridges, a settlement. It's called Ma'ale Adumim. 35,000 people live there.'

Julia does not look or talk like a hard-nosed settler intent on re-establishing an enlarged *Eretz Izrael*, the biblical land of her forefathers. She is a liberal, enlightened, secular Israeli. She must see the confusion on my face. I don't need to ask her why.

'It's cheaper,' she says simply. 'Jerusalem is horribly expensive. Even with my husband's and my own salary we could never find a decent place to live in the city. When Ma'ale Adumim was first built the state handed out financial incentives to encourage people to live there. It doesn't any more, but it's still much less expensive. The children have good schools and all the modern conveniences are available. There are shopping malls, community centres, sports facilities, performing arts theatres, youth clubs, health clinics. It's clean and new and affordable. Try finding all that in Jerusalem.'

And what about the people who live there, I ask. For a moment I have a picture of the Hilltop Boys in mind. They are a particularly violent bunch of young religious Jews who take over hilltops in the Occupied Territories. They sing, pray, smoke dope, live in tents and violently defy anyone, Arab inhabitants or Israeli soldiers, to remove them.

Julia seems to have read my mind. 'I'm afraid we're a very dull, well-scrubbed lot,' she says. 'There's not a religious zealot amongst us. We're almost all new immigrants – Russian, American, European, Ethiopian. We're all there for the same thing, a better, easier life.' She shrugs. 'I'd move if I could. But why don't you go and see for yourself? It's easy to get there.'

'Bus number 174,' says Ashraf. 'You can catch it just down the hill, at the corner outside the Hyatt Hotel.' He's been quiet at his desk until now and I haven't known he's been listening at all. Now it dawns on me: Ma'ale Adumim is the place he has wanted to point me to all along.

'It will cost you 17 shekels and takes about twenty minutes,' he continues. 'You can have lunch out there at the shopping mall.'

I leave Ashraf and Julia poring over photos and brittle copies of little poetry magazines sixty years old, and head down the hill, past the Hadassah hospital, to the bus-stop.

The Number 174 leaves behind it a cluttered cityscape, burrows into the base of Mount Scopus, and emerges from a long tunnel into what might be another world. It's bone dry and colourless. At the end of a long, merciless summer only the skeletons of scrubby plant-life now remain – the sparse dead grasses by the roadside are weightless, tossing back and forth in a whoosh of air as the bus rushes by. The sun bounces off rocky hillsides and eroded ravines, and the glare through the window discourages curiosity. We pass two small Palestinian villages perched, as are all old settlements in this part of the world, on hilltops. Otherwise there is no human presence, nothing but a ribbon of bitumen running through a dead and barren landscape.

Not yet thirty-five years old, Ma'ale Adumim is a modern city, but it too is built high on the spine of a long ridge. The bus, winding upwards, enters the town by an armed checkpoint and is waved through. And suddenly we really are in another world. If the desert surrounding Ma'ale Adumim feels alien and slightly hostile, inside everything has been brought under control. It's not just the natural elements that have been eliminated, but time and place themselves. Human history and geography, and all they entail, are gone. The site's essential Middle Easterness itself has vanished, every last trace of original identity erased. A snapshot photo of the town would not reveal where in the world it lies. We are in some anonymous, anodyne, sunny place. It could be a bedroom community in California or a resort-town on the Costa del Sol. Certainly we are a long way from the place which lies between the Mediterranean Sea and the Jordan River.

New Japanese cars cruise along the smooth four-lane strip that winds along the ridge-top. Recently repaved, its traffic-lane stripes and pedestrian crossings are white and newly painted. The grass on the raised median dividing the road is freshly cut and regularly watered. On either side of the road broad sidewalks are dotted regularly with wooden benches and glass-sided telephone booths, shady palm and bright sprays of bougainvillea. Everything is clean and crisp and glistening. I haven't seen a graffiti-free bus-shelter in years, but now I do. After the shabbiness of Arab East Jerusalem, Ma'ale Adumim is a minor miracle. Purpose-built, it looks like it's been assembled somewhere else and gently lowered onto the ridge-top from the air. From its lush, irrigated gardens to its polished, dust-free cars, Ma'ale Adumim denies the nature of the desert. It simply might as well not be there.

School must be out, for suddenly there are kids in shorts and baseball caps skateboarding past us in the opposite direction. The bus goes through a retail shopping zone of stores and wide parking lots and malls, past commercial office space and on into residential areas. The villas and bungalows, roofed with red tiles and built to the same standard designs, are pleasant and without distinction. Set closely together on small plots, they recede into the distance with geometrical precision. One street looks exactly like the next. We drive through a town that's long and thin and without a nucleus, a town that everywhere sticks to the hilltops.

This gives each householder his own plunging, million-dollar view, but the panorama is more than just a consideration of aesthetic design. Like Mount Scopus, like the two Palestinian villages we've passed on the way out, Ma'ale Adumim retains the high ground through a regard for self-protection. In this part of the world strategic principles of territorial defence have not changed in 3,000 years – you're safer when you're more elevated than any potential enemy.

And for the town's architects and residents the principle remains as important as ever. Ma'ale Adumim, for all its peacefulness and mod-con functionality, remains an illegal settlement in the eyes of Palestinians and the rest of the world. Arab residents of the nearby town of Abu Dis continue to claim the land as their own. Not only has Ma'ale Adumim's growth required the expulsion of pastoralist Bedouin families from their homes; Palestinians protest that plans for further extension of Ma'ale Adumim, along with the development of two adjacent settlement blocks, will cut East Jerusalem off from its Palestinian hinterland. And that will make its establishment as the capital of a future state impossible. Backed by determined right-wing political parties, pro-settlement groups fully expect Ma'ale Adumim to remain in Israeli possession in any future dispensation.

The bus drives on, dropping people here and there until I am the only passenger left. We arrive at the end of the ridge – without warning, the lush California-style gardens and shady palm trees cease to exist and the drab dullness of a Middle Eastern desert takes over. On a slope far below I can see two small Arab boys and half a dozen sheep foraging among the thorn bushes. Then the bus swings around and heads back the other way, picking up passengers for the return journey to Jerusalem.

I jump off at a multi-level shopping mall. I flip through CDs at Tower Records, try on a pair of Lee Cooper Jeans, and consider for one ill-advised moment a pair of bright red Crocs. Apart from the security check at the entrance, mall life in Ma'ale Adumim is exactly the same as mall life anywhere else on the planet. As far as I'm concerned the desert outside is less barren. After twenty minutes of wandering I decide to skip a mall lunch, to hop back on the bus, and have a falafel at the Damascus Gate instead.

And this return, too, like the return from Mea Shearim, is a relief, really. Ma'ale Adumim may well be a community of advanced technology and secular material progress, a haven where hard-pressed Jerusalemites can find affordable housing. But there is something wrong here. It doesn't matter whether you're focussing on a four-decade-old contravention of international law or on two shepherd boys scrabbling around in thorn bushes. Not only does the town itself feel physically displaced; it is inhabited by people who shouldn't be here and inaccessible to people who should.

I've never given any thought to the proposition that the absence of something that has no existence anyway can be felt more acutely in one place than another. But now, on the return home to Jerusalem, I know it's possible. God may not exist, but there is altogether too much of him in Mea Shearim. And in Ma'ale Adumim there isn't enough of any spirit at all.

Six

I have an occasionally recurring dream in Jerusalem. It only comes when, before going to sleep, I walk out onto the roof of the Maison d'Abraham to watch the stars and moon wheeling above the city. At those moments the bright silver sliver above me is not the only moon riding over Jerusalem. It is a model for a thousand others – the crescent moons, made of beaten metal, that rise from the top of every domed mosque and minaret here. And whether I want them to or not, both real and imitation moons seem to work their way into my sleep. For invariably in the dream there is a journey, one that originates here on earth, in Jerusalem, and ends up high in the whirling night sky.

The dream begins not at night but in the broad light of day, on a esplanade that is blinding white with sunlight and summer heat. I am a small boy in shorts once again, and walking beside my father. Both of us are following an Arab in a long robe, a guide, I suppose, because he is reeling off a history of names and battles and dates. I am not listening very hard but patiently biding my time, for on this visit the guide has promised me a magical horse.

In the middle of the esplanade we come to an eight-sided building with a burnished golden cupola for a roof. Like a second sun, it is so bright it hurts my eyes. We walk around the base of the structure, gazing up at geometrically tiled panels, at complex colour patterns of lapis, turquoise and cobalt, at arches and marble columns and capitals. Running above doors and below cornices are markings the guide says are writing. I know the alphabet because I've already learned it at school, and this is not writing. The marks are too delicate and wispy – they are like the scratches of tree branches on a frosty window or the tracks of beetles in sand. But I nod anyway, as if he's right, because I want him to show me the horse.

The guide leads us inside the building and after the fierce heat of the day outside it is suddenly dark and cool. In the dim blue-grey obscurity there are golden mosaics and carved ceilings floating above our heads. Also rising far above us, directly beneath the vault of the dome, is a solid mass of black rock. There's a deep, dark cave beneath it, says the guide, which is called the Well of Souls. It's a place of echoes where the voices of the dead merge with the rumble of the rivers of paradise as they plummet to eternity. I don't know what it means, but it scares me. The rock above the cave, the guide goes on, is the place where Abraham pleased God by making preparations to sacrifice his son. It also marks the centre of the world, the very spot where Mohammed arrived in Jerusalem and left it.

He leads us up to a small, deep indentation on the rock's side, a hole about the width of a hand. It's Mohammed's footprint, he tells us. It was here where he mounted his horse Buraq and sprang away from the earth on his night-ride to heaven to meet God and his prophets.

I am less interested in God and his prophets than in Buraq – the idea of a horse galloping away into the sky is bewitching. He was a very beautiful white horse, says the guide, with a golden bridle and feathered wings. And very strong, too, to have carried a man on his back through thin air. Where, I ask, is Buraq now? Gone, of course, says the guide with a smile and a mannered, upward flick of his hand. Flown to heaven.

But is the footprint not enough? he asks. It is enough for thousands of pilgrims. Touch the place, he tells me. The rock is hard and cold, and when I withdraw my hand my fingers are perfumed with the smell of a sweet, musky scent placed there by worshippers.

For me it is not enough. I am disappointed. I want the horse itself, not belief in the horse. Then, with all the naturalness that dreams bestow on such transitions, it is late at night and suddenly Buraq appears. We are alone in a starry, moon-flooded midnight. No father, no guide, just the two of us.

And I know that all human marks, the strokes of writing and the imprint of feet, are irrelevant now, because this horse is real and magic and there is no need for mere signs. Buraq is indeed a beautiful horse, highly-strung and richly-caparisoned, his nostrils dilated and puffing with excitement at the coming journey. He is also an inviting horse. He stands patiently as I scramble up onto his back, and then we are away with a rush of air and a steady beating of wings, until the buildings of the dark city are tiny below us and we are rushing upward into the luminous sky above Jerusalem.

I am always a little disappointed when I wake from these dreams to find myself back on earth, lying in bed on the rooftop of a pilgrim's hospice. Perched up here but earthbound still, it seems to me before I become fully conscious that I really would like to get away skyward. And I sometimes wonder whether Buraq is the spiritual belief I don't have but would like to if I could possibly believe in it all. I cannot, though, so earthbound I remain.

But part of the dream, the first part, is no dream at all. When I was a small boy I really did visit Jerusalem with my father, and we really did enter the Dome of the Rock to hear of the story of Mohammed's night-ride to heaven and see the footprint in the stone there. Was it this first visit to the city that's given me an enduring curiosity about the place? I have no idea, but the dream remains, vivid in my mind, and one morning I set out to see the rock under the golden dome again.

I arrive early, and am one of the first tourists to mount the ramp that climbs the Western Wall to the esplanade above – the place Jews call the Temple Mount and Muslims know as Haram al-Sharif, the Noble Sanctuary.

As I'd hoped, the Haram is almost deserted at this early hour. Raised above the surrounding bustle of the city, wrapped in a soothing greenery of lawns and cypress trees, dotted here and there by domed pavilions and kiosks, the broad esplanade is quiet and peaceful. Such tranquility is surprising, perhaps, but not without a logic of its own – in a city around which a dark tornado incessantly swirls, what could this place be, if not its calm dead centre?

At the top of the entrance for non-Muslims a few small boys sit around, bored and waiting to pester the coming morning's tour-parties for money. There's a man washing his feet at a sunken stone trough where a long row of water taps await ritual ablutions. Another old Arab walks the esplanade alone, his cane tapping the stone flags as he takes his morning constitutional. Enjoying the morning sun and their own chatty company, a group of Arab women sit on a low wall at the far end of the esplanade. Moving slowly around the perimeter of the complex, past the Iron Gate, the Prison Gate and the Gate of the Cotton Merchants, a pair of Israeli soldiers patrol the Muslims' public entrances to the Haram.

I stroll for a while, gazing from different angles at the Dome of the Rock and the sun bouncing off its surface. It sits there as magnificently as it's sat in my head all these years – the columns and capitals, the geometric designs in a dozen shades of blue, the graceful arabesques of calligraphy bearing the message that God is great. It is not an hour of Muslim prayer, and I'm surprised when I see a Palestinian woman round the Dome to the building's high main doors – daily prayer on the Haram al-Sharif usually takes place under the dark lead roofs of the Haram's second great building, the Al-Aqsa mosque. But this woman has come for unofficial, impromptu communion. Young and slim in long black robes, her face invisible in its surrounding scarf, she stands straight and still beside the mosque's marbled entranceway. Her arms clasped, her head lowered, she prays silently. Sinking to her knees, she then bends gracefully forward and prostrates herself, touching forehead to ground. The gestures of this lone woman are different from those of the men who gather in countless rows outside the great mosques of the Middle East in Friday prayer. Yet contained in her deep, silent reverence, in her devotion to a sacred place, there is the same fundamental impulse found in all religion – her desire to find completion in something larger than herself.

Lourdes, Benares, Mecca, Bhodgaya... Jerusalem, of course, isn't the only holy place in the world. They all leave me bemused. What is this need to convene around natural sites – groves of trees, peculiar rock formations, river confluences, mountain tops – and ascribe to them a sacred nature? Why the compulsion to create a spiritual topography we then seek to become part of? Presumably because in their beauty or strangeness these spots evoke another kind of existence, the presence of something other than ourselves. In such places, it seems, we become aware of a category of being that is larger and more important than mere human being. Is this the significance of holy sites, that they are places where we become aware of ourselves as part of some great, central, unanswered mystery? And where, by connecting with that mystery, we can rise above the isolation of our own separate lives?

It's as close as I can get to the enigma of holy places. And maybe at one time they really did help us climb towards the place we call heaven. But as I watch the young woman with her face pressed to the ground, I can only reflect that there's a problem with sacred geography in Jerusalem today. The surveyors of the soul are working from different bearings and the divine chart-makers have lost their way. All of us, Jew, Christian and Arab, have been issued different maps of the same place.

It's with these thoughts in mind that I approach the entrance to the Dome of the Rock. I'm a little hesitant. Is there still place inside for a boy, now long grown, to wander around dreaming of flight on a magical horse?

I'll never know. At the doorway itself stands a fat, unshaven Arab. He is the door-keeper of the Dome, and a deeply unpleasant character.

'No foreigners!' he shouts, his voice horse from shouting the same message to a hundred others like me. 'Muslims only! Go!' He bats the air in front of him as if he's swatting flies.

I try to explain that I was here once years ago. How long has it been, I ask, since non-Muslims have been barred from entering the mosque? 'Many years,' he answers, as irritated as if I had started the first Intifada myself. 'Since Sharon walked up here to make trouble.'

And when, I cannot help asking, will we be allowed in again? This man is so nastily bad-tempered I don't mind making him even more irritated than he already is.

'Never!' he roars back. 'Never! Now go! Go!' And with that he retreats into the mosque and slams the door behind him.

Even dreaming, it seems, is becoming difficult in the heart of Jerusalem these days.

Take, from one side, the ancient sense of sacred destiny proper to a chosen people. From the other, add the burning sense of resentment that belongs to the newly disenfranchised. Combine them in a pressure cooker, keep the lid screwed down tight until the mixture is simmering, and what have you got? You've got El Wad Street in old Jerusalem on a Friday evening.

It is just such an evening and I'm lounging over the street on the garden terrace of the Austrian Hospice. It's a delightful place in the heart of the Muslim Quarter, a Catholic hostel that's been here since the glory-days of the Austro-Hungarian empire. A bit like the Maison d'Abraham, it's run on much grander lines – once inside its fine old stone building you expect to run into the Emperor Franz Joseph himself. There are gilt-framed mirrors on the walls, a chapel with terrific paintings in elegant Germanic counter-reformation style, and a genuine Austrian café where you can get strudel and coffee, each loaded with small mountains of whipped cream. Outside on a terrace raised well above the street there are gardens with lawns and shady trees – an unimaginable luxury in this densely-packed city – and comfortable chairs where you can look down on the passing scene. In its Teutonic, well-ordered way it's sublime, an escape from the noisy confusion that lies just outside the doors.

I've been sitting back, reading the paper in true Viennese café style for some time, when I notice the young man at the table beside me. Using a video-camera mounted on a tripod he's been filming the street. There's nothing unusual in that. The Hospice has a superb view down El Wad, one of the busiest thoroughfares in the Old City; lots of tourists come here with cameras for its colour and movement. But this man has been filming continuously for more than an hour. I can see him occasionally check-ing the camera's illuminated monitor to make sure it's all being properly recorded. He never moves the camera, and when one cassette is full he simply replaces it with another.

Another half-hour passes. I've read everything including the want ads, and still the man is recording. As far as I can see there's nothing special happening down there – it's the usual mix of every race and people on earth. Finally I can stand it no longer, and ask him what he's up to.

Simon James, it turns out, is not a tourist. He runs a small production company called Front Line Film and is working on a project for Cambridge University. He is looking at tense situations in small spaces – the study known as 'Conflict in Cities' studies the ways in which everyday life in urban settings is affected by ethnic and religious conflict. The effect is reciprocal; the project also investigates the ways in which conflict is influenced by everyday urban life. That's not the only duality of the project. It's in cities that are physically divided that these phenomena are especially crucial: Jerusalem aside, Belfast, Beirut, Nicosia and Mostar are also included in the study, and from Israel Simon James will eventually be moving on to Kirkuk in northern Iraq.

James looks like a pretty easy-going fellow, and I ask him if he himself gets agitated in these places. Jerusalem, he tells me, is easily the tensest, most anxiety-producing place he's worked in. At the same time he acknowledges the four-hour filming sessions he sits through each day are not relentless, action-packed thrillers. That's not the point. 'What we are looking for,' he says as he removes yet another full cassette from the camera, 'is the complex relationship between human behaviour and physical space. Sometimes it's tiny things – the distance at which members of different communities pass each other, or how long they hold eye contact. Sometimes it's bigger things – the way entire cities physically restructure themselves to cope with unsustainable situations.' Back at Cambridge, in an effort to understand how people might better find resolution in trying circumstances, James' films will be reviewed again and again for analysis.

I look down the street once more. I suggest that after a few re-runs of this particular four-hour segment the analysts might be holding their eyes open with toothpicks. Simon James only smiles, but before he slides a fresh cassette in the camera he can't resist showing me a short section of video he's taken from precisely this place a few days earlier. Looking at the little monitor, I find myself zoomed in to an unobtrusive doorway a hundred yards down the street. It's the entrance to an old synagogue, and outside it are gathered some thirty young Ultra-Orthodox Jewish men. At a first, casual glance they appearing to be having nothing but a good time – they are singing, waving flags, dancing in the street.

'Pure provocation,' sighs James. 'In fact they are blocking the street, making it difficult for Arab residents to get by. They're deliberately disrupting the normal life of the quarter – they are both frightening and angering people. And they get progressively more antagonistic as time goes on. It appears to me that they are purposely looking for a reaction, pushing and inciting until they get some kind of response. And indeed things do get a good deal rougher a few minutes later and the police move in.' He fast-forwards, and in the tiny, illuminated oblong in front of me I see miniature Jews and miniature Arabs shouting, shoving and slugging it out in a silent, reduced-size drama. James shrugs. 'I can't tell from the cassette if the Jews later blamed the Arabs for causing a violent incident. But it's often the case.'

I don't spend much longer on the terrace of the Austrian Hospice, for as sunset approaches there is more and more pedestrian traffic in the street below. Usually foot traffic flows along in a slow, confused rip-tide of opposing movements. But now it's coming in from the Damascus Gate, fast and purposeful, and headed in the direction of the Jewish Quarter. I am too curious to sit still. Leaving Simon James to his filming, I head out into the street. This is not any old day of the week. Once again, it is Shabbat eve.

First I head upstream, against the flow of pedestrians, in a five-minute walk to the Damascus Gate. On a roundabout on the road outside an army jeep is parked and redirecting motor-traffic away from the Gate. There's a blue light flashing on its roof and two armed Israeli soldiers leaning against its bonnet. Arab drivers – there are no Jewish ones about now – are having to find other routes home. There is another jeep and more flashing lights and soldiers at the Gate itself. In the gathering evening darkness Ha Neviim Street is no longer the province of its usual inhabitants, muscled young Palestinians hefting crates of fruit. Instead the sidewalks are busy with Jewish men, women, and children, dressed for Shabbat as if they'd just emerged from the eighteenth century. Gone are the everyday black hats, black suits, white shirts. There are fur hats brushed to a glistening sheen, satin brocade gowns, white hose leggings. The women and children, too, are dressed in their Friday best. All are walking to a single destination on the far side of the Old City. For Jews close enough to walk from nearby Mea Shearim, there is nothing more important on the eve of Shabbat than to pray at the foot of the Western Wall.

How do the Ultra-Orthodox feel as they set out from the confines of their own quarter to walk through the Muslim Quarter to their destination? I don't know. I'm not an Ultra-Orthodox Jew and haven't got centuries of violent racism and the ghetto existence of eastern Europe behind me. How do Arabs feel when hundreds of Jews come striding through their quarter each Friday night, their faces set, their eyes wavering neither left nor right, the presence of the quarter's inhabitants determinedly unacknowledged? I don't know that either. I'm not a Palestinian and haven't experienced, within living memory, an entire people's dispossession. But from the faces alone I can infer both states of mind.

The inhabitants of Mea Shearim don't have to come this way – they could just as easily enter the Old City through the New Gate in the Christian Quarter. This walk through dark Arab streets is a symbolic undertaking – it's not difficult to see that it produces fear and defiance on one side and feelings of injustice and indignation on the other. It is the running of a gauntlet, a perilous high-wire act of faith, a weekly parting of the Red Sea.

Slipping in behind a knot of Hasidic Jews, I join a continuous stream of Shabbat worshippers on their way to the Wall. They move wordlessly along El Wad Street, striding fast, heads down. They keep to the middle of the passage, equidistant and as far away as possible from the Arabs who stand silent in doorways and shop entrances on either side. It is a situation made for anxiety, as good an example as any of the sustained undercurrents of tension which keep the city constantly off-balance and at odds with itself.

The stream of Jewish worshippers marches on. There are foot patrols of soldiers every hundred yards; dark, covered sections of the route through which the column moves especially quickly; an Israeli flag hanging defiantly above the road at the end of the Muslim Quarter. Then there's an arched tunnel, a security barrier of metal detectors and soldiers rifling through bags, and finally the Western Wall Plaza, broad and filled with evening strollers. At the bottom of the Plaza, brightly spot-lit and colonized here and there by tufts of resilient plant-life, fifty feet of solid stone wall rise into the night sky.

What is a non-believer to make of the faith professed there? I'm not sure. Once I've passed down a stone ramp, and put on the cardboard *kippah* all bareheaded visitors must borrow if they wish to approach the Wall, I've passed over a frontier of rational thought. This is a different kind of territory – it's a place so old, with a topography receding so far back in human thought, that the baggage of modern skepticism we bring along these days is useless. It's not that I suspend my religious disbelief – it simply stops providing me with any answers. Whatever's at work here isn't amenable to doubt.

There is no free space at the foot of the Wall. Every inch of it is occupied by devout, bobbing, chanting worshippers. There are no women – they have their own partitioned section of the Wall – but scattered across the Plaza, facing the Wall and praying, is every kind of Jew. There are black Jews, white Jews, and all shades of Jew in between. There are Jews who look Jewish, Jews who don't look Jewish, Jews who bear every resemblance to the Arabs with whom they co-habit the city. There is barely a people on earth that does not have a genetic foothold in Judaism, and they are all praying fervently here this evening.

It is at the Wall itself, though, where worshippers stand plastered flat against the stone surfaces, where hand-written messages to God are stuffed into chinks in the blocks, that the level of devotion is most fervent of all.

It's as if some of the celebrants simply can't get enough of the place, as if there is some precious essence in the very substance of the stone that with sufficient will and effort might be extracted. I watch one man, sitting on a chair six inches from the Wall, put his hand up against its smooth stone and stroke it sensuously, as if he were stroking the flatness of a woman's back. At one point he seems to want with his fingers to penetrate the surface of the Wall itself, to become part of the Wall.

And at the same time he is talking aloud, constantly and eagerly, as if to a living listener. Most church services I've ever sat through have left me thoroughly unconvinced that the congregation really thought there was someone listening. The prayers they were offering up, the supplications they were making were rote, simply part of an approved liturgical formula. The odd feeling I have here is that each worshipper fervently believes he is in direct and intimate communication with somebody else. Someone whose presence I'm not aware of, but he is.

It's not the kind of performance you can fake. I find myself standing next to a red-haired Jew, an open Torah in his hand, whose long beard and swaying side-curls are bold, fiery exclamations in copper. But there is no need for his hair to say anything at all – all his expression is in his face. Great emotion has pulled the features there into a twisted rictus. His eyes are narrowed, the muscles around his mouth are pulled back and his head sways rhythmically up and down. It is an expression so intimate, so personally private, that I find myself embarrassed to be looking. Occasionally he switches his movement from side to side, or pounds the text he holds with a clenched fist. But the physical rhythm and the words he is intoning are never abandoned. As he bends repeatedly from the waist his whole body seems to be jerked violently around by some potent and uncontrollable force inside him.

Is it, as is sometimes described, the sacred words of the Torah igniting the soul the way a match ignites a candle? Is it, in consequence, the body moving like a flame? It may be, but it doesn't make the act of prayer at the Western Wall appear any less strange to me. In an uninterrupted row hundreds of other worshippers are also involved in their own equally intense and private discourse with God. As I stand there watching, I have to admit I find the whole process a little alarming.

Packed three or four deep, the worshippers form a dense, corporal mass. At the same time they are so distant, so removed from their immediate physical surroundings that they hardly seem present at all. They are far away, somewhere else. This is the kind of intense, inner-directed awareness that is usually visible only in jazz players, transcendental poets and heavily stoned individuals. Spiritual flames these worshippers might be, but what are they burning for? How do people so exclusively tuned to an internal voice form opinions or take decisions in the external world – this world? Individual identity usually implies individual will and responsibility. What happens when that identity is absorbed by another will, higher and more authoritative? How do such worshippers cope with other worshippers who listen to other inner voices, different than theirs but equally undeniable?

I watch a non-Orthodox Jew praying a few yards away from the wall. I can't see his expression, for he is hunched over in a chair and his face is obscured by his long hair. But I can see the back of the black T-shirt he's wearing. It shows an outlaw biker on a Harley-Davidson motorcycle straddling the centre-line of the highway. The caption beneath it reads, 'Yes, I do own the road.'

God, of course, does not manufacture motorcycles, and Jews are not bikers. Neither are Christians or Muslims. But it doesn't matter who you are – provided you believe zealously enough that God has sanctioned your road-trip, you're capable of riding just about anywhere.

There's a sudden blaring noise, a sort of wild, errant siren, issuing from an open space fifty yards back from the Wall. It's different and distinguishable from the many other siren-sounds in Israel – it's a *shofar*, that Old Testament instrument made from a curled ram's horn and used on ceremonial occasions.

It's the same sound I heard in my first hour in Israel, and for a moment I am back in the arrivals hall of Ben Gurion airport. In the milling crowd a team of victorious Israeli athletes just off an overseas flight have dropped their bags on the floor, gathered in a knot, and with arms held over each other's shoulders, begun circling. As they turn they sing, expanding their bodies and voices outwards as they make space for themselves in the crowd.

Is it a welcoming father or brother who has brought a *shofar* to the airport and, raising it to his lips, blows long and hard? The singing grows louder, the faces of the boys as they continue to circle grow flushed and ecstatic. I have seen this dance once before in an old photograph, a picture of Jews dancing for joy on a Haifa dockside following deliverance from a displaced person's camp in war-ravaged Europe. This return is scarcely as dramatic, but somehow these young men, too, make their dance not merely the celebration of one small group. With no apparent effort they have contrived to make it the dance of an entire people.

Once again now, in front of the Western Wall, the rough, ancient rasp of the *shofar* rings out repeatedly over the heads of the crowd. And once again, too, a circle of young men forms. They are not athletes, but young conscripts in uniform. The exultation that rises in their cheeks as they begin to circle, though, is the same.

But there is something more, someone I recognize in the middle of the circle. Beating out the time as the men move rhythmically around him is an American from the Old City tourist office at the Jaffa Gate. Like the Frenchman I met in Mea Shearim, he too is named David. He works as a student volunteer there, and if he can't write upside down on maps like his full-time colleagues, he's more sincere and engaging than they are. I drop in from time to time for bus schedules or the opening hours of obscure monasteries, but David offers me something more – he tells me how it is to live a new-found Judaism. In Phoenix, his family is Jewish by name only; religion for them means nothing more than polite meals at Passover. In Israel, his life has changed. A two-week 'birthright trip' organized by the rabbis on his campus has turned into something more serious: study in a yeshiva and a decision to remake life in Israel. David has, he rejoices to me, reconnected.

Now I watch him as he joins in prayer and dance. If he was ever unconnected, if he felt directionless and out of place in the past, you wouldn't know it now. His face glows. His hands move faster as he claps in time to the movement of bodies. Yes, his hands and face say, this is a dance of worship, of spiritual engagement with an invisible god. But having seen this dance before, I recognize in this newcomer, this young man who has found his place, something else as well.

It has not so much to do with invisible spirit, but with the land that spirit is now attached to. David's dance, as unmistakably as any airport athlete's or dockside refugee's, is a dance of belonging, a celebration of triumphant homecoming. And thinking of that long, risky walk performed every Friday in the shadows of El Wad Street and across the Muslim Quarter, I see something more in it, too. It is jubilant and tribal and defiant, a dance of victory.

Seven

Frère Jean and Frère Paul, the gnomish Breton clerics, may be a couple of jokers, but they are serious students of the Bible as well. Either that or they have run out of Asterix albums to read. For one morning in the Maison d'Abraham's library they ask me if I wouldn't like to visit a rather more famous library with them – the library at the *Ecole Biblique et Archéologique Française de Jerusalem.*

I accept immediately, not because I have decided to devote myself to scriptural study, but because the *Ecole Biblique* is a world-class institution with a rip-roaring reputation. Through its efforts some of the Middle East's oldest and greatest secrets have been revealed. Its researchers may look like humble Catholic clerics, but they come from a school of daring scholar-adventurers who for more than a century have risked everything to get to the bottom of complex archaeological mysteries. They don't need felt hats and bull-whips; they're real-life Indiana Joneses in soutains and dog collars. The only problem is that they do much of their work shut tightly away from the rest of the world. The *Ecole Biblique* lies behind the high walls of Jerusalem's Dominican Convent of St Stephen, and without prior arrangement you don't stand a chance of getting through the door. In fact, without a degree in Biblical Studies, without ancient Hebrew and Greek, without modern English, French and German, it's not even worth trying.

Somehow Frères Jean and Paul have wangled an entrance usually reserved for eminent scholars. I suspect they have been exploiting an old-girls' connection, sweet-talking our own Dominican nuns at the Maison d'Abraham into pestering their confreres for permission to visit the library. Certainly if Soeur Azucena pestered me for anything, I'd cave in immediately. However they've done it, I'm right behind them as they present themselves at the convent gates on the Nablus Road an hour later.

In the library we are received by Janusz Kaczmarek, a tall, dark Polish priest, who issues us with a stern warning of silence and leads us into the stacks. The library is not vast, but it houses great treasures that are today consulted by scholars from all over the world – most of the desks scattered through the library are occupied by solemn grey heads bent over rare manuscripts, leather-bound vellum or the library's own monographs and reviews. And as we are conducted from one collection to another, Frère Janusz whispers the origin of each in a low, sibilant voice.

The *Ecole* has conducted field research all over the Middle East. It covers diverse specialist topics of ethnological, linguistic, historical and archeological interest, and its learning has been amassed by men with one great principle in mind – the verification or dismissal of biblical traditions by scientific study. The impetus for such an ambitious programme, we learn *sotto voce* as we walk on, came as long ago as the 1850s. It was then that Protestant explorers and archaeologists, largely from the English-speaking world, began applying the methods of modern empirical investigation to age-old stories and beliefs. Digging deep into the Middle Eastern past, they started coming up with such astonishing discoveries as the Babylonian cuneiform tablets recording the 'Epic of Gilgamesh', the world's first literary account of a great flood. The Catholic establishment's reaction to such material revelations was to hunker down and resist – so heavily invested in by Rome, the myths of the biblical past had to be preserved from contemporary interpretation at all cost.

The Dominican order of priests, however, took a different stance. Educated, well-travelled and progressive in outlook, they decided to join in the search for biblical pre-history. Equipping themselves with archeological technique and equipment, they fanned out in expeditions to the Holy Land and across the region. And soon, in archaeological digs from Tripoli to Arabia, in exploration from Turkey to the Yemen, they began bringing in results. Much of it is contained in the written word; other evidence is stored in 18,000 negative photographic plates archived in deep wooden drawers here – the largest collection of early Middle East photos in the world.

We look at a few. Held up to the light, I can see dark, ghostly date groves, monumental desert excavations, priests in solar topees, frail-looking Model T Fords mired deep in sand. Some plates are so old they are held in original boxes marked 'Frères Lumieres'. We gaze at the Leica camera that was first used to photograph the Dead Sea Scrolls by translators at the *Ecole Biblique*. We discuss the literary and linguistic problems encountered by *Ecole* scholars who at these desks made the first modern translation of the Bible – the Jerusalem Bible, used in much of the world today.

Frère Janusz's disquisition continues. But looking around the hushed library at men who have given their whole lives to biblical study, who come to Jerusalem to spend spend day after day sifting ancient truth from legend, I become lost in my thoughts. In men like these the impulse to return to the biblical past might well be a healthy and positive thing – having no material stake in the land and its inheritance, they can afford a cool historical objectivity. In others, though – Christian, Jew or Muslim – such a return can be entirely compulsive, a pathology which from time to time becomes delusional. I am thinking of that mental aberration which spectacularly afflicts unsuspecting visitors to the city, the disorder known as the Jerusalem Syndrome.

It is a relatively rare condition – there are only three or four cases a year – but it is well documented. And given the kind of furore a white-robed, self-proclaimed Jewish Messiah might ignite if he chose to preach on the Haram al-Sherif, the Jerusalem Syndrome is not a phenomenon the authorities can afford to ignore.

The onset of the delusion is in most cases surprisingly similar. After a short while spent in Jerusalem the foreign tourist experiences a generalised emotion of anxiety or nervousness. He or she then goes on to feel an imperative need to visit the holy places. First there is ritual purification

– bathing, the shaving of body hair, the cutting of nails. And before setting out, the victim dons improvised white robes, almost invariably made from sheets taken from his hotel-room bed. He heads for one of any number of biblical sites in and around Jerusalem and then, loudly singing, chanting and praying, begins preaching to the world at large to reform its ways and follow him.

In the case of Jewish tourists the Jewish Messiah is the most commonly assumed character, although Moses is a close runner-up. Christian men seem to favour Jesus, Christian women the Virgin Mary. John the Baptist is also very popular. In recent years Israeli police have apprehended no less than six John the Baptists stalking eastward though the Judean desert. Wrapped in bedsheets – at least one, though, managed to dress himself in wild animal skins – they were determined to baptise themselves and their followers in the Jordan River. Muslim tourists would have their own congeries of sacred figures to emulate, but we don't know who – such tourists have never been permitted on Israeli soil.

According to medical authorities, there are three categories of visitor who suffer this kind of psychotic reaction to Jerusalem. The first are those with previous histories of mental illness. The second are those with no case history of mental instability, but a past marked by an extensive religious education and lifelong faith. But it is only the third category of sufferer that specialists regard as genuine victims of Jerusalem Syndrome – those who have no psychotic history nor any past of religious conviction. Their delusions arise for reasons as yet undetermined by science, and usually disappear within a few days of their being returned home. It is, to say the least, a bizarre condition.

The library visit concludes and we are ushered out, back from the subterranean gloom of biblical mystery into the sunlit world of crowds and traffic and noise. On the far side of the gates the Breton clerics spot and run for a bus home. I am left standing for a moment in front of the convent, still contemplating the vagaries of the religious imagination, when I am approached by a young woman. She has seen me coming out of the *Ecole Biblique,* and tells me she absolutely must get in.

I am a little taken aback. This is no weedy, bespectacled academic. She is an attractive, well-shaped blonde in dark glasses, somewhere in her late twenties. She is wearing a red-and-white Arab *keffiyeh* headdress foulard-style around her neck – a hip young fashion for backpackers around Jerusalem – but at the same time there is a well-groomed look of ease and money about her.

She tells me she needs to consult the best West Bank maps and reference books available because she is planning a prolonged stay out there. I tell her it's impossible, that any good bookshop would have adequate material. But she won't give up and I can't make out what she's really after. She trails after me. For a moment I even consider the possibility that this desirable young woman has been cruising the sidewalks, seeking an erotically-charged encounter, and of all the thousand possibilities at hand has opted for this one – me. It is a brief and highly creative moment, I admit, but clearly she doesn't want to be alone. We head to the nearby café terrace of the Jerusalem Hotel. I suggest we sit outside, but she opts for an inside table. It's so dark after the glare of the streets that we can hardly see where we are walking. When she takes off her glasses her pale eyes are puffy and swollen – I can see she has been crying.

I order coffee. She asks for soda water and then, impulsively, orders a vast lunch, saying she hasn't eaten anything for two days. Waiting for the food to arrive, she begins to talk about herself.

Her name is Nadine. She lives in Paris and a week ago, without warning, she left her husband and two young daughters to come to Jerusalem. She has spent the last four days travelling by bus and communal taxi across the West Bank, staying in Nablus, Ramallah, Tulkarem and Bethlehem along the way. She has never done anything like this before, and it scares her so much that at the sight of each military patrol, each military checkpoint on the road, she became physically ill. 'Touch my hand,' she says, holding it towards me. I touch her hand. It is trembling. But her Arab fellow travellers have been kind to her, she says, and she is still in one piece. Terrifying as it all is, she feels compelled to go out there again.

She hardly needs more than a nod of the head or a quiet word of affirmation from me to continue. I feel like a psychiatrist beside a divan as she gets further into her story. Why Jerusalem? I ask. She shrugs. She's never considered the place before in her life, she tells me. Has she ever had any involvement with Palestinians, with Israelis? She shakes her head. Politics have never interested her, not even at home, and certainly not in the Middle East. She just watches the television news like everyone else.

It's her own home, finally, that she knows more than anything else about. She is miserable in Paris. She hates her job. She hates her car, her tennis club, her sophisticated *chi-chi* friends, her spacious flat in a good *arrondisement*. She is no longer interested in her husband, a man who is more involved in his business than with her. Not even her children, although she misses them, are a source of deep satisfaction – they cannot make up for an unhappiness she can no longer tolerate. Her own small-town childhood in Normandy was cheerless and without affection, she says, and she remembers being repeatedly told she was not put on earth to be happy. Now she knows that lesson was wrong and she wants to prove it, in Palestine.

The food arrives. Nadine pushes it around, barely touching it. The more she talks the more I see how fragile she is. She is looking desperately for a break with her past. And deliverance, she is positive, will come for her soon, and through the agency of one man – the celebrated Gideon Levy. Occasionally appearing in the foreign press, Levy is a columnist who writes for *Ha'aretz,* Israel's left-wing national newspaper. He is a controversial figure, a traitor to some and a hero to others, much admired and much despised for his Palestinian sympathies.

Nadine cannot stop talking about him. 'He is a man, a real man,' she repeats with conviction. 'He has principles, energy, integrity, guts. He is brilliant.' She does not know him outside of his columns, but she will soon. She has telephoned him, she tells me, and he has agreed to meet her before she goes out to the West Bank again. Maybe they will go out together.

Is it all part of a larger fantasy? Despite her enthusiasm Nadine has no specific idea of what she really wants of the journalist – nor of the West

Bank itself – if not some sort of dramatic resolution of her life. Gideon Levy is a saviour.

Nadine, it seems to me as I sit listening, has evolved some sort of modified, updated form of Jerusalem Syndrome. She is not walking around in bedsheets. She does not take herself for the Virgin Mary. Instead, she is going to sudden, extreme lengths to become a militant, pro Palestinian activist. She wants to write about Palestinians. She wants to defend them, protect their persons, efface their humiliations, put right their wrongs. She wants to become the scourge of the Israeli establishment and see justice come to the land. For the moment she doesn't know how to give her fantasy concrete substance. Will she move on from the ritual purification stage, from the sloughing off of family and job, to full-blown delusions of personal transformation? Will she join Gideon Levy? Will she, in the way of fellow syndrome sufferers, become a Gideon Levy?

Somehow I doubt it. She might well go out to Hebron or Jenin. But once there, what then? Even half a dozen John the Baptists only thought as far as submersion in the Jordan River. Looking at Nadine, febrile, strung-out, running on nerves, I find it difficult to imagine her own rebirth. I see her eventually returning home deflated, dispirited and sadder than ever. She hasn't got the self-confidence, the high-flying exaltation for a real *folie de grandeur*. She is one more of Jerusalem's victims.

Later, recounting my day to Ashraf Noor, he is amused that I might for a moment have imagined some kind of erotic sidewalk encounter with Nadine. From time to time, he admits, he and I might meet slightly eccentric characters over plates of Daube Provençal at the Maison d'Abraham. But however flamboyant they appear, I am assured, they remain among Jerusalem's more sedate visitors. The city attracts all sorts of much more troubled individuals for all sorts of truly desperate reasons. It is a place where people seek to realise on earth, in the here and now of daily life, every manner of heavenly fantasy. And sometimes they do. But they hardly ever involve attractive young blonds throwing themselves gratuitously on perfect strangers outside prestigious institutes of bible study. That, I realise with just the slightest disappointment, is strictly my own Jerusalem fantasy.

In this emotionally-charged city, religious delusions are not necessarily limited to unbalanced individuals. They can creep up with the most astonishing vigour and stealth on entire groups of unsuspecting visitors. Why bother, I ask myself one morning after my encounter with Nadine, staying up to watch Linda Blair in *The Exorcist* on late-night TV? It's just as easy to watch a dozen Linda Blairs rolling on the ground and fighting devils in the plain light of day. All you have to do is show up at the Garden Tomb.

I don't actually go to the Garden Tomb to see evil spirits being thrown *en masse* out of writhing bible-belt charismatics. I go there because, along with a couple of other places I've discovered in the city, it offers a kind of relief. There is something about Jerusalem that is physically draining – more often than not I climb to my rooftop room at night feeling limp and wrung-out. At first I thought it might be the altitude, or the sheer, frenetic denseness of the place – the reduced personal space that Jerusalemites must live in within their Old City walls. But it has little to do with natural reserves of energy or how much one runs around on any given day. The fatigue is more insidious than that, and it hangs there in the air over the city for everyone to breath. It finds its source in that almost limitless bank of tension, built from countless acts of mistrust over decades. And so instinctively does that strain come to citizens now that it exacts a price in carrying out even the simplest task.

So when I need a break, the places I tend to gravitate to in Jerusalem offer simple things – calm and quiet and repose. I am an atheist who's come to like churches.

One is an Ethiopian church – not the celebrated collection of huts, run-down and tourist-ridden, on the roof of the Holy Sepulcher, but a cupola-topped building in Ethiopia Street guarded by a stone-carved Lion of Judah. It is little visited and barely a century old. But it is dedicated to an ancient proposition: that Ethiopia's most celebrated woman, the Queen of Sheba, received the emblem of the Lion of Judah from King Solomon when she visited Jerusalem 3,000 years ago. The spiritual vision of the Ethiopian Copts is a strong, simple, bright one, and their church is a wonderfully refreshing place. You take your shoes off at the door and wander along sunlit carpets, through wreaths of fragrant incense smoke and past brightly-coloured naif paintings of Abyssinian saints. High above, on the underside of the cupola, vivid stars scintillate in a painted heaven of deep blue. Rarely is there anyone present apart from a barefooted monk who chants endlessly under his breath as, a solitary wanderer, he strolls about his domed and starry domain.

A second refuge of mine is the Monastery of the Cross, set in a sloping valley on the far side of town. Run by a small community of Greek Orthodox monks, it too commemorates an ancient belief: that this is the precise spot where the tree used to make Jesus' cross grew. Not only that – the tree is purported to have grown from wooden staffs given to Abraham by heavenly angels. The building is terrifically solid and a thousand years old; thick-walled and heavily buttressed, it is built around a ponderous double-barreled church vault. But the decoration reposing on these massive stone structures is their absolute opposite; elegant, airy, ornate and complex. There are detailed floor mosaics in geometrical patterns of red, black and white; dozens of burnished silver oil lamps hanging from 30-foot chains; 12-foot high candelabras striped blue and white like barber's poles; a bald-aquinned patriarch's throne in red velvet and gilt, all fretwork friezes and heraldic shields. Better still, high on the iconostasis dividing the nave from the altar, is a lustrous painting of God, wild-haired and bearded, surrounded by flocks of hovering cherubim and looking down on the world below with the pride of ownership on his face. But what I like most about the church is the magisterial quiet that comes with all this splendour. The place is so rich, it glows so lavishly in the candlelight, that even the bus tours that sometimes show up are left silenced and without words. Once I watched a man with his small daughter alone in the church. Standing with flickering tapers in their hands, they remained before the iconostasis perfectly still and in absolute silence for twenty minutes. If that doesn't sound like a very long time, try it yourself one day, in church or out.

The third haven for me in Jerusalem is the Garden Tomb. There's no more empirical evidence that Christ was crucified here than that the Queen of Sheba visited Solomon in Jerusalem or that the cross of Jesus grew from angel's staffs. But it's not proof that is Jerusalem's common currency, of course – it's faith. It's this same faith that convinced Major-General Charles Gordon – the imperial commander later struck down by the Mahdi's spears at the celebrated Siege of Khartoum – that at last he'd found Jerusalem's real Golgotha.

These days Gordon would need faith in spades to believe that the rocky little outcrop that sits not far outside the Damascus Gate is the genuine Calvary. When I first visited the Garden Tomb I was surprised to find that the far side of this same outcrop forms the back of the East Jerusalem Arab bus station, the depot where I catch the Number 36 to the Maison d'Abraham. Just metres from the spot where a divine being redeemed all mankind buses now rev and roar, waiting passengers spit pumpkin-seed shells onto oil-stained tarmac, and the air is blue-grey and acrid with clouds of diesel fumes.

It's hardly a hill you'd imagine to be revered by millions of worshippers. Even a century and a half ago, though, it would have been difficult to posit this place as an alternate crucifixion site to the Holy Sepulcher inside the Old City. Helena, mother of the Emperor Justinian himself, had made her own claim there millennia before. But then Charles Gordon was a man who admitted that everything he did, in his service to Queen and country as much as in his service to God, was driven by his militant Protestant faith. And Protestants, excluded from the resurrection rites of the Holy Sepulcher by their ideological differences with Catholics, had nowhere to go. A place was needed and evidence, however circumstantial, was sought. A place was found.

My great-grandfather, Methodist Superintendent of North-west Missions on the godless Canadian frontier, was himself equipped with formidable Protestant zeal. A young missionary to the Indians when Gordon was still alive, he might, if he'd found time to slip out of his canoe and make his way to Jerusalem, have found some sort of presence here. I certainly feel a presence when I come to the Garden Tomb, but my own uplift grows out of what is green and cool and botanical. If one side of the Protestant's Calvary is a bus station, the other has been transformed into a minor paradise.

There are stands of tall shade-trees, massed banks of shrubbery, narrow and intimate footpaths that wander here and there through well-watered greenery. It's cool and dim and humid, peaceful and serene and comforting. The attempt, I think, is to create a private, miniature Garden of Eden where worshippers feel close in spirit to the Jesus they perceive here.

And it works. It works to the point, in fact, where some adepts really do just that – perceive Jesus. The droves of Protestants who visit the Garden Tomb today have inherited all of Gordon's evangelical ardour and more. I imagine that even he, Victorian exemplar of constrained manners and the stiff upper lip, would find himself aghast at some of the loony fervour regularly let loose and on display here.

I sometimes arrive in the mornings before the Holy Land tour-groups get there. Even then it's not completely tranquil. Already present are buttoned-up Zwinglians from Zurich, sedate Lutherans from Oslo, soulful but polite Presbyterians from Accra. They walk the paths in quiet meditation and, murmuring softly, pray together. They might even indulge in a little song, faint and tremulous, before the tomb of Jesus, a dark, rock-carved hole in a wall before which worshippers wait their turn for entrance. And then, smiling in the satisfaction of a pilgrimage completed, they take photos of each other at the tomb's sill and leave.

But each day also sees the arrival and departure of busloads of those limitlessly expansive pilgrims, evangelicals from the robust churches of the American South. There are Baptists and Methodists and Seventh Day Adventists, Congregationalists, Anabaptists and Restorationists, Trinitarians and Pentecostalists and Episcopal Zionists. Occasionally there are various obscure sects of fundamentalist Holy Rollers who make even the most rambunctious of these celebrants look like demure maiden-aunts at a church pot-luck dinner – so boisterously joyous and loud are they you'd think Tina Turner and an entire rock-gospel entourage had showed up with them. Then the Garden Tomb ceases to be a garden. It becomes a Big Tent in a Revivalist travelling show, a theatre, spectacle, a drama so physically gripping it leaves its participants literally gasping for breath. The staff at the Garden Tomb try to encourage jubilation of the etherial rather than the raise-your-hands-and-roll-your-eyes variety, and when the tour-buses pile up and the Garden Tomb overflows with exultation they scuttle from one group to another, shushing and fussing and calling for just a minimum of decorum, please. But however much they urge restraint (New Orleans jazz trumpets, they will impress upon you, are *not* on their approved list of instruments of celebration) things often just get clean away on them.

One day I listen to a slick-tongued pastor from Tennessee who, instead of moving human spirits, sounds like he's moving vehicles off a second-hand lot. On another day I watch a snake-oil salesman from Oklahoma who struts and gestures, thunders and rejoices as if he's auditioning for celebrity-host employment on God TV.

'Yes!' 'Amen!' 'Praise the Lord!' I hear a congregation of Virginians shout as their pastor, evoking the glory of the coming of the Lord, works them to an ever higher pitch. What is said hardly matters – what counts is the persuasive verbosity, the patter that's always self-assured and quick-footed, the insistent, driving rhythm that never misses a beat. If it sounds like the word of God, if it's backed up here and there by biblical page references – Paul to the Corinthians, Chapter two, Verse six – well, then, it must be the word of God. And it sells like hot-cakes. There's even a skinny little Briton in khaki shorts, a Yorkshireman with a not-so-sonorous voice, who's sure enough of himself to try it on, American-preacher style. Conducting a party from Nevada through the Garden he peppers his talk with 'You all' and 'So help me, folks' to move things along. And it works – in no time they're clapping and singing aloud:

They pierced Him in the side
They pierced Him in the side just for me
One day I was lost

He died on the cross
And I know it was done just for me

But my favourite pastor is Pastor Joe from Amarillo, Texas. On the day I watch him give holy communion to his flock I have already seen another group fall to pieces with a rousing sermon by their own pastor. There is trembling; the laying on of hands; shouting out in foreign tongues; a man who writhes and moans through spittle-flecked lips and must be restrained; another man lying apparently unconscious, only his heels alive and drumming on the ground in a frenzied tattoo; a woman who collapses and is revived by the application of a large crucifix to her forehead. It all ends with cheers and applause for the pastor and hugs of Christian love liberally distributed to all around. Not only am I embraced, I am given Jesus' blessing and one of the little wooden cups, not much bigger than a thimble, in which the sacrament of his blood has been administered. I still have it on my desk, wine-stained ruby red inside, a souvenir of Jerusalem.

So, between one thing and another, I am more than primed for Pastor Joe. And you have to be, for Joe, it must be said, makes claims that even the most powerful representatives of God on earth might shy away from. Not even the Pope, I believe, claims he can raise the dead. It's all the more surprising, as Joe is such an average-looking guy. No bedsheets for him. Jeans, running shoes, a fresh white shirt, a little goatee – when you have the power, you don't need the props.

It all starts modestly enough, with Joe telling the group that on the previous night, their first in Jerusalem, he's had words with the Holy Spirit.

'I couldn't sleep,' he says, 'knowing that I was here in the City of God. I lay there, tossing and turning until the Holy Spirit just jumped out at me. Didn't He, Jackie?' Jackie, Joe's wife, has jeans too, and big hair. She waves to the congregation, tinkling her fingers as if she's playing the piano.

Joe continues. ' "I'm here! I'm here!" the Spirit of the Lord said. And exhausted as I was, He wouldn't let me be until I rose, and dressed, and walked out into the dark streets of Jerusalem after him. Did I know where I was in this strange and fearful place? Of course I didn't. Did the Holy

Spirit know where he was leading me? Of course He did! I walked for hours until I came to a high wall. And the Spirit said "Climb up!" and I climbed, and where do you think, folks, I found myself? Why, right here, where I stand before you now, beside the tomb where our dear Lord died and was resurrected. Such is his power and the strength of our belief in him. And look at me. I'm fresh as a daisy. Isn't that incredible?'

I tend to think that it is incredible, but who am I when it comes to faith? There are shouts of wonder and approval from Joe's congregation. 'Praise be!' 'Amen!' 'Hallelujah!'

There is a good deal more Christian boostering of various sorts, and then Pastor Joe turns to the main point of his sermon. You don't need proof, he hammers away at us, to believe in and receive eternal life.

'In any other religion you need proof. They'll take you to some place where they'll show you their leader's bones. You go to Mecca and you'll see the bones. You go to Lhasa and you'll see the bones. You go to Jerusalem and what do you see?' Pastor Joe swivels around, gun-fighter style, and points towards the tomb entrance in the wall behind him.

'Nothing!' he shouts in triumph. 'Nothing at all! Not a femur, not a collar bone, not the tiniest little pinky finger. And why is that? Because Jesus has risen! Yes! He is no longer here, but gone to heaven! How could there be bones? Who needs them? We have faith in God's love and the life everlasting instead.'

But Pastor Joe is not content with abstract theory alone. Just in case there's the slightest lingering doubt about what we see before us, he's happy to give a practical example as well. He's seen resurrection before, flesh and blood resurrection, with his very eyes. Why, acting as God's earthly agent, he's even performed it himself.

'Two times in my life, folks, two times I have assisted the Lord in bringing the dead back to this world. In fact it happens all the time in Africa, where I and my outreach team have often conducted God's work. The last time it was a boy lying sick in a hut. There were no doctors, no medicines for him, just witchcraft and mumbo-jumbo. He was covered in ju-ju beads, shaking with fever for days, when at last his bowels let go and he died. But the outreach team did not give up. Hands held together, we surrounded that boy on his bed, filthy and stinking and diseased as he was, and began to pray. And you know what? We broke the curse of darkness that surrounded him. In less than an hour he came to life again, and soon was well. He became the first Christian in his village, and I do believe today he is responsible for the lifting of gross ignorance and superstition there. Such, my friends, is the power of faith made manifest.'

At this point there is an interruption. An elderly woman, diminutive and blue-rinsed, works her way to the front of Pastor Joe's congregation and holds up her hand until he asks her what's wrong. Her ears are hurting, she replies. She can't hear what Pastor Joe is saying. Pastor Joe approaches her, takes her head in both hands, and stares intently into her face.

'There's an evil spirit blocking your ears,' he says so softly the rest of his flock can hardly hear. They lean forward. 'He doesn't want you hearing the word of God.'

Suddenly Pastor Joe shouts – 'WAAAH!' – and violently expels all the air in his lungs into the woman's face. People nearby jump back in consternation. The poor woman is so startled she nearly faints, and needs to be supported. But if she's not scared entirely out of her skin, the devil is. He is gone and will not return. We know that's so because Pastor Joe tells us. Dazed but smiling bravely, the woman receives a reassuring pat on the head and totters back to her place.

The show goes on and by the time Pastor Joe gets around to communion, not even his Christian ad-speak can surprise me. As he breaks out the wine and wafers he assures us that the blood in which we are about to partake is not like the blood of the Old Testament. No, that's just a cosmetic substance – it merely covers over sins. The blood we are about to receive is the purifying blood of the New Testament. Not only is it new, it's improved – it is the most powerful cleansing agent ever known to man, and guaranteed to permanently remove all stains of sin.

'Do this, then, in God's name,' says Pastor Joe, lifting his cup to his lips, 'and you and I shall have the peace that passes all understanding. Together we will share a thousand-year reign in Jerusalem.'

They're the last words I hear – I don't stay around for the end of the ceremony because, frankly, the idea of reigning a thousand years with Pastor Joe is not on. Just one minute more is too much for me. Even the tiniest chance of being once again hugged clean by sinless, stainless, devil-free Christians from Amarillo, Texas causes me to seek the exit gate and the street outside.

On a little mature reflection, in fact, Pastor Joe is quite enough to make me think about changing tack altogether. As I stroll down the sidewalk I am thinking of putting religion aside. The world of secular Israeli politics might not offer nearly as much peace as the peace which passes all under-standing. But at least it's got to be more understandable than the lunatic proceedings that unroll every day in the Garden Tomb. Then and there I make a mental note to see what Ashraf Noor might think of the idea.

Eight

I hunt Ashraf down in one of his favourite hideaways, the garden at the back of the Maison d'Abraham. Beyond the fountain and the rose bushes, near the little block where the staff washing machines are housed, rises a stand of tall, shady pines. There's no spectacular view of the Old City from here, but it is quiet and cool and on hot afternoons Ashraf likes to haul a garden-table here to write.

He is sitting at it now, his old tweed jacket hanging on the back of the chair, his bulky black leather case, open and bulging with papers, posed on the carpet of dry red pine needles beneath the table. I don't mind bothering him, for at the moment I can see he is more meditative than productive. Occasionally he bends his round, close-cropped moon-head over the lecture he is preparing on the aesthetic theory of the Jewish-German thinker, Walter Benjamin. But more often he sits back to contemplate the nuns as they hang their habits up on a washing-line to dry. Pegged at the shoulders, their arms hanging limp and empty, the habits flutter in the deep shade of the trees like pale ghosts. When it comes to nuns' underthings, Ashraf and I feign complete indifference and look away. But honestly, it's hard not to steal a peek from time to time. Where else but in Jerusalem are such mysteries brought to light?

Other mysteries, though, remain dim and unrevealed. I don't seem to have made any headway on religion in Jerusalem at all. In fact, I have to admit to Ashraf, religion makes me feel more clueless about the city than ever, and I'd like to duck the whole murky subject if I could. I still haven't consulted any of the Christian clerics on the list Father Michael offered me. I haven't phoned a single priest, pastor or patriarch, haven't dropped around presbytery, parsonage or priory. And if Christian divines are not perplexing enough, I tell my companion, Jewish and Muslim holy men seem even more distant and obscure. I'm finding it increasingly difficult to consider any clerics at all as guides to the hidden inner world of the city.

Ashraf slowly nods his head as I talk. The gesture seems to imply that perhaps I'm right, that this is not where I should be looking in the first place. But when I tell him I think that maybe I should make a new list of names, that politicians and other public figures in secular life might be a better route to understanding, he begins to move his head the other way. He's shaking it in doubt.

I can see he strongly believes there might be even more humbug and duplicity in Jerusalem's politicians than its evangelical pastors. In the end, before the next wash-cycle is over and new batches of nuns' habits are being hung out to dry, Ashraf has talked me into a compromise. I will talk politics and public life, but not with politicians. I will look instead to those who approach the reality of Jerusalem through the written word. But they won't be any old writers. They certainly won't be journalists. By this point I've had my fill of dissemblers, sophists and visionaries. They must speak the truth.

It's a tall order anywhere at all, much less in a city like Jerusalem. After some judicious debate I come up with two names: Jeremy Leigh, a British-born Jewish writer who decided to remake himself by moving to Jerusalem as a young man, and Yiftach Ashkenazy, a young Israeli-born novelist who instead has chosen through his writing to remake Jerusalem. I'd be happy to meet other writers as well, but Ashraf, never one for excess, urges a wait-and-see approach. He doesn't seem overly optimistic about my new undertaking – two outlooks on Jerusalem, he hints, might already be sufficiently confusing.

So just two outlooks, then, and only one café. When I phone Leigh and Ashkenazy they say they'd be happy to talk. Curiously, when I ask them to suggest a rendezvous, they both name the Café Kadosh, a place on the Jaffa Road.

Does this mean central Jerusalem has a limited choice of places where writers might congregate? It might, I conjecture as I walk to my first meeting. For despite its status as the *de facto* political capital of the most dynamic country in the entire region, Jerusalem's city centre feels distinctly provincial. Perhaps it's only that the streets are tired and somewhat paw-marked after the long, hot Middle Eastern summer. Or that since the late 1990s two Intifadas have acted as brutal brakes on business confidence and new investment in downtown premises. Or simply that modern Jerusalem is not that modern; restricted by city ordinance to constructing traditional facades of tailored local limestone, the city cannot look as up-to-date as other cities of steel and smoked glass.

In fact Ben Yehudah Street, the city's pedestrian mall and busiest thoroughfare, is lively enough; if its scuffed-up sidewalks, down-at-heel street-musicians and not-quite-fashionable shops give it a dowdy, parochial air, there are other signs of Jerusalem's engagement in a larger, global existence. There is an exotic contribution in the large numbers of Jewish American students, come to Jerusalem to renew their roots on year-long study programmes. There are French restaurants, Irish pubs, and New York-style delis where you can have your own bagel sandwich built to order from endless different fillings. And in Israelis themselves, also a composite built to order from a thousand different elements, there are also hints and suggestions of every continent in the world.

For all that, though, the centre of Jerusalem doesn't feel central to anything, and for a simple reason – it *isn't* central to anything. Jewish West Jerusalem is only half an entity, and it sits not in a middle, but on an edge. The city's other half, Arab East Jerusalem, lies across an invisible line of division that allows no organic connection to it. If the downtown area feels oddly inanimate and without vitality, it's because it lacks the essential element that creates urban vitality. In a city in which there is virtually no exchange between different parts of the population, there can be none of the dynamism that comes when human elements meet and combine in new and different ways. For all the drive of Israeli society, for all its physical energy and intellectual variety, Jerusalem remains an eerily static place with little to pull it forward.

Is there anything that *could* pull it forward? It's the first question I put to Jeremy Leigh after we've ordered coffee and pastry at a sun-splashed table near Kadosh's big picture-window. The café is trendier than most, and apart from a clientele of fashionable twenty-somethings has its share of academics and creative types. Leigh is nonetheless easy to pick out. He may be casually dressed, but there's nothing casual about his eyes. They are set beneath lustrous, dark eyebrows, two heavy half-moons that look like they've been stenciled onto his face in black ink. The regard below is quick, intense and incisive.

Leigh engages with my question immediately, and I'm pleased because he provides me with what I hoped he might: an attempt to sort out surface effect from underlying reality. Direct in manner, he has a restless, searching intelligence that likes to see things straight-on, no matter how dark they might look. And he sees no small amount of darkness ahead.

Of course the polls are right, he assures me. Most Israelis would be delighted to get rid of the problem of the Occupied Territories – they'd sign them away tomorrow. More telling, many would also be willing to abandon any claim to the Temple Mount and East Jerusalem. Not gracefully, perhaps, but because the price of not doing so is simply too high. But like many other Israelis willing to move forward, Leigh draws the line when it comes to the question of security. Jews will not give up anything at all, he affirms, unless they have absolute confidence that they are going to come out of a peace deal with Palestinians safe and unharmed. If there's peace, it's going to be peace on Israeli terms.

All that is obvious and has been gone over endlessly, Leigh says. But what's not so obvious and preoccupies him is how far Jewish insecurity extends past any possible agreement on the West Bank and Jerusalem.

'On a gut level,' he says, cutting into a slice of strudel with his fork, 'Arabs don't like us now, and whatever we might agree to they're not going to like us any more in the future. They would like to wake up one morning and discover that we are no longer there. We, too, would like to wake up one morning and discover that the Syrians and Jordanians and Egyptians are no longer there. But that's not going to happen.'

Leigh sips his coffee and is silent for a while, then frowns. 'Perhaps Zionism was a huge mistake. Perhaps Jews would have been better off in multi-cultural societies spread around the world. We might have been more creative, more productive as a people. But the point is now that there's no going back. If we don't want to discover that we have gone down a historical dead-end, that the world's twelve million Jews have made a mistake of unimaginable proportions, we have to carry on. We just have to make the most of it.'

He sips again, and sighs. 'In my darker moments I see no solution at all; we will always live in a state of tension with our neighbours. The question is, where does the dissonance that makes up Jerusalem become destructive, pushing its communities apart, and where is it potentially positive, making use of creative tensions so that change might come? It's hard to know just where that point is, but we have to make the effort to get on the proper side of it.'

As Jeremy Leigh continues to talk, I am stuck by the theme around which all his ideas and conclusions are organised – fear. Its not the kind of punctual fear which you deal with and move on; it's a deep, visceral, underlying fear which, while not at the forefront of every thought, never entirely goes away.

Leigh is the author of *Jewish Journeys*, a literary tour of Jewish heritage. In a work which sees journeying as the central thread of Jewish experience, he calls on biblical journeys, journeys of exile and return, journeys into the past, biographies of travellers and chronicles of voyages. With a focus on Jewish suffering and survival, Leigh uses travel as a metaphor to write about the dilemmas of being Jewish.

No journey, however, has been as crucial in developing his view of the world as his own journey. The son of a rabbi, he grew up in Stanmore, a London suburb which, he says, offered him neither romance nor revolution. Too small and staid to contain him, Stanmore was swapped for

Jerusalem, a move which eventually provided more excitement than he was looking for. In the mid-nineties, while jogging on the roadside not far from his home in the suburb of Talpiot, an Arab suicide-bomber detonated an explosive charge on a bus as it passed near by him. Leigh was uninjured in the blast, but the shock of the experience changed his outlook on the prospects of an eventual solution to the Arab-Israeli impasse.

'We came close to making another journey at that point,' he says ruefully, 'a journey of emigration from Israel. My wife wanted to leave – she was afraid of more bombs. If someone has to prove to the world that Jews are the idiots of history, she asked, why should it be us?'

Our conversation is temporarily suspended for a moment as a young woman enters the café and approaches Leigh. 'I saw your eyebrows through the window,' she says, and they both laugh. As well as conducting cultural tours in Europe, Leigh teaches Jewish cultural studies in Jerusalem, and this is one of his students. I watch their good-humoured banter as they discuss an upcoming outing; at the same time I am visualising a bus explosion, ambulances, blood on the sidewalk, body parts, the whole horror as Jeremy Leigh saw it. If it had been me, what would I have opted for, I wonder – fight or flight?

When his student is gone Leigh turns back to me and provides his own uncompromising answer. 'We stayed,' he says. 'The biggest mistake made by Arabs again and again is to think that suicide bombs can soften us up. They only harden us, and in the end make us determined we are not going to make any dangerous concessions to them again.'

Leigh continues to profess a reasonable, enlightened and liberal attitude even today. He's willing to seek political compromise. He believes an effort in relations between Arabs and Israelis should be made. The proof of his good will is right there in his personal life – at her private school, he tells me, his daughter is a member of a soccer team that regularly plays with teams of Arab children. But he acknowledges that it's largely symbolic, that he continues to be sensibly pessimistic. The apprehension remains profound and anchored.

'First let them deal with their crazies, the rocket-launchers and the bomb-vest detonators, and then we'll start talking,' he says of Palestinian demands for an independent state. And, he says, in a not-too-distant future the crazies may well be induced, for the sake of expediency, to enlist in mainstream political activity. Some sort of patched-up independence agreement, the product of international pressure exerted in an American-engineered overall regional peace agreement, might be hammered out. But real peace? That's tougher. Jeremy Leigh's peace is one that finally dissolves the gut-level anxiety that has been gnawing constantly at Israelis for the last sixty years. As yet, he's unconvinced that peace is a place towards which Jews will ever find themselves journeying.

Yiftach Ashkenazy is a traveller of sorts, too, and his voyages have made him far more familiar with violence than Jeremy Leigh. Regularly he also makes cultural journeys of his own, to a Jewish past which for systematic barbarity has no parallel in history. For the last few years Ashkenazy has worked as a guide at Yad Vashem, Jerusalem's Holocaust Museum. Where his overwhelmed charges gaze just once at the sights on offer there and walk away stunned, he lives with them repeatedly, day after day, until they have become part of him. The piles of broken eyeglasses from Treblinka, the Belgian death-camp railway car, the continuous-loop film of naked Jewish women, their hands held protectively over themselves, running through the sand dunes at Liepāja towards their own burial pits... all this he has seen a thousand times. Nor is his own personal past any less filled with violence. Barely thirty today, as a younger man he was a front-line soldier and saw active service in Lebanon and the West Bank.

Neither experience, though, has made him consider either fight or flight as options. Jeremy Leigh, a non-Israeli-born Jew, made a conscious decision through immigration to undertake his Jewish journey. But for Yiftach Ashkenazy journeys are much less of a paradigm of the Jewish experience. For the native-born *sabra* there is no choice. This has always been home and there's nowhere else to run. If Israelis are going to change anything at all, Ashkenazy is convinced, they must begin by changing themselves. Their journey will take place inside their own heads.

Ashkenazy is not at all as I picture him when we meet at Kadosh just a few hours later on the same day. He is not a soldier-patriot, tight-lipped and battle-hardened. Neither, even though his latest novel is entitled *Birkenau My Love,* is he the tortured, memory-of-the-nation obituarist I imagine a Holocaust guide might be. Instead he is open and enthusiastic and engaging, a tall, thin, pale young man with full lips, liquid eyes and a head that is already losing its hair. He speaks softly, and if Leigh has the searching, never-still eyes of the restless intellectual, this young man seems to see the world through his senses and emotions. Nor is he adverse to a little self-indulgent enjoyment. We sit outside Kadosh at a sidewalk table so he can smoke, and we drink strong, dark, German-style beer from half-litre steins.

But Ashkenazy is no soft touch – when it comes to attacking the conventions of Israeli society he is, in his own way, as uncompromising as Leigh. An iconoclast, he sees it as his moral duty to deflate all that is sacrosanct, taboo and untouchable in Israeli life – without shocking Israelis out of the complacent and self-deluding beliefs they've grown up with, he says, they'll never see the truth. When I tell him I'm having a hard time getting through to any kind of reality in Jerusalem's spiritual life, he says he's not surprised. In this city there is no single reality, spiritual or otherwise. What interests him, he says, is not reality at all. What grips him instead is the appearance of reality, and the ways in which that appearance is misused.

Ashkenazy stands somewhere out on the left, but quite where I can't see. Not even the pantheon of Israel's Old Guard left goes unscathed. When I mention Amos Oz, internationally-acclaimed doyen of Israeli letters and a peace activist for more than two decades, Ashkenazy is dismissive.

'Oz supported the second war in Lebanon,' he says. 'as did our other prestigious writer of the left, David Grossman. Later Grossman lost a son in that war – only then did he become critical of its conduct. Oz talks peace, but peace on our conditions; when it doesn't happen he turns around and supports the right. When it comes to Nobel prizes it's literature rather than peace he's looking at.'

Épater la bourgeoisie – is that Ashkenazy's role as a young lion, ambitious writer and critical representative of a new generation? Where, I wonder as he continues to attack the hypocrisy of the Israeli establishment – politicians, media personalities, military leaders and religious figures as well as older writers – does this deep vein of anti-authoritarian rebellion spring from?

In the West, and in America especially, it is difficult to criticise Israel publicly without risking howling accusations of anti-Semitism from pro-Israeli lobbies. Our discreet silence extends even to our choice of language – we are sometimes hesitant to use the noun 'Jew' at all, proffering instead the adjective 'Jewish' in describing an Israeli. It's as if we're afraid to be seen trading in racial insults or dirty words. This is the hold our past and our collective sense of guilt maintains over us. In Israel itself, of course, it's different. On all questions of Jewishness, Jews criticise other Jews, openly and often viciously. Barely a day goes by without an article in one of the country's daily papers questioning the most fundamental principles of what it means to be a Jew. But in one as young as Yiftach Ashkenazy I can only imagine some traumatic origin, and one that is personal rather than ideological, for such self-assured and critical convictions.

And as Ashkenazy continues in a monologue that centres more and more on attitudes to conflict with Arabs, the wellspring for his rejection of Israeli morality becomes clearer – it is war itself. As another tray of beer arrives, Ashkenazy describes for me his youth in Karmiel, the setting for his first novel, *Tales of a Dying Town*. It is a new, purpose-built town east of Haifa, a place surrounded by old Arab villages that were absorbed into Israel and Israeli life at independence. Growing up there, Ashkenazy and his friends saw it as quiet, conservative, and provincial – they only wanted to get away. But it was when they did get away, as conscripts in the Israeli Defense Force, that Ashkenazy says he began to recognize his hometown's real nature. 'Karmiel may look like a sleepy, peaceful place,' he says as he demolishes the frothy head on his beer and wipes his mouth. 'It was only after military service in Lebanon and the Occupied Territories that I realized that Karmiel too is an occupied territory, with all kinds of hidden tensions and conflicts of its own.'

The novel is highly critical of the Israeli army and military service and what it does to young men. Even the left and the self-proclaimed peace sympathisers, Ashkenazy tells me, are guilty of hypocrisy. 'They go to war, they fight and they kill, and afterwards, when they return home, they say it's very bad, that Israel is living an unavoidable tragedy. Nobody says what being in the army is like, what happens to young men who kill.

'In fact it's exciting.' He puts another cigarette to his lips and lights it. 'When you are twenty years old and in the company of other twenty-year-olds there is something you find in killing – something satisfying. This is what war does to young men.' He says it with such simplicity and quiet confidence that I'm sure he knows what he is talking about. 'It is more important for soldiers to recognise and admit this than to say they feel sorry afterwards. This is how war deforms Israeli society – it brutalises whole generations. We must know this, and publicly say exactly how it works, even if nobody here even wants to think about it. If we don't learn this lesson, we will never get along with the rest of the world. There are so many things badly wrong with Israeli society, and the world must know that we are going to change.'

Yiftach Ashkenazy is making his own personal effort to ensure that the world knows that Israel *can* change. Not long ago, in the company of half a dozen other Israeli writers, he took part in European Union-sponsored ten-city book tour of Germany. Of all the European languages, he tells me with a smile, Israeli writers have their best chance of getting their message to the outside world in German. It is thanks, once again, to the German-Israeli 'special relationship', a link emerging from the past efforts of one group to wipe the other group from the face of the earth.

How did the tour work out? I ask. 'Very well,' answers Ashkenazy. He considers his glass. 'It's where I developed a taste for beer. I was very nervous at first about the book-reading and questions afterwards, but I discovered a trick – you have a stein or two before you go on. Not too much, of course, but enough for a Jew on his own to face a room of 200 Germans.'

In fact, Ashkenazy insists, he had some wonderful conversations with older men, ex-Nazis who'd never before had a chance to talk to the objects of their former obsessions. It was good for him, too, he says, in dealing with other concepts of victims and victimisers — the ones that live on in Israeli today.

At first I find it hard to imagine this good-willed young man trading army reminisces with hoary old Nazis, but in the end I see it. What I like most about Yiftach Ashkenazy is his ability, while confronting the deepest, least attractive parts of human nature head on, to celebrate humanity. Jerusalem is not a normal city – Ashkenazy is saying that it, too, like an older Germany, is a place deformed and riven by its own religious and racial obsessions. But somewhere in Jerusalem's life he also manages to find ordinary life and make the most of it. A few years ago, he tells me, Jerusalem's Gay Pride parade, its most blatant symbol of the non-religious life, was cancelled because of virulent Ultra-Orthodox protest. Furious, he says, he considered moving to Tel Aviv for good. 'In the end I stayed. I cursed the city with every name I could think of, but I stayed.' He loves and hates the place at the same time, he says, but could never give it up.

And now, some time after dark, Yiftach Ashkenazy guides me on my own mini-tour, not of Yad Vashem, but of downtown Jerusalem. It's to show me that the city, for all its wounded and incomplete nature, has a capacity for regeneration.

He takes me down narrow alleys to Katz Square, a backstreet alternative to Zion Square, the better-known rendezvous of night-time Jerusalem. Like debaters in an amphitheatre, city teenagers are seated here on a series of step-like concrete tiers, talking in the dim streetlight and smoking Arab water-pipes. 'Here,' says Ashkenazy, smiling. 'I'll show you one of Jerusalem's tried-and-true seduction techniques.' He places me on a certain spot on the square's pavement and points me to face a central section of the rising tiers.

'Now talk,' he says. I talk, and by some weird law of acoustic dynamics my voice comes back to me with a fraction of a second's delay. It's an odd effect, like listening to electronic feedback without headphones. 'It's useful for impressing girls when you need to impress them,' Ashkenazy chuckles. It's not exactly high-tech Tel Aviv clubbing, he admits. But this is, after all, Jerusalem.

He leads me down another quiet alley to a low, broken wall and, on the far side of it, the Mamillah cemetery, a Muslim burial ground stranded in Jewish Jerusalem since independence. 'This is where Jerusalem kids come to have sex for the first time after getting drunk on Katz Square,' he says, pointing at the stone grave-markers that stretch away into the gloom. As a rendezvous for young lovers' trysts it sounds a bit grim. For Ashkenazy, it's simply proof of life's irrepressibility. We ourselves do not get drunk on Katz Square, but go to a bar instead, a place a bit like an Amsterdam café from the 1970s, and have another beer. But it's too quiet and only gets going after midnight, so we end up in a place called the Stardust. There's a crowd there, young and noisy, watching a wide-screen TV basketball game between Jerusalem and Tel Aviv.

'I don't have to tell you our two cities do not love each other,' Ashkenazy says over more beer and loud, hurled shouts of insult and encouragement. 'Basketball, unlike clubbing, is something Jerusalem is actually quite good at, so we tend to get excited.' He's enjoying the noise, the simple, strong emotions that have nothing to do with race, or religious faith, or murderous conflict.

'Do you like football?' he asks me a little while later, after a triumphant Jerusalem victory has nearly brought the house down. 'Have you heard of Jerusalem Appolon? No?'

It's a fourth-division Israeli team and not very good, he says. But some Jerusalem fans are so disgusted with the money scandals and corruption of larger teams that they have gotten together and collectively financed their own team. 'You must come and see them; they are getting better,' he says with conviction. 'They draw 5,000 fans a match, an unheard-of number in Jerusalem. I own some shares in Appolon myself. One day they might be champions.'

Israeli football is not my forte, but I've had enough beer that by this stage Appolon, sight unseen, sound very good already. I happily insist that soon they *will* be champions. The real cause of my happiness, of course, stems from something larger. In the company of basketball and football players I have managed to outrun the men in beards – all of them, Jewish, Muslim and Christian. Yiftach Ashkenazy's enthusiasm for life's ordinary little pleasures has helped me escape, for a couple of hours at least, the incessant demands that faith places on Jerusalem. As I leave the Stardust to walk home through the Old City, I feel more moral uplift than any religious service could possibly provide.

But the elation gradually fades as I cross the Mount of Olives and in a midnight darkness approach the Maison d'Abraham. There is a comment that keeps echoing in my head. It's the novelist's admission, made hours before, that he no longer seeks reality in Jerusalem. As I stand before the gate, weaving slightly as I press the buzzer for the night watchman to let me in, it is a preoccupying thought.

Have I spent the last weeks chasing after phantoms, seeking answers to questions for which there is no real basis? Do appearances so crowd out reality in Jerusalem that it cannot be found? The more I think about it the more alarming the idea becomes: I cannot find the defining note I am looking for in Jerusalem because from the beginning it might as well not exist. Incessant as all those demands of faith on the city are, they lead to nothing coherent. As I make my way down the drive, along empty, echoing hallways and up stone stairs to my rooftop room I feel my own faith in myself scattering out behind me like so much seed from a grain-bag. By the time I finally climb dizzily into bed there is only one certainty I can count on, and it's a Dominican one. It's Soeur Marta – she'll be after me in the morning for not telling her I'd be out for dinner.

Nine

The day dawns, as it has dawned in Jerusalem every day since my arrival, serene and cloudless. The nuns are as bright at breakfast as ever, and even Soeur Marta forgives my minor transgressions. Everything looks new and remade in the morning light.

At this time of day the old, worn stones of Jerusalem themselves radiate an improbable freshness. There's a kind of clean, regenerated newness to them that suggests they've just been quarried, that they are innocent of the the long, dim past. Is it the clarity of the thin air, the dryness of the high desert hills that makes for such an effect? The Jerusalem light, with qualities both hard and soft, is like light nowhere else. At noon it causes each contour, each edge of hill and building, to stand out in sharp, hair-line distinction. At dawn and dusk the sun is different, touching the city in gently suffused horizontal light until the entire place glows, soft and rich. Generation after generation Jerusalem may fail to resolve its other differences, but these are contrasts that every day it negotiates with natural and nonchalant ease.

If only I could do as much. Wandering into town, not quite sure of where I'm going or why, I feel as if I've come to a dead end. I've tried everything – the Mount of Olives; Jewish markets and Arab markets; the different quarters of the Old City; godly places like Mea Shearim; godless places like Ma'ale Adumim; the Dome of the Rock, the Wailing Wall, the Garden Tomb, the cafes and bars of the new city. I've talked to priests and pilgrims, shopkeepers and soldiers, writers, academics and cranks. Some are desperate, others bursting with righteous self-confidence. None of them have given me the feeling I'm any closer to knowing what lies at the heart of Jerusalem. Are there other city places I should have gone? By this point I know there is not one, neither gate nor garden nor grotto, that is going to enlighten me any further. I'm at an impasse, and don't know how to proceed.

Walking aimlessly outside Old City walls on the edge of East Jerusalem, I end up at a building on Sultan Suliman Street. What draws me is its eclectic style, a look that's unusual for this part of the world. Built of white limestone and topped by a high hexagonal tower, this is the city's Archaeological Museum. I enter it, if for no other reason that a place concerned with beginnings suits my mood just now. Having failed to understand what Jerusalem is all about, I feel compelled to start all over again.

Built around a garden and central reflecting pool, it's a superb structure, Byzantine, Islamic and Art Deco all at the same time. Erected at vast expense by John D. Rockefeller just before the Crash of 1929, the building is also an unsuspected storehouse of treasures. There's a portion of the Dead Sea Scrolls, those oldest codices of ancient Judaic life. There are gorgeous, ninth-century wooden polychrome panels from the Al-Aqsa mosque. There are intricately carved Crusader stonework lintels from the portico of the Church of the Holy Sepulcher. No matter that they derive from different traditions – there's nothing jarring in seeing them brought together here. Considered as component parts linked together in a whole, they only add to and compliment each other. They sit together in this building, itself a blend of harmony and proportion, in calm resolution.

Where else in Jerusalem can you find such synthesis? But no matter how happy a mix this is, no matter where in the museum I stroll or what I look at, I cannot find much satisfaction in it. Attempts at finding similar synthesis myself have brought me to the edge of my very own Crash.

Is Jerusalem all that different from other places in the world? Even in cities of the most extreme variety and contrast you can find, somewhere beneath the surface, balance, correspondence and connection between disparate elements. From a hundred different voices, opinions, and points of view you'll be able, sooner or later, to draw out a single, coherent reality.

With a little persistence most places begin to make some sense. But not here.

I abandon walking through the galleries, and sit overlooking the clear, reflecting pool at the heart of the building. And when it too refuses to give me any answers, showing me nothing but the empty sky above, I make my way out of the doors and across the city.

More despondent than ever, I cross from East to West Jerusalem where the old pre-unification transit point, the Mandelbaum Gate, once stood. There is no added value in retracing routes I have followed a dozen times before, but I walk on towards King George Street. The noonday sun is hot and the glare off the sidewalk bright. Finally, in the not-so-cosmopolitan heart of West Jerusalem, I give up and come to a halt among the travel guides, fictions and histories of Steimatsky's Bookshop.

It is blessedly cool inside and I move among the shelves with relief, grateful not just for air-conditioning but the familiarity of books. I cast my eyes over the titles. Unlike the city just outside the door, this is a world I'm comfortable with. There's escape here. Then I spot, close to the floor in the politics and biography shelves, a small, thin, hardcover volume by Amos Oz. It is titled *How to Cure a Fanatic*. Thinking of my conversation with Yiftach Ashkenazy the previous day, I pull it out for a quick flip-through.

And immediately, from the very first page, and heedless of the young writer's disregard for the older, I am hooked. Instead of riffling, I take myself off to a quiet corner for the next three hours; unaware of the passage of time, I read the book from cover to cover. And when I have finished and raise my head to find myself once again in Jerusalem, it is no longer quite the same place. Nor, in the way I look at the city, am I quite the same pilgrim in it.

The little book is a revelation for me. In choosing to assess Israel's prospects for peace Oz has done nothing new – Steimatsky's shelves groan with the theme. But in writing in such a calm, simple, focused manner, in writing not about conflict, but how to perceive conflict, Oz forces me to examine how I've perceived Jerusalem from the beginning.

We labour under the illusion, says Oz, that it is religion which lies at the heart of the Arab-Israeli problem. Wrong, he pronounces. This is not a battle of faith or ideology. This is not a war between two irreconcilable cultures. This is, very simply, a turf war, a squabble over real estate.

In many ways Jews and Arabs in the Middle East, Oz insists, are the same. They both have historical claims to the same patch of land, and both are valid. Both peoples have been exploited and kicked around, the first subjected to prejudice and atrocity by European society for centuries, the second to false promises and arbitrary division by the British empire. Both Israelis and Palestinians are products of cultures that see themselves as victimised, and as a result both are self-righteous, paranoid and insecure. That makes it all the harder for them to see the truth of their situation and the only solution to it. It lies in compromise. This small patch of land must be split up and shared.

The idea that Jews and Arabs might eventually come to the realisation that love conquers all is nonsense, says Oz. Old enemies like these are not going to suddenly repent and throw their arms around each other. Nor is there any need to. What is required instead is a pragmatic and realistic attitude, a willingness to give up what before has seemed wholly impossible to give up. It can only be a very difficult, very painful process, and there is no way around the problems to be overcome.

Oz likens the conditions for division to the most challenging of divorces – one in which former husband and wife will remain on in the same small apartment because there is there is nowhere else to go. They will live in Room A and Room B. Who will get the kitchen? he asks. How will they agree over the use of the bathroom? Only one thing is certain, says Oz. To successfully carry out such difficult compromises both sides must change. They must adopt different attitudes, and move away from that fanatic insistence which has dominated the conflict from the beginning: the uncompromising view of each side that it is entirely right and the other is entirely wrong.

The minutes tick by, the afternoon wears on. There is a change of staff. Customers come and customers go. Occasionally I have to move a step to left or right to let browsers browse. But throughout I remain riveted to the page. Of course most outsiders to the conflict and many Israelis, too, argue the need for a two-state solution. But what impresses me about Oz is his utterly calm and common-sense attitude, his refusal to be side-tracked by the emotional passion that for sixty years and more has radiated outward from Jerusalem. As a place where religious considerations must be added to claims of land ownership, it can only be the most difficult part of the problem. But there is nothing mechanistic about Oz's view – he takes a human, individual approach to the essential problem of rigid and unwavering conviction. There are ways around fanaticism, he says, attitudes we can promote to help cure the fanatic who resides in others and in ourselves.

One of them is humour. Oz has never met a fanatic with a sense of humour, he says, for a simple reason – humour requires an ability to see oneself as others do, and to laugh about it. Another is imagination. A capacity to imagine the other, to put yourself in his place, says Oz, immediately extinguishes the desire to kill.

Oz tells the story of a friend of his, a poet, who on a taxi ride strikes up a conversation with the Israeli driver. The driver is an Arab-hater who says that all Arabs, whoever they are, should be killed. Men, women, soldiers, civilians... the lot. They do not deserve to live. The poet, a gentle man, asks the driver who exactly would do all this killing. It's not a question the driver has ever considered. It doesn't matter who does it, he replies; the important thing is that it's done. But the poet insists, obliging the man behind the wheel to see that it might be he himself required to carry out such exactions. What if it were you? he says. And what if you came into an Arab family's house at night, and in that house a babies' bedroom? Could you murder the children as they lay sleeping in their beds?

Forced to face such a picture, the taxi-driver cannot bring himself to say yes. All he can offer, turning to the poet after a long, thoughtful silence, is remonstration. 'You are a very cruel man,' he says at last. But the cruelty he has confronted, of course, is his own.

It's a wonderful story, and one that emphasises the kind of personal empathy that Oz stresses throughout. If he has learned to use imagination, he says, it's because he's had to. Earning a living as a writer of fiction, he imagines himself as someone else every day of his life. Not everyone writes, but everyone can do this same thing through their daily relations with the world. Each individual must become what he or she is naturally made to be, says Oz. We individuals are not islands, wholly cut off from our history, our culture and race. Nor are we continents, wholly merged with and part of that exclusive existence. Instead, we are peninsulas. Sometimes we turn inward and act in common cause with others like us, and sometimes we face outward to meet and join with the larger world.

When I come to the last page of *How to Cure a Fanatic* I continue to stand there for some time. I am thinking about Jerusalem. There is no need, I realize at last, to stalk the corridors of archaeology museums. I don't have to discuss the minutiae of Status Quo agreements with Christian clergymen. It's not necessary to thrash things out with hard-line members of the Knesset. I have filled my eyes and ears with plenty enough already – the ordinary sights and sounds of the city. What I need is my own understanding, my own calm and common-sense approach to Jerusalem. What's essential from the beginning, Amos Oz maintains, is perspective – the ability to see through to the simple truth at the centre of things.

And the simple truth about the city that's evaded me all these weeks is this – there is nothing at the centre of Jerusalem. We'd like to imagine that here, in a city which time and again proclaims itself the world's spiritual nexus, all things might come together. But this is not a place where life overlaps at the middle – here separate things gather on separate peripheries, and the centre is dead and neglected. It is an empty void. It's not quite a vacuum, because a vacuum carries no sound, and Jerusalem is one of the noisiest places on earth. There are many voices here, all of them vying for attention, all interpreting one particular version of the city.

So it doesn't matter how hard you listen. Other cities may have signature notes; Jerusalem doesn't. The fact is that there is no single, unified narrative that contains everyone's Jerusalem, no concert of voices that together offer any coherent idea of the whole. And so there is no possibility of understanding Jerusalem in one way. A splintered, fragmented city can only be understood in a splintered, fragmented way.

It's a realisation that comes as a relief. I can stop beating my head against the wall. If there's no coherent whole making up Jerusalem, then I'm free to pursue the fractured, free-floating bits of existence that do make up the city. It's a change I look forward to.

There are other changes as well. So preoccupied have I been that I only discover them after slipping Amos Oz's little volume back into the shelves. Just outside Steimatsky's Bookshop, Jerusalem lies beneath a torrential downpour. Where before the sky was blue and endless it is now low and black. Where streets were dust-dry and sun-filled, they are now dim and drumming with rain. Where pedestrians once sauntered, they now streak, newspapers over their heads, from one place of cover to another. After months of unending heat and glare, the autumn rains have at last arrived in Jerusalem.

It's coming down hard. Exiting Steimatsky's, I stand outside in the doorway of a small jeweler's shop. I gaze at rain pelting down onto the top of white Jerusalem taxis, see shop-lights reflected in shiny black tarmac, watch a nearby kiosk make quick sales of cheap Chinese umbrellas to Jerusalemites surprised by rain. And when it becomes clear that it's not going to let up anytime soon, I step out into the deluge and begin walking home.

In West Jerusalem, water flows in horizontal torrents in the gutter. In the Old City, it goes vertical, cascading noisy and splashing down long flights of stone steps. It forces shopkeepers to haul down hangers loaded with sopping dresses, remove crates of rain-spattered crucifixes, push broom-handles up into plastic awnings heavy and stretched with accumulated rainwater. Bedraggled groups of pilgrims mill in trinket shops, unable to leave, obliged to buy. But the rain doesn't bother me. It's not quite immersion in the River Jordan, but there is something purifying in this drenching. If I'm soaked to the skin by the time I reach the Maison d'Abraham, I am also elated – I feel I can start anew.

So when, at dinner in the refectory that evening, I explain my afternoon at Steimatsky's to Ashraf Noor, I am just the slightest bit disappointed. It is as if Ashraf has been patiently waiting for this all along.

'Ah ha,' he says, nodding in less than astonished acknowledgment and spooning up soup at the same time, 'at last we are getting somewhere.'

But where in fact am I getting? All I know now is that there is no over-riding truth, nothing to be pulled from the city as a whole. And if I cannot see the whole, I ask him, which of a thousand separate bits should I be looking at?

Ashraf finishes his soup, dabs at his mouth with a napkin, and gives a smile of thanks to the volunteer who collects our bowls. And then, as he always does, he urges patience and reflection. Could it be, he suggests, that I've been trying too hard? Maybe I shouldn't try at all. Instead of running off in all directions to find Jerusalem, I could try letting Jerusalem come and find me.

But there is something Ashraf adds then that comforts me. Maybe I haven't got it completely wrong from the beginning. When I first arrived I felt the need to step back a little for that all-important perspective. Perhaps, he says now, I haven't stepped back far enough. Could it be that perspective also means seeing Jerusalem not in isolation, but as a product of something larger? Can any city be properly seen without also seeing all the things – the lives, the places, the conflicts and contradictions – that surround it on every side? To get a real idea of what Jerusalem is made of, Ashraf suggests, perhaps I must leave it altogether.

Ten

The autumn rains continue to fall, and three or four soggy evenings go by before Ashraf Noor and I are joined at dinner by a new arrival at the Maison d'Abraham. Sylvia is an occasional pilgrim in Jerusalem and a full-time pilgrim at home. She works, she tells us, in a religious hospice in the city of Lourdes in southern France. In an institution of more more than 500 beds, her own duties involve looking after pilgrims whose needs are the greatest of all. For the chronically ill and severely disabled Lourdes is a last, desperate resort.

How utterly and unrelievedly grim, I think, and as we settle down to dinner my mind is full of wheel-chairs and arthritic fingers, back-braces and colostomy bags. But it isn't long before I begin to feel ashamed and begin to revise my opinion of this woman's life. There is nothing grim or institutional about Sylvia. In her late thirties, she is quick of mouth and mind, a bright, funny, unconventional woman with mobile expressions and sudden bursts of amusement that light up her face. She's a great joker, and immediately she and Ashraf have established an ongoing, teasing banter between themselves that makes depressing conversation at the table impossible.

From the beginning Sylvia defends her elderly charges. Far from depressing her, they actually rejuvenate her – they arrive in Lourdes tired and dispirited and leave revived and stimulated. It's no miracle, Sylvia says. She is sure in her Catholic faith, but the dramatic change has nothing to do with the the divine presence, and everything to do with the human one

– when you see people in far worse situations than you doing their best to cope, you do your best too. This may be true, but I suspect it's Sylvia who's the biggest coper of all, and a bright point in the pilgrims' lives.

Sylvia has not come to Jerusalem to get away from it all. From time to time she returns to Israel to tour the Holy Land near Galilee, a place she's grown fond of. She also comes to visit a childhood friend who has been living in Jerusalem for several years. We will be meeting Pierre very soon, she says – she's invited him to dinner at the Maison d'Abraham. But now, with the first course already cleared and Pierre still missing she's afraid he might have had car trouble.

Earlier in the day Sylvia and her friend drove out to a ruined monastery in the desert near Jericho, and even if Pierre took the precautions necessary to desert travel the ongoing rain gave them trouble – in the *wadis* they bogged down badly in heavy, water-soaked sand. On the road back to Jerusalem the engine stalled and died twice, due, thinks Sylvia, to a clogged air filter. Now she sighs, theatrical but only half-joking, with the air of someone who has borne unnecessary tribulations with good patience. You can see she is happy to have returned in one piece.

Pierre, when he turns up a few moments later, is not the brawny, desert-driving roustabout I imagine him. In fact he's not just plain Pierre, but Frère Pierre. Tall, thin, pale, and none too robust, he is a monk dressed in the full regalia of the Russian Orthodox Church. As he enters the refectory his black robes, flowing, voluminous and soaked with rainwater, swish rhythmically against the stone floor. His hair, long and tied at the back of his head in the Orthodox ecclesiastic manner, runs down between his shoulders in a pony-tail. Framed beneath a tight black brimless hat that pins back his ears, his face is suitably ascetic. His cheeks are bony and prominent, his beard wispy, and the eyes behind their wire-rimmed glasses are narrow and half-closed as if in permanent contemplation. There is something more than simply Slavic, something eastern and born of the distant Asian steppe in the aspect and manner of this Russian monk.

Which is all the more surprising, in that Frère Pierre, for all his devotion to the Russian Orthodox Church, has never been anywhere near

Russia. He's a Breton, born and raised, as was Sylvia, in a tiny inland farming village near Rennes. They've known each other all their lives. If rural Brittany, I think as introductions are made, is disproportionately represented at the Maison d'Abraham, it's because it is the most traditional and fervently Catholic of all the regions of France. It only makes me wonder why Frère Pierre has abandoned Brittany for Jerusalem and an Orthodox church.

But at dinner it's Sylvia who's asking the questions. Having spent time with a Russian monk when he's not a Russian monk but a small French schoolboy tends, I imagine, to minimize the sacerdotal drama of swishing black robes. What Sylvia wants to know is what's happened to their vehicle.

It is no more the robust, all-terrain 4-by-4 I have pictured than Frère Pierre is a desert adventurer. Instead it's an aging Volkswagen Jetta belonging to Frère Pierre's church and shared by all the monks who live there. Mechanically dodgy, infrequently driven, it has been handled for most of the twenty-five years of its existence by men not entirely of this earth. Innocent in the arts of the oil change and the brake-job, they know far more about praying for things than fixing them. When I ask Frère Pierre what measures he took to ensure safety in the back-stretches of the Judean desert, Sylvia hoots with laughter – Pierre has deflated the tyres for better traction in the sand. He has read about such techniques and hotly defends them, but admits he may have let out just a little too much air. The trouble now is that on the drive back to Jerusalem the steel rims of the Jetta's wheels may have damaged the tyre-walls. All this is a little preoccupying for Sylvia, for together she and Pierre are planning to use the Jetta once more for a trip north to Galilee.

For all the car-talk – Sylvia seems to know a lot more about these things than her friend – I can see that Frère Pierre is articulate, eager in his embrace of Russian Orthodoxy, and quite happy to talk about being a monk. It's a rare combination, and I would like to talk more. But I am hesitant at dinner, especially as Frère Pierre seems to be enjoying his evening out. The Russian liturgy is superb, he says, the church unparalleled in beauty, and the Russian monks and nuns who serve there exceptionally devoted. The food, though, he admits, is unremittingly lousy – meals revolve mostly around dried, smoked fish and boiled potatoes. How can I ask Frère Pierre about Russian Orthodox dogma and theology when I see him so thoroughly enjoying French Catholic roast chicken and *petit pois*?

It is only at the end of the meal that I ask him which monastery he belongs to – if he is preparing to leave on foot it cannot be too far. His answer surprises me. He lives on the pine-forested grounds of the Church of Mary Magdalene just ten minutes away across the Mount of Olives. It is one of the most beautiful places in Jerusalem, and I have often wanted to visit it.

Frère Pierre seems to know what I'm thinking. 'Come and see me tomorrow,' he says, collecting a dripping overcoat from a corner near the door of the Maison d'Abraham. Outside it is raining harder than ever. 'But don't come to Mary Magdalene,' the monk adds as he slips the coat on. The nuns are jealous of their privacy. 'Instead,' he says, 'meet me up the hill in the Tomb of the Prophets.'

It seems an odd spot to meet. Who, ghouls aside, fixes rendezvous in subterranean tombs?

But Frère Pierre insists. 'It's a good place – you can't get wet underground. Besides, I've got to be there tomorrow. In fact I'm there all day, every day.'

'Why?' I ask. Frère Pierre is being just a little bit morbid.

'It's simple,' he replies with a smile. 'I am the Keeper of the Tomb.'

And with that he bids us farewell and steps out into the dark, rainy night.

The Tomb of the Prophets and the job that goes with it are not as gloomy as they sound. The burial place near the top of the Mount of Olives, a prime site for internment in ancient Jerusalem, is indeed dry, a series of deep, inter-connecting tunnels reached from the surface by a stone-carved stairway. And if there isn't much light down there – Pierre operates with the aid of long, thin wax tapers brought up from the church – there is at least company. Haggai, Zachariah and Malachi might not be the most famous prophets in a city replete with doomsayers, but tradition attaches a burial site to few other Old Testament figures. So at least a couple of times a day Frère Pierre, his hand held protectively around a flame continually threatened by draughts of air, walks visitors through the tombs.

We meet at the bottom of the stairs, and the pony-tailed monk lights tapers for each of us to show me around the galleries. As soon as we have turned a corner or two all hints of daylight and the outside world disappear. By candlelight we inspect, one after another, the rock-hewn chambers in which the bodies of the prophets once lay. Frère Pierre is talking to me about conceptions of fate and the afterlife in Jewish ritual burial as it existed long ago. But my mind is not on it. I'm more interested in my own immediate fate, for as we round another corner there are stronger, more sudden gusts of air. Abruptly our candles are snuffed out. Pierre has left the matches at the bottom of the stairs, and in the pitch black the tomb complex's rough walls and uneven floors are difficult to negotiate. It takes an eternity to work our way back.

In the middle of the darkness my shins hit hard on an unmoving object. I suppress an obscenity and instead, in a level and controlled voice, ask the monk a question. If the Church of Mary Magdalene is the custodian of the Tomb, couldn't it see its way to laying on an electric torch or two? It would make life a good deal easier.

But Frère Pierre is not interested in an easy life. Torches have been offered to him numerous times, he replies. It's he who has refused them. They would only ruin the mystery, the world of flickering light and shadow that makes these tombs so alluring. Frère Pierre, in a picture gradually emerging from the obscurity, is not just a divine; he is also a romantic, a man who values imagination above practicality.

Mystery, it will eventually become apparent to me, is a key word in Frère Pierre's lexicon, not just in his subterranean working day, but in his deepest religious beliefs as well. Mystery is the reason he left the Catholic church and the French countryside in the first place. For all the depth of Brittany's spirituality, it was not deep enough for him.

Back at the stairs, we light new tapers and sit on the bottom step. The stone is frigid under my backside, but Frère Pierre doesn't appear to notice the cold at all. More interested in the life of the spirit, he seems to exist in some place beyond such material concerns. He is explaining the more important matter of faith, and why he traded his in.

His father, he tells me, as he drips wax onto the stone and fixes his candle in place, was a devout Catholic, a farmer, and deeply attached to the land. He kept sheep, prayed, never travelled, and expected his own son to be a keeper of sheep as well. As childhoods go, it all sounds pastorally biblical to me. But in its spiritual scope it was a life too small, too restricted for Pierre. It was too restricted, in fact, for the entire community, which in some strange and unexpected gust of divine wind was carried away to new and different pastures. The whole village, Frère Pierre tells me, underwent a mass conversion to Eastern Orthodoxy.

In an age of doubt and cynicism, in a country that can barely hold on to the few genuine Catholic believers it has left, it seems an astonishing event. 'A mass conversion, out in the heart of Catholic Brittany?' I marvel. 'How many, exactly, converted?'

'Seven,' replies Frère Pierre grandly.

'Only seven?' I ask, a little let down. 'That doesn't sound like very many.'

'It depends on the size of the village,' Frère Pierre reasons. 'It was virtually the entire congregation.'

'But *Orthodoxy*? Why?' I continue. There are a dozen more popular spiritual choices on the French market these days, everything from California-style Buddhism to the Church of Scientology.

'Perhaps because we're Bretons,' Frère Pierre replies a little mournfully. 'We longed for deeper mystery.'

I can see this is not a conversation that is going to resolve my deepest theological questions in the next five minutes. In less time than that my backside will be a frozen block of ice, so I suggest we climb the stone stairs to the world of light and warmth. Pierre looks at his watch and blows out the tapers – it's almost time for his lunch at the monastery at the bottom of the Mount anyway. Outside it has stopped raining and the sun has appeared. After being underground it makes my eyes ache. The view, though, is magnificent from up here, and after Frère Pierre locks the tomb's iron gates we start down the hill, gazing at Jerusalem spread out glistening before us after the rain.

We don't get too far down before Frère Pierre pulls me off the road for a particularly famous view of the city. Dominus Flevit is a better-known site than the Tomb of the Prophets, and apart from its own tombs has a church, Franciscan-built, with a wide, panoramic esplanade in front of it. I admire the city from here, but am distracted by a large flag, swaying in the breeze, that's flying from a pole by the church. Printed bright red on white, it shows the Jerusalem Cross. One large cross with four smaller crosses lodged in its interstices, it's the same symbol I bought in olive-wood from a small, angry Christian woman a few days after my arrival. Zipped into a pocket of my day-pack and forgotten, I have it still. I thought it just a symbol of the city, I tell Frère Pierre. What is it doing flying on a flag here, and what does it mean?

'It *is* a symbol of the city,' says Pierre, gazing upwards. 'But it is also the emblem of the Franciscan Order. In the 14th century the Franciscans were named by Rome as *Custodia Terra Sanctae*, the guardians of all Christian sites in Palestine, and they adopted the Jerusalem Cross as the Custody's device. All over the Holy Land, wherever Franciscans are in charge of churches and sacred sites, you'll find this cross.'

But Pierre, devoted Orthodox monk that he is, is not going to give up the Jerusalem Cross to the Franciscans too easily. 'Of course, it's a very old symbol,' he says. 'It predates the Franciscan presence by centuries. It was popular during the Crusades. You'll find it on shields in paintings of Godefroy de Bouillon, leader of the First Crusade in the late 1100s. You'll find it scratched in stone by bored night-sentries in Crusader castles. Many of those foot-soldiers had it tattooed on their arms as souvenirs. The Cross may even pre-date the Crusades. Some say it comes from the very earliest Christian times.'

I ask Frère Pierre what the Cross means. Here, he is on even less certain ground. 'The big cross symbolises Jerusalem, the Mother Church – that I know for sure. And I'm pretty certain the little crosses represent the four early churches under its protection: Antioch in the North, Alexandria in the South, Rome in the West, and Constantinople, of course, in the East.' Frère Pierre is careful to put special emphasis on the last city, spiritual home to the Eastern Orthodox rite. 'But then again,' he continues, as we turn away from the church and head back down the hill, 'you hear all sorts of things, different, conflicting versions of what those little crosses represent. I don't think anyone really knows for sure.'

Now, it's a small thing, the meaning of five crosses arranged in a particular pattern, and Jerusalem has more pressing concerns to deal with. Normally I would forget the matter with my first lunchtime falafel at the Damascus Gate. But for some reason I don't. Is it because, from the day of my visit to Frère Pierre, I start finding the Jerusalem Cross in every place and on every route I follow in the Old City? It is displayed in tourist-shop windows, carved over front doors in private homes, etched into stained-glass, hung on silver chains around women's necks, graffiti-chalked on walls and sidewalks, embossed on sacramental silverware and stitched on the coarse brown robes of the Franciscan monks who wander the alleys beneath city walls. Suddenly the Jerusalem Cross is there where I haven't seen it before, and I'm curious to discover what it's all about.

'Yes, the big cross stands for Jerusalem. And yes, certainly I know what the four little crosses in the corners are. They are the four Crusader countries sent to fight the Arabs in the Holy Land: England, France, Spain and the Holy Roman Empire.'

I am standing in a busy bazaar street in the Christian Quarter and talking to a jeweller polishing his display window. On the other side of it, in a tray lined in black velvet and illuminated by overhead spotlights, are a dozen gleaming silver Jerusalem Cross pins, the kind you attach to the lapel of a jacket. They are beautiful little things, as fine and precise in their detail as Persian miniatures, and not cheap. The jeweller, surrounded by lesser bazaar tradesmen, mere vendors of vulgar and worthless knick-knacks, considers himself a connoisseur; he is put out that I might question his erudition. His merchandise is high quality, and so is his knowledge. 'Of course this is so,' he says, 'Everybody knows the meaning of the Cross. Everybody.'

But everybody doesn't know the meaning of the Cross. Or at least everyone I've asked in the last hour knows a different meaning for it. Most people I've met are adamant in their pronouncements. Some attempt objectivity, citing what they know to be the truth and adding alternative versions, obviously erroneous, they've heard bandied about. But few Christian Jerusalemites will tell you they don't know the meaning of their own city's cross.

Almost everyone agrees the big central cross can only stand for Jerusalem. A few random examples, then, of what those four little crosses represent:

A nun perusing a roadside pile of aubergines near the Greek Praetorium: 'Everybody knows that – they stand for the gospels of the four evangelists, Matthew, Mark, Luke and John.'

A Saint Francis Street shop-assistant emptying a newly-arrived carton of plush red Santa Clauses from Taiwan: 'We learned that in convent school. They are the four mini-kingdoms ruled by the Crusaders in Palestine – Edessa under King Baldwin, Tripoli under Raymond of Toulouse, and... And I can never remember the other two.'

A sandaled monk of the Franciscan Order of the Friars Minor, emerging from the doors of Saint Saviour's Monastery: 'Of course – they were the first four priories of the Province of the Holy Land under Franciscan administration – Mount Sion, Bethlehem, Beirut and the Holy Sepulcher.'

A beringed Christian Arab businessman in a pearl-grey suit, imitation alligator-skin attaché case in hand, swinging up David Street: 'Yes, it's very simple – they are the cardinal points of the compass, north, south, east and west, with Jerusalem at the centre.'

A waiter squeezing oranges at a juice-bar in the Christian Quarter Road: 'They are the four different Christian faiths of Jerusalem – Catholic, Armenian, Syrian and Orthodox. You want juice?'

The very reverend Michael Sellors of Saint George's Anglican Cathedral, East Jerusalem, buying postcards from a stall at the Jaffa Gate: 'Well, you'll hear this and you'll hear that. But what the Cross really represents is the five wounds of Christ. The four little crosses are his two hands and two feet pierced by nails, and the big cross is the spear-wound in his side. This is the absolute truth. I guarantee it, and don't let anyone tell you differently.'

By the time I have wandered past the Coptic Patriarchate on my way the the Holy Sepulcher I am thoroughly flummoxed. How can anything so central to the history of Christian Jerusalem, a symbol of the city for millions around the world, be so variously understood? But by now I have learned my lesson – even in this tiny matter it's not the truth that counts in Jerusalem, but what people believe to be the truth, and there is no reconciling the differences.

All the same, I reason as I carry on walking, it's worth going straight to the source. I can make my last enquiries at the place in Jerusalem where the whole thing, for Christians at least, is supposed to have started. Ahead of me, across a wide, stone-flagged courtyard filled with a tourist group of Ukrainian pilgrims in bright orange baseball caps, stand the open doors of the Church of the Holy Sepulcher. If I cannot get a definitive version of things here at the site of Christianity's seminal event, the Crucifixion, I can't get one anywhere.

Things do not start well. At the church porch a small knot of Ukrainians is clustered around a man wearing glasses, a blue blazer and an Astrakhan hat of soft grey lamb's wool. He is holding forth knowledgeably in English, and occasionally pointing upwards to the massive wooden doors, high and carved and scarred with age, that make the church entrance. In his hand he holds a key. It is a odd object, and resembles no key I've ever seen before. Hand-made of beaten metal, almost a foot long, its working end is composed of a broad triangular flange with a hollow ring at its apex. Judging by the gazes of the Ukrainians it's an important object, and its holder a man of some consequence. I hang back until they have filed inside the church, and then approach.

At first the the man is a little touchy. He's a church official, not a tour guide, and he doesn't pose for photos, he insists. When I assure him I am not looking for a snapshot of him and his key he warms up. 'I will help,' he says. 'I know everything.' No one, he affirms, as he pulls a business card from his breast pocket, knows more about the Holy Sepulcher than he does. The place has been in his family's blood for generations, and it's in his blood too.

I look at the card. *Abed A. Joudeh*, it says. *Key Custodian Of The Church Of The Holy Sepulcher – Jerusalem.* 'I am the only man in the world authorised to hold the key to the church,' he tells me with dignity. Apart from the few moments at the beginning and end of each day when the doors are locked and unlocked, the key is entirely his responsibility. It is a sacred trust, he sighs, and one which weighs heavily. Whether he is eating or praying, watching television or alone with his wife he must always be aware of it – even in his sleep, he claims, he knows the exact whereabouts of the key.

I look at the name again. Is it Christian? I ask. Of course it's not Christian, he protests – do I think the great Saladin would have trusted Christians with such an important object? The Keepers of the Key have always been Muslims.

And this, I discover, is why Abed Joudeh is so proud – the Keepers of the Key have always been Joudehs, too. When the Muslims conquered Jerusalem in 1187, Abed Joudeh says, it was the father of his fathers who rode into the city at Saladin's side. Ten days later the Sultan approached him and asked him to become the official Keeper of the Key.

'And why was that?' the present Keeper asks rhetorically, flourishing the symbol of his office like a magic wand. 'I will tell you. Because Saladin, a gracious man who did not slaughter his enemies, knew there would be trouble and fighting among the Christians. You think the big cross of the Jerusalem Cross stands for the city? Ha! It stands for England, the most powerful of Christian nations. It was the English who wanted the key, and the other little crosses, Spain, Italy, Germany and France, who would fight them for it. That is why Joudehs have always held the key. We are keepers of the peace among the Christians!'

Things are not getting simpler, but cloudier and more complex. I am just about to ask Abed Joudeh for clarification when I am nudged in the ribs from behind.

I turn around. 'Come with me,' whispers a man with a large round face and a bristly mustache in the middle of it. 'There is something I must show you.' Taking me by the arm he leads me around the great doors to a place where we cannot be seen by Abed Joudeh. And there he dives into his back pocket and pulls out his own business card.

I look at it in the dim light of the church interior. *Wajeeh Y. Nusibeh*, it reads, *Custodian and Door Keeper of the Church of the Holy Sepulchre*. Mystified, I look up at Mr Nusibeh.

'You must not listen to Joudeh,' he says, jutting his chin in the direction of the man behind the door. 'He is old and foolish. He keeps the key, yes. But he is not allowed to touch the door or the lock. Never. I am the only one who can do that.'

'Look,' he says, holding up a strange cylindrical object. Bound with metal bands, it is attached to something that looks like a piston rod and is gleaming with oil. Wajeeh Nusibeh's lock is even odder looking than Abed Joudeh's key.

'Do you know how foolish that Joudeh is?' the Keeper of the Door asks. 'He tells tourists the lock and key are Chinese. Chinese! I know they are Ottoman. Everyone knows they are Ottoman. But Joudeh has to be different. He doesn't know what he's talking about, and you must not believe anything he says.'

I have the feeling I've fallen into the middle of a very old and very jealous feud between families. 'Are your people Arab?' I ask. Wajeeh

Nusibeh nods. 'Have they been door- and lock-keepers since the beginning?' He nods again. 'Of course. But our job is more important than the Joudehs' job.'

'Come see this,' he says, taking me around the door and pointing at a stone column that acts as a door joist. Abed Joudeh has disappeared. 'I am responsible for that, too; do you see where the stone is split?' I look and see a deep fissure in the marble, as if the column has been hit by lightning. 'It is where the church received the holy fire from heaven,' says Nusibeh. 'It is very important every Easter. But I, too, am very important every Easter. It is I who must certify that there are no matches, no candles in Christ's tomb before it is sealed and the holy fire visits it. If I do not put my wax stamp on the door just before Easter, there is no Easter.'

Nusibeh pulls a mobile telephone out of his pocket and turns it on. 'Look, I'm the one who meets the important people. You think Joudeh has a picture like this?' And there on the screen of his telephone is Wajeeh Y. Nusibeh standing in front of the Holy Sepulcher with Pope John-Paul II. He hasn't quite got his arm around the Pontiff's shoulder, but you can tell he'd like to have it there, if only to spite Abed Joudeh.

'Well, then,' I say, growing tired of all this one-upmanship, 'you must know all about early Jerusalem. 'Naturally,' he says with a gracious smile.

'What is the meaning of this, then?' I ask, pulling my little Jerusalem Cross out of my own pocket. 'What do all these crosses represent?'

Wajeeh Nusibeh gazes down at the object as if, like holy fire, it has just fallen from the sky. Then he looks up at me. His face is a complete blank and he shrugs. 'Who knows?' he says at last.

It's probably the most accurate answer I've had all day.

Inside the Church of the Holy Sepulcher it is damp and dark and noisy with excited voices, a bit like the reptile house at a zoo on a Saturday morning. Just ahead of me through the doors there is a large crowd and a constant popping of camera flashes. In a rambling building which over the centuries has amassed a uneven collection of monasteries, sacristies, tombs, and chapels (at least fourteen of these last), there are some corners that are rarely visited at all. The Stone of Unction, though, embodying all the drama that religious sites can evoke, is a star attraction and rarely sits unattended.

The Ukrainians have moved on; a large Philippino party now surrounds the Stone, and like all other groups stopping at the raised slab of red rock they have come with a specific purpose – they want an energy top-up.

That, at least, is what the Philippino lady crouched beside the Stone tells me. She is waiting her turn to place her hands on its polished surface, an act by which she will absorb the holiness and divine power stored inside it. This was where Christ was laid out after he was taken down from the cross, she tells me, indicating a stairway packed with visitors slowly moving upwards to the crucifixion site. But before he was buried – she points in the opposite direction, towards the Sepulcher itself – Jesus rested here. This is where his body was washed, anointed with oil, and wrapped in shrouds. So of course the holy spirit is in the stone, she tells me. And it flows into everyone who touches it, into everything that is laid on it. It is a blessing and an energy that you can take home with you. I watch as Philippino pilgrims lay religious objects, just-bought and with price tags still attached, onto the red granite. Crucifixes, rosaries, candles, icons, bundles of incense, prayer books, all get the same treatment. Back home in Manila or Luzon they will end up on walls or in family shrines, the centrepiece of a pilgrimage to Jerusalem. There is even a mobile phone or two laid on the stone for a quick charge.

The woman invites me to lay my own hands on the smooth rock, but I am not looking for energy. I am looking for a Franciscan priest. Around me I can see Armenian clerics, Greek Orthodox churchmen, Copts, Ethiopians, Syriacs, Russians, all dressed in the elaborate garb of their office. They are difficult to tell apart. The Armenians have beards, black robes, and short cylindrical hats with soft brims, I think, and the Greeks beards, black robes and tall cylindrical hats with stiff brims. But where is a Franciscan when you need one? There isn't a cowled brown robe in sight.

Slowly, with crowds of other visitors, I make my way up the heaving stairway to Golgotha. There is a clogged mass of pilgrims at the head of the stairs, successive tour groups pressing forward on each other for their turn at the site. It takes a good while, for each pilgrim must squeeze his or her way into the small space beneath an altar, there to kiss the silver rim surrounding the spot where the cross once stood. There are some women too bulky and wide-hipped to get in without a struggle. In the meantime, milling, mingling, flowing one way and another, the crowd surges beneath a hundred suspended silver lamps, each reflecting a hundred bright camera-flashes.

It used to be that pilgrims carried inoffensive objects – staffs or scalloped shells or holy water sprinklers – as symbols of their mission. Why is it that the digital camera has become the indispensable piece of pilgrims' equipment in our times? It is no longer sufficient to see the holy sites; we must be seen in the holy sites. It's not enough to adore; one must be recorded adoring. Never mind Christ; what we really want to bear eternal witness to is ourselves with Christ.

'No photo! No photo!' roar the priests who stand before Golgotha like policemen handling an unruly crowd. When one man loses his patience and shoves forward, I see one priest lose his patience and shove back. But for all the cleric's forcefulness, the crowd pays no attention, and the cameras continue to erupt, lighting up the sweaty, body-heated chamber, the lamps, the icons, the pressing crowd, the angry priests. On again, off again, an incessant alternation of darkness and light, it's like watching a disco under strobes or aerial footage of night-bombing over wartime Europe. But why not? I think. Lasting split-seconds and unlinked by connecting narrative, Jerusalem itself is only made up of a thousand separate images.

Downstairs, a long line of tourists snakes away from the mouth of the Sepulcher and disappears around the corner into the dim distance. Slowly it moves forward as, two or three at a time, a priest leads visitors into the crypt to the rock-carved tomb of Christ. On the far side of the waiting line I find what I am looking for – the Franciscan chapel and, standing at the bottom of the aisle near the doorway, a monk.

His name is Brother Andrew and he is Ghanian. Apart from a pair of blue suede shoes – the stone-flagged floors of the Church of the Holy Sepulcher are too cold for long stints of sandle-wearing – he fits the image of a Franciscan to a T. His robe is brown and coarse, the fastening around his waist is suitably rope-like, and stitched over his heart in bright red thread is a Cross of Jerusalem.

I explain my confusion and ask Brother Andrew for help. For a long moment he looks at me, as if trying to gauge my intent. I fear the worst. Perhaps, like Wajeeh Nusibeh, he has nothing to say at all. Or perhaps his answer is so theologically complex I am unqualified to hear it. 'Follow me,' he says at last.

We retrace the line of tomb-visitors to its head, and at the entrance to the Sepulcher veer off into the church-nave that faces it. It is a large, open, almost empty space, and Brother Andrew's voice echos slightly when he talks.

'Come right into the middle. Here. This is a special place. It is called the Centre of the World,' he says. He leads me to an object so insignificant compared to the soaring heights of the church all around me that I haven't even noticed it. It is a squat little column about a foot across, rising no higher than my shins, sculpted from rose-coloured stone. The top of the column is bowl-shaped, and in the centre of the bowl two lines have been carved at perpendicular angles to form a cross. The place where the lines meet is marked by a black disk.

'This,' says Brother Andrew, touching the intersection in the stone, 'is the Cosmic Cross, the centre of all creation. And it tells you that every different story you've heard about the Jerusalem Cross, each and every version, is true. All of them. True to the extent that all these stories place a supreme truth in their centre.'

I put my own hand on top of the column. It is cold and moves a fraction of an inch under my touch. Not only is it a bit wonky, it is anchored to the floor by a length of cheap and none-too-substantial looking chain. Are the Church authorities so uncertain of the cosmic centre of existence that they have to tie it down?

But Brother Andrew, for one, is confident. 'I cannot say exactly when the Jerusalem Cross originated,' he says, 'but the idea behind it is very old. It dates to Old Testament times. In those days the Temple of Solomon was the centre of Jerusalem, Jerusalem was the centre of the kingdom of Israel, and Israel was the centre of the world.' He points to the Sepulcher lying at the end of the nave. 'We Christians have taken up that idea. Jerusalem is central to our view of the world because our Saviour was crucified and resurrected here.

'But does that leave the rest of creation out in the cold?' the Franciscan asks. 'Of course not. On the contrary – Jesus didn't die for Jerusalem. He died for the sake of men everywhere, and without the message of salvation spreading out from the centre in all directions Jerusalem would have no meaning. So it doesn't matter whether it's England, France, Germany and Spain, North, South, East and West, or Antioch, Alexandria, Rome and Constantinople. Without the centre there is no periphery. If Jerusalem lies at the heart of the world it is because it is wholly connected to the world.'

There is more in Brother Andrew's account, a history of the Franciscan role in spreading the good word to every continent, but I don't absorb it fully. I am thinking of what Ashraf Noor was saying about stepping back even further, about leaving the city entirely. See Jerusalem as part of a larger whole – is that what Brother Andrew is also saying?

There's a note waiting for Ashraf and me when I arrive back at the Maison d'Abraham. It's from Frère Pierre. He would like to talk to us. Would Vespers at the Church of Mary Magdalene be convenient? He has left instructions with the Russian nuns to let us in. They don't speak English. 'Just say Frère Pierre sent you,' the note ends cryptically.

As Ashraf and I stand ringing the buzzer at the Mary Magdalene half an hour before sunset it all seems rather mysterious. A nuns' Vespers service is a rare thing. There may be twice-weekly public tours of the church, but the convent attached to the church is home to one of most cloistered communities of nuns in Jerusalem, and it does not share its life with outsiders easily.

There is a sudden crack in the gate, and a face whose expression is creased with doubt. But at the mention of the word 'Pierre' the face disappears and the gate swings open. By the time we walk through it the nun has disappeared into the evening shadows already gathering in the trees and gardens beyond.

Alone, we walk up a steep, winding lane bordered by tall pines. There are banks of flowers and, peeking through the shrubbery, small roadside oratories holding figurines of the Virgin Mary. Above us we can see the ornate white turrets and golden onion domes of the church, bright now as they catch the dying rays of the sun. Only when we climb a last flight of steps do we see a knot of nuns gathered on the stone terrace before the church. They are clothed in voluminous black habits and all wear the same headgear, peaked wimples that cover foreheads, necks and temples. The hems of their robes touch the ground and their sleeves are so long that their hands remain hidden. Only the nuns' pale faces are exposed. It is impossible to say how old they are, what shape they have, or what kinds of lives have propelled them into this strange existence. They ignore us, and we hang back at a respectful distance until the church doors open and we file in behind them.

There are three rows of hard benches at the rear of the church, the only place to sit in an otherwise open and uncluttered building. We head for the last row, backs to the wall. Before taking their own places in front of us, the nuns glide here and there about the church kissing wooden-framed icons. For a minute or two the absolute silence of the church is broken only by the the sounds of the basketball court. I cannot see the nuns' feet, but they must be wearing rubber-soled shoes. They squeak their way across polished stone floors from one saint's image to another. When the icons are too high on the walls to kiss with their lips, the shorter nuns kiss their fingers instead, then reach up and touch them to the image. In one distant corner of the church they kiss a glass-topped, coffin-shaped box. It must contain a real saint, for under the domed glass at the far end of the box I can see the tips of a pair of shoes protruding. For women who have forsworn the company of men they go in for a lot of kissing.

But it is the church itself that really captures my attention. It is simple and elegant at the same time, a large, open space that focuses all the viewer's attention on the iconostasis, the partition that separates congregations from the hidden sanctuary that lies behind it. If the sanctuary and its altar is too sacred to be seen by ordinary mortals, the iconostasis forms a kind of celestial curtain upon which the worshipper may dwell. Through contemplation and prayer, he hopes, a tiny corner of it may eventually lift to partially reveal to his purified heart the tremendous secrets which lie concealed beyond.

I feel no need to see eternity on the far side of this particular iconostasis, though – with its arches, flickering tapers, brass candleholders and chain-suspended oil-lamps it's tremendous enough by itself. As the sun sinks and the light streaming through the church windows fails, candle and lamp-light illuminate the tall façade in their soft dazzle, and turn the worshipping nuns standing before us into dark silhouettes.

There is an odd moment, so precise it might be timed, as a choir of a half-dozen nuns emerges from the dark recesses of the church. Suddenly their shoes are squeaking noisily across the floor, birds in the trees outside burst into a night-roosting song, and imams from surrounding mosques announce the evening prayer in loud and wailing voice. There is complete chaos for a brief while, and then, out of the last remnants of subsiding noise, the high voices of the nuns' choir break into Russian chant and the office of Vespers begins.

Pierre has not appeared. But as the chanting progresses, sometimes in multiple voices, sometimes in a high, clear, single voice, I can once again see his face as in the Tomb of the Prophets as he describes for me the mystery of the Russian Church. It's all here in this service. The nuns in front of us sit, stand and bow low from the waist in veneration, their sleeves touching the floor. We imitate their gestures. Two bearded monks in glittering capes appear through the central arch of the iconostasis. One carries a candle on a tall staff, the other a billowing censer. Together, they make the rounds of the icons, enveloping each saint in a mist of sweet smoke. The nuns sing on, their voices rising and falling, falling and rising in haunting Slavic harmony. The monks disappear behind the iconostasis, re-emerge from a side-entrance, then disappear again as if through stage flats in a comic theatrical production.

But it works. The dramatic suspense is kept high and our attention is riveted upon the goings-on we sense behind the sacred screen. Of all the secret, unknowable things that take place in the universe, who can imagine which ones are taking place right there, right now, just an arm's-length beyond our reach? Not I, certainly. The whole grand performance is mesmerising, and I doubt anyone in the church has been aware of the passage of time. I only come fully to when, one by one, all the candles in the church are finally snuffed out. We are left in a profound darkness illuminated only by the tiny flames of lamps over the icons. And somehow, too, by those etherial Russian voices. Then they also fade out and the service is over.

The effect is supernatural. In the Bells and Smells department no one does it as well as the Orthodox Russians. As I sit there, relishing the afterglow, I am barely aware of Frère Pierre sliding onto the bench beside us. He apologises; he has been praying, he says, and finished too late for Vespers. But that doesn't stop him making the offer that he's had in mind all day.

He is smiling, for the news is good. By a miracle the wheel-rims of the church Jetta have not been damaged. The tyres have been re-inflated, the air-filter cleaned, and their bags are packed. He and Sylvia are ready to go to the Sea of Galilee, passing through Nazareth, Mount Tabor, Tiberias, Tapgah and the Golan. They are leaving tomorrow morning at eight o'clock. Would we – Ashraf and I – like to join them?

For once I see Ashraf waiver. He is tempted to telephone the university, plead illness and take off in the rattly old Jetta. But in the end his conscience and his students win out, and he says he must stay.

I, on the other hand, have no commitments, and no one to teach but myself. Will a few days away from Jerusalem tell me something about

Jerusalem? I have no idea, but the opportunity is too good to miss. By the time we are through the church doors and out into the cool night I have signed up for a Holy Land road trip.

Eleven

The Jetta shows up early next morning, and it's even dodgier-looking than I imagined. Once midnight-blue, its paint-job has faded over the decades and now resembles something more like six o'clock on an overcast morning. It's scratched and banged up all over, and the front left fender has had a run-in with a large, unmovable object. But the great advantage, Frère Pierre says as I bundle my myself into the back seat behind Sylvia, is that it's 25 years old, one of the earliest Jettas on the road. They built things simply back then – there's not much to go wrong.

'Look,' Pierre says, grandly sweeping his hand over the dashboard. 'There's on and off, up and down, left and right, blue and red. That's about it.'

Frère Pierre may be right about simplicity – I haven't seen a manual pull-out choke for decades. But that doesn't mean things can't go wrong. The Jetta's sliding heater lever is stuck at red, so the heat is permanently on maximum. Frère Pierre's window may wind up and down, but mine doesn't, so it quickly gets hot in the back. Turning left on the Jericho road towards the Old City and the main highway north, the French monk depresses the turn indicator. *Tic-tac-tic-tac-tic-tac*, the indicator light on the dashboard flashes on and off at high speed, making me wonder if the turn signals are burning out or even working at all. But Frère Pierre has supreme confidence in our vehicle. The monastery, he tells us without a flicker of irony, bought it years ago from a little old lady, a congregation member who only drove it to church on Sunday. He seems so sincere in his pronouncement that even Sylvia does her best to suppress a guffaw of incredulity.

Highway No. 6, the Yitzak Rabin Highway leading to Haifa, is no different than any four-lane freeway you'd find in the West: once down off the Judean hills, we shoot along over the top of the countryside, never getting much of a sense of the land we are travelling through. Not that there is a great deal to see out there – the coastal plane we're heading north on is flat and dull and browned off by months of blazing summer heat. Mostly it is stubbly, harvested fields, a broad swathe of agricultural land squeezed between sea and hills, crossed by high-voltage power lines and dotted here and there with modern Israeli towns and shopping malls. These, however, are better-looking than the towering obstruction we drive alongside for a short stretch. Israelis call it the separation or security barrier, Palestinians the racial segregation, or apartheid, wall. It dwarfs everything else on the plain, a great zig-zag vertical slash in a countryside of horizontals. Made of 25-foot-high slabs of concrete, it is part of the system of fences, walls, observation posts and electronic sensors winding along for more than 700 kilometres and dividing Israeli territory from the occupied West Bank.

It is one of the more dramatic details of topography in this part of the world, but for the moment I have little time for the kind of eye-popping attention it gets from most foreign visitors. There may be few other symbols quite as emotionally evocative of the Arab-Israeli dispute, but what I am more concerned with for the moment is Israelis themselves – especially their driving behaviour – and one particular foreigner's reaction to it.

As he tootles down the freeway at no great speed, Frère Pierre doesn't seem to notice the insane way drivers are roaring up behind him, leaning on their horns, pulling out and then cutting sharply back in front of him to avoid even faster drivers coming up behind. Israelis love to jockey their cars at high speed and close distances between as many lanes as possible, and they are unhappy about Frère Pierre. He's cramping their style. Pierre, on the other hand, doesn't even seem to notice their existence. Blithe, carefree as a spring-break sophomore on his way to Daytona Beach, he worries me the way he's constantly looking around, gazing at the passing scene. He might as well be a front-seat passenger sitting beside some other person doing the driving. This is the first time I begin wondering if Frère Pierre lives entirely in this world, but it's not the last.

Take, for instance, Pierre's impromptu roadside wardrobe change. Not only is the car heater blowing full blast, but it's a good deal warmer down here on the plains than it is in the high hills of Jerusalem. Frère Pierre, still in the heavy black ankle-length robe that is the only thing I've ever seen him wear, is also getting a touch over-heated; monks, it seems, wear clerical robes over already adequate sets of clothing. Suddenly and without warning, in the middle of an interchange where the freeway broadens out into six lanes, Frère Pierre blunders into the right-hand lane of departing cars and parks the Jetta on the approach to an exit ramp. It's his idea, apparently, of an ideal place to change outfits.

With drivers shouting out of their windows at the perilously parked monk, Pierre struggles beside the open boot of the car to extricate himself from his priestly apparel. It's not an easy job, and sightless, the garment still bunched up over his head, he wanders along the wrong side of the car – the side facing angry, swerving traffic – to ask Sylvia for help. We hold our breaths. When he finally slides back into the driver's seat, smiling triumphantly and sporting a lightweight cotton robe in natty blue-grey, he is still oblivious of any risk; he can only remark on how the new robe makes him feel festive and summery and relaxed.

If Frère Pierre relies heavily for survival on his guardian angel of physical safety, there are plenty of other examples of his peculiar brand of unearthly detachment. There's his reliance, for example, on his heavenly ward of personal finance. Frère Pierre doesn't seem to have to worry about the same irksome pecuniary details of life the rest of us are weighed down with. They are mysteriously taken care of. I first notice this when, about half-way to Haifa, Frère Pierre tries to alter the reservation he has made in Tabgha on the Sea of Galilee. He and Sylvia have reserved accommodation in a Franciscan hospice there for the following day, but now I need to be added to the booking, too.

Back on the freeway again, straying haplessly between lanes, the monk roots around in the pockets under his robe until he finds his mobile phone. Without a penny to his name, Frère Pierre doesn't actually own the phone. He owns little more than a pet cat and the clothes he stands in. But the nuns have made a permanent loan of the phone to him, for even humble monks need more than heavenly connectivity these days. What Frère Pierre apparently doesn't need, though, is to keep track of billing. Halfway through the call the phone goes dead, its credit exhausted. Frère Pierre is undismayed. He merely asks Sylvia for the use of her own mobile, thumbs in a Jerusalem number, and speaks to a certain Ibrahim. The next minute his phone is vibrating on the dashboard, its credit topped up and ready to go.

I am intrigued. Who, I ask, is this distant, invisible, but powerful Ibrahim? He's some sort of terrestrial fixer, it turns out, a lay-employee back at the Russian church who assists the monks and nuns in their more complex daily transactions with the here and now.

And does Ibrahim pay the freeway tolls for monks as well, I enquire?

'What tolls?' asks Frère Pierre. There's nothing to pay on this road, he insists. It's free of charge and always has been. But the next time we drive past an exit ramp I point out the yellow sign by the side of the road that reads: 'Exiting toll road – Bill will be sent by mail.'

'That's funny,' says Pierre after a quiet moment's reflection, his brow wrinkled. He's perplexed. 'I've driven this road a dozen times and never paid a shekel. I had no idea.'

God, or at least his agent Ibrahim, works in mysterious way. But none of them, I discover a few minutes later, are as mysterious as the ways of the Jetta. We have left the freeway, and are on a hectic main approach-road on the edge of Haifa, when hell breaks loose. One moment we are whistling smoothly along in heavy traffic, gazing out at anonymous and ever-denser urban build-up. The next there is a bang and a clatter and the Jetta takes a little gazelle-like leap into the air. We all hit our heads on the car's roof. With the driver in the truck behind us honking and gesticulating, Frère Pierre rolls another fifty yards before putting on the brakes.

We have driven over our own front bumper. In an instant the holy man is out of the car and streaking back down the road, robes flying. Oncoming cars, having swerved around the bumper, fly past him and then swoop down on us with horns blaring. It is a fraught moment, and my least concern is for the bumper.

'Do we really need it?' I ask Sylvia as, looking behind us, we watch Frère Pierre stoop in the road to retrieve it. But as he jogs back I can see we do – the bumper holds the vehicle's front license plate. Without it we'd be picked up in minutes.

'It's nothing,' says Frère Pierre, his lungs heaving, when he gets back to the car. 'It happens all the time. It's just a question of proper attachment.' He jams the bumper back onto the front of the car and gives it a savage and determined kick with the heel of his shoe. Reaching in through the window to the car ashtray, he opens it, selects a long screw from the reserve pile lying there, and pushes it through holes aligned in the car's bumper and body. 'If I could get the same kind of hole drilled on the other side of the bumper it would fix things for good,' he says. 'I must speak to Ibrahim.'

There's no screwdriver, of course, and with drivers yelling at us to get our rattletrap off the road he uses the first thing at hand. It happens to be the car key, and when Frère Pierre is finished with the bumper he has some difficulty getting it back into the ignition. But throughout he remains supremely unfazed and cheerful. These are minor details, and have nothing to do with the really crucial matter in life, the piercing of the great mysteries of the spirit.

Besides, Frère Pierre, I can see, is looking forward to lunch in the old Crusader port-town that lies just north of Haifa, Saint Jean d'Acre. At least that's what he calls it. My own map calls it by its modern name, Akko. But Frère Pierre does not work by modern names or modern maps. He navigates instead by a book that never leaves his side during our trip. It is small and red and worn threadbare. Entitled *Le Petit Guide de la Terre Sainte* – The Little Guide to the Holy Land – it is not entirely up to date. Written by Benedictine monks in Jerusalem, it was published in 1953. No wonder Frère Pierre is surprised that the routes it advises are not all that time-saving – a lot of them no longer even exist. But that is not important, he says as we slowly work our way around the sweep of Haifa Bay, away from the modern city and towards the old port-town. Time doesn't matter.

In fact time, from Frère Pierre's point of view, is the enemy, and the modern age it has foisted on us brings doubt where no doubt used to be. What Pierre likes about *Le Petit Guide* is its unqualified certainty. There is no prevarication in its accounts of biblical places and events. There is no fiddle-faddle, none of the current mania for hypothesis and theorising. There are no milk-toast apologies for the possible inaccuracies of religious tradition. If the *Petit Guide* says that Jesus walked over this hilltop or spoke to his followers from that riverbank, well, then, that's good enough for our expedition guide and leader. The unresolvable debate over factual detail simply isn't relevant. What counts is the immutable reality, indivisible and without substance, that lies behind the details. Frère Pierre is not at all like the researchers at the *Ecole Biblique de Jerusalem*. Focused on a search for the eternal, he is uninterested in the trivia of history.

There is plenty of history in Akko, much of it more than mere speculation, for its ancient centre is littered with solid stone remains of the past. Some of them are Arab and Ottoman. Others, older, were left behind by Christians who used Saint Jean d'Acre's harbour as a main staging post for their Holy Land crusades. Frère Pierre would like to give us the full conducted tour of the city's encircling walls, its Crusader halls, its land and sea gates, but the heavens intercede. Walking along a high, crenellated stone sea-wall facing Haifa Bay, we spy a dense black curtain of cloud fast approaching from far out in the Mediterranean. It is closer than it seems. By the time we have reached the end of the wall and protective cover, we are soaked to the skin.

The winter rains, which have already launched their first assault on Jerusalem, have at last reached the north, and we spend the rest of our time in Akko sheltered beneath the drumming canvas awning of a harbour-side restaurant. Sylvia and I have little silver fish cooked crisp on a grill. But for Frère Pierre, having escaped the dreaded smoked herring that makes up much of the Orthodox ecclesiastic diet in Jerusalem, no modest little fish will do. He is on holiday. Feeling expansive, he splurges. His large, single fish arrives at the table, expensive and as ugly as sin. It is almost as round as his plate, has a severely recessed chin, and a back and tail covered in long, nasty spines.

Why order such a hideous fish? we ask. But the monk makes a conspicuous point of enjoying it, taking a long time to consume every last morsel of flesh he can scrape off its bones. Before dissecting it, though, he has us note the large dark spot on its side.

'Do you see that?' he says. 'It's a thumb-print, or at least that's what Holy Land Christians used to say. It was left by the fisherman who caught it and pulled it from his nets. Any idea who that might have been?'

Sylvia is way ahead of me, for she has known the holy man long before he was a holy man, at a time when he was a simple village boy with jug-ears and the name of Eric, the name his parents gave him.

'Of course,' she says confidently, smiling at the pleasure suffused over her friend's face. 'That fish is a St Pierre.' The monk nods. He is celebrating himself through his own chosen bible-name. Immersed as he is in the infinite, the impersonal and the divinely inscrutable, Frère Pierre still has his little pleasures and vanities. It is what makes him human and likeable.

It continues to rain all the way into the country behind Haifa, the low, dark clouds scraping Palestinian villages perched atop hills that rise as they march eastwards. Israel is not a large place. You could drive its length and breadth in a day, and although we doddle along the way, by sunset we have climbed the looping road to our first night's destination, Nazareth.

When it comes to economy travel, hanging out with Christian monks in the Holy Land is as good as collecting air miles – you're eligible for exclusive special offers. In the centre of town, a stone's throw from the towering Basilica of the Annunciation, we park the Jetta in a narrow street outside the Convent of the Sisters of Nazareth. Nazareth is the largest

Arab town in Israel, but these are not typical Middle Eastern Arabs. Almost all of them are Christian. Much of their livelihood comes from the pilgrim tourist-trade, and Nazareth offers a fair choice of hotel accommodation. But Frère Pierre has phoned ahead and instead arranged a stay with the Franciscan nuns of the convent.

Clean, spartan and institutional, the visitors' quarters are like boarding-school dormitories. But on this particular night we are their sole occupants. The convent is dead quiet, and through the dorm windows we see only brief glimpses of robed nuns as they flit across an inner courtyard. The nuns, and the tall palm trees that steadily drip rainwater to the stone flagging there, at least make it an exotic kind of boarding school.

After dumping their bags Frère Pierre and Sylvia immediately head off to pray at the Basilica. It's the most important place in Nazareth, the spot where the Virgin Mary announced her willingness to bear the world's saviour. At the end of a long and often harrowing day of driving I enjoy my atheist dispensation; instead of going to pray I stroll in a gentle drizzle through Nazareth's still busy streets and at a small grocery store stop to buy a bottle of aniseed-flavoured arak. When I ask the man behind the counter about the best local tipple, he advises Golden brand arak, distilled in Ramallah. Not all the customers in the shop agree, and a long and lively debate ensues. I enjoy chatting with Christian Arabs. They have all the garrulous Middle Eastern sociability of their Muslim brothers, and at the same time a long cultural history whose sensibilities overlap Western ones. It's a kind of sharing which on a personal level often allows for immediate closeness. This, I suppose, is my own form of Christian communion for the evening, and when I return to the convent I am content to sit on a bed until my friends return, sipping watered arak and watching the rain fall into the brightly illuminated courtyard outside. Streaming across every surface, the water glistens on the stone pavement, the sodden palms and the sculpture of Jesus, Joseph and Mary that sits beside them.

The night is long and the convent not so quiet after all. Frère Pierre, the gentlest of men awake, does not make the best of dormitory companions. Asleep, he is a restless and violent snorer. Even when I move to the empty dorm next door – there are two for men and one for women – I can hear him through the thin partition. He is almost as loud as the constant sound of rain falling on the roof and the on-again, off-again rumble of thunder echoing through the hills beyond the town. And when I finally do succumb, my sleep is laced with odd dreams. Perhaps I've spent too long contemplating the courtyard sculpture, or perhaps I am unused to sleeping in a convent full of nuns. Somewhere out there a drainpipe is emptying water onto the flagging, making a sharp, noisy splattering. In my sleep the sound becomes the clatter of rosary beads falling incessantly to a hard floor, and by the time they have stopped bouncing it is morning.

Frère Pierre has not been entirely truthful about smoked fish for breakfast. From time to time well-wishers and visitors to the Church of Mary Magdalene leave him foodstuffs they have brought from home. Not all of it is delectable. The packaged Russian food – instant noodles with synthetic bacon and tomato flavouring, for example – is sometimes challenging. Other items, like the vials of essential herb extract left him by a Californian nun, can be plain weird. But by the time I am up and dressed Pierre has hauled a large cardboard carton of these goodies from the back of the car, and is producing a breakfast porridge of oats loaded with honey, almonds and raisins in the visitors' kitchen. It is his favourite breakfast, he says, the only thing that permits him to rise, day in, day out, at four-thirty a.m. Without it his morning schedule – three hours of pre-dawn prayers with the Russian nuns, followed by a long underground stint as the Keeper of the Tombs – would look fairly grim.

In fact we all need such energy-producing sustenance, for the monk has a full day planned for us – he wants us to see the most important places Nazareth has to offer. So, full of porridge and armed with a New Testament Bible and *Le Petit Guide,* we step out into the streets of Nazareth.

But that's not all we carry. Frère Pierre is also equipped with a formidable force that can't be contained in a food-care package or the pages of a printed book. It is his own profound sense of the invisible, sacred mystery that these biblical sites embody. If I'm moved at all when we look at oil paintings or sculpted stone or billowing incense in these places, the spirit that moves me is not the same spirit that moves him. Much as the monk loves the rich sensual nature of these things, they are merely instruments of evocation, doors which, if pushed, open the way into something much deeper.

For Pierre, life's real dramas occur in some ineffable place way down inside ourselves. Cosmic, revelatory, without boundaries, they are in fact the same boundless place which which I last glimpsed hiding behind the iconostasis in the French monk's adopted Church of Mary Magdalene. It is this underlying mystic strain in Pierre which, in fact, attracted him to the Russian Orthodox Church in the first place. The plainly visible, the cut-and-dried, is not for this holy man. For him the Latin Catholic church is too scholastic, too categorical in its views. Its answers are too simple.

Frère Pierre, of course, can explain his embrace of Orthodoxy rationally. He can talk about the Latin church's drift, as he sees it, away from the original credo of Christianity. He can discuss the Great Schism which has separated Catholic and Orthodox Christians for 1,000 years, or more recent attempts by the Vatican to bring them closer together. But Pierre cares little for rationality. What he loves in the Orthodox faith are its intimations of the divine presence in the here and now, its rapt attention to that central, burning mystery around which the candles, the incense, the chanting and bell-ringing, the meditations and sudden illuminations all revolve. For Pierre religion is a well whose depths cannot be seen, a divine source which has no bottom. The only way to plumb the godliness he seeks there is with high-torque, deep-dive, all-consuming passion.

In the end Frère Pierre and I see two completely different Nazareths. It may be that we all have some kind of inner eye that longs to penetrate far past the dull and banal surface of everyday life. But mine is not directed towards the transcendent. For me the Basilica of the Annunciation, a site both Pierre and Sylvia are happy to return to once again for further contemplation, is a rather ugly, modern structure. Nor is the ancient holy site over which it is built any more attractive to my eye – it looks as if it were tailor-made for a low-budget Roman movie epic.

The subterranean shrine is not in fact the home recognised by biblical tradition as the original dwelling of Mary and Joseph. That particular structure, built onto caves dug into the Nazarene hillside, was long ago whisked away. The Crusader-period story that it was carried off by flying angels to a safe place is doubtful; today, nonetheless, you can visit Mary's miraculously relocated home in a Gothic church in the Italian town of Loreto. What we are gazing at instead is a reconstructed model built on the same underground cave site. It seems ersatz and gaudily overdone. The stone facade with its arched doorway, temple-like pedimented roof and carved columns, jaggedly broken to suggest great age, look like they might be constructed of fibreglass. I've seen antiquity better imitated in hokey Neapolitan pizza restaurants.

But no matter. This is the place where Mary, invited by the archangel Gabriel, accepted the divine invitation to become the mother of God on earth. Like the knots of other worshippers gathered in silent adoration around the shrine, Sylvia and Frère Pierre sink to their knees and for the next quarter hour remain outside human communication. It is only when they return that Pierre begins the routine he will follow at such places for the next few days. This might first involve an historical explanation of the site as laid out by *Le Petit Guide*, or perhaps a short reading from a relevant chapter in the Bible. But always there is Frère Pierre's own commentary, a detailed elucidation that leads always inward to the mystery of the divine nature of all things.

In Pierre's book, material reality, however it is interpreted, is of little importance. What counts is the sacred meaning it contains. This is the reason, Frère Pierre insists, why the Holy Land is so important. Isn't this the place where in an ordinary daily existence Jesus led two lives, one as a human being and the other as a divine being? And although that seems to me already quite a large undertaking, it's not all. Mary is not merely a virgin who accepts an invitation, literally out of the blue, to be impregnated by an invisible god. Her acquiescence, Pierre marvels, permits the until-now unthinkable. The greatest of human facilitators and a gateway to humankind's redemption, Mary becomes the agent who allows heaven to descend to earth.

I suppose in the end this kind of talk must have some kind of value, for its mystic purpose has transformed my friend from back-of-beyond farm boy into soul-palping theologist. As acts of transubstantiation go, that's fairly impressive. I have to admit, though, that after about fifteen minutes of chasing the divinely etherial my mind goes blank and still. It's as if some deep, white, clogging substance, cotton bolls, or heavy snow, or vanilla ice-cream maybe, begins to blanket a landscape of once bare and exposed thought.

So when after the third or fourth time I hear an introductory phrase beginning, 'Now, the real beauty of this gospel passage lies in...' I have to steel myself. It's the kind of thing that could go on forever. But what can you say to a monk as he stands before some celebrated object, flushed and exultant, delivering to you a key piece in the great jigsaw-puzzle of existence? I simply grin and bear it.

Luckily, there are enough places on our list that we change bible-land themes regularly through the morning. Not far from the Basilica we pay homage to the world's most celebrated woodworker at the Church of St Joseph's Carpentry. Close by, in the Church of the Synagogue, Frère Pierre shows us where Joseph's presumptuous young upstart of a son, Jesus, angered the Scribes and the Pharisees by preaching his own brand of religion to local crowds. A few minutes' walk up the hill in the old town, we enter a Franciscan church to gaze upon the Mensa Christi, a flattish slab of rock where Jesus, risen from the dead, shared a meal with his disciples. There we share a little meal of our own, eating crumbly sweet-cakes pressed upon Pierre by the wife of the Mensa Christi's Christian Arab caretaker.

Also nearby is the Church of St Gabriel, which Orthodox believers treat as the true site of the Annunciation. Here Brother Pierre's Orthodox robe and circular, flat-topped hat is recognised, and many of the pilgrims lay their hands on their hearts and and bow to the monk. He responds in kind. All part of the seriousness and dignity of his calling, it's not the kind of attention he'd get if he stayed on in his sheep-bleating, rain-soaked village in Brittany. Once again I think to myself that he is human enough to enjoy it.

Around noon, our tour is interrupted by another outbreak of heavy rain. The dark skies open up and miniature tidal-bores rush down the steep streets of Nazareth's outdoor market, carrying straw, rotting oranges, broken sandals and other refuse before them. Shoppers huddle in shop doorways and stall-holders rush to rescue merchandise laid out to the open sky. Not yet entirely soaked, we jump from one narrow awning to the next until we find what we are looking for, a shop selling umbrellas.

Sylvia and I go for the cheapest, most basic ten-shekel models. Her collapsible umbrella sports a garish tartan plaid pattern in blue and red. Mine is even more lurid, a loud number in nasty swirls of purple paisley. Frère Pierre, conscious of clerical decorum, cannot bring himself to buy either. Although every shekel represents a major effort on his part, he splashes out on a more expensive full-size model in sober and dignified black. Although the ferule and handle are plastic and only imitate real wood, he considers his new umbrella a superior sort of instrument of office, and walks beneath it with all the poise of an old-time country curate. He obviously likes the effect – within a few days, even when there's a not a single cloud in the sky, he's become fond of walking along with his umbrella furled, planting it firmly in the ground with each stride. Every now and then he gives it a jaunty little twirl, flipping it in a 360 degree circle with a casual twist of the wrist.

Frère Pierre's enthusiasm never flags. Early afternoon finds us straddling a barbed-wire fence behind a shopping mall on the edge of Nazareth. Once over it – no mean task for a monk whose robes are flapping crazily in a high wind – we climb from the back of Toys 'Я' Us, up a barren, treeless hill, to a ruin overlooking the town. This is Our Lady of the Fright, an abandoned, little-visited Franciscan chapel built over an older Crusader church. It is cracked and crumbling, with stones falling from its cornices and wild fig trees growing from its foundations. We gaze in through a wide breach in its apse that lets in wind and weather, and inside see walls blackened by fire and scored by crudely scratched graffiti.

Yet it is the site I enjoy most in Nazareth. I like it because there is no one around but ourselves, and none of the pious sanctity you find at religious sites. I also like it for its name – this is the place, tradition says, where Jesus' mother stood terrified as she watched her son being hauled away by the Pharisees for preaching in their synagogue. From here we can also see what Mary saw in the distance – Mount Precipice, the craggy hill they intended to hurl Jesus from.

But most of all I like the place for the image it leaves me with, that of Frère Pierre climbing the steep slope to the chapel. Hunched and silhouetted against a ragged, flying sky, his robes streaming out behind him, he grasps his new umbrella in two hands as he holds it firmly into the fierce teeth of an oncoming wind. If he directs the umbrella just a few degrees off course it will catch the air and its destruction will instantly follow. It's not quite the starkly silhouetted hillside dance of death in Bergman's *Seventh Seal*, perhaps, but there is a certain cinematic drama to it all.

Half an hour later, having checked us out of the convent, Frère Pierre has driven the Jetta to the summit of Mount Precipice. The drop-off into empty space is sudden and the panorama vast. But even if the patchwork plain of olive groves and wheat fields below is rich and fertile, it fails to inspire. Everywhere it is being rapidly eaten away by real estate developers. Here there's a shopping mall, there a housing tract or parking lot or warehouse zone. And tracing its way through it all runs a network of new roads and freeways. The land in 'Holy Land' is fast disappearing around Nazareth.

And yet there is still room for a measure of biblical drama here. In the end Mary's worst fears were not realised and the Pharisees did not succeed in throwing Jesus into the void which now lies at our feet. How exactly he did this is not clear. It sounds as if he simply slipped free of them and escaped. 'They led him to the brow of the hill that they might cast him down,' Frère Pierre intones moodily, reading from the gospel of Mark as we stand looking out. 'But he, passing through the midst of them, went his way.'

It's hardly a gripping passage, and you'd think perhaps Frère Pierre would be more attentive to his physical surroundings than to his New Testament readings. But as he talks he walks in a meandering, erratic kind of way, and comes perilously close to falling off the hill. It is only when Sylvia, becoming another Lady of Fright, shouts out loud, that her friend comes to a halt just inches from the edge of the drop-off. He can't understand why we hustle him into a car and suggest we get a move-on to our final destination. At 700 feet below sea-level, there's not a great deal of falling that Frère Pierre can do in Galilee.

But there's one last holy site the monk insists we see before we head down there: Mount Tabor. It is the place, Pierre informs me, of the Transfiguration, another hilltop site where Jesus, accompanied by three disciples, revealed himself as a divine being. Transfigured before their astonished eyes, his body becoming bright and radiant, it was on this hill that he held conversations with the prophets Elijah and Moses. There was another voice here, too – the booming voice of God himself, who spoke out of a cloud and commanded the disciples to obey his son.

So off we drive to Mount Tabor along a muddy, bumpy road, up slopes that rise so high and steeply out of the surrounding plain that Tabor makes its own weather – while the rest of the sky has cleared, its summit remains wreathed in cloud. We spend only few minutes in the church gardens up there, but it is not just the bitterly cold wind that drives us down. We, too, hear voices coming from out of the clouds. No longer are they just low, rumbling growls – they have transformed themselves into deafening claps of thunder.

It's only four o'clock in the afternoon, but the daylight is steadily draining from the sky. Sylvia is terrified of electrical storms, and getting more nervous by the second. It's as if the same storm has been pursuing us across the Holy Land since yesterday, she says. She herds us into the Jetta and urges a quick descent. It is not quick enough. As we head down the narrow switchback road we see successive forks of lightning streak down from the heavens to hit the plane below. We are hypnotised – they are a strange purple-white colour and unnaturally bright. Then with a loud crack, lightning strikes the hill a hundred metres behind us.

Sylvia squeaks with fear and elbows Brother Pierre hard in the ribs. '*Fonce! Pour l'amour de Dieu, fonce!*' she screams. She may be putting it a little more politely, but it's not far from 'Hit the gas, for Christ's sake!', which is what I'm screaming. The monk floors it, bucketing around the sharp bends far too quickly. Soon enough the Jetta, aged, infirm and not used to such treatment, gives at its weakest point. Abruptly there is another bang and a clatter, we hit our heads on the roof one more, and again the bumper is lying in the road behind us.

It takes much longer to attach it back onto the car this time, and Frére Pierre and I grow sopping wet in the deluge that follows the lightning. This time, Sylvia allows no more stops, no more bible readings, no more lengthy exegesis. She won't even give us time to change our clothes. But before darkness entirely envelops the Holy Land we come to a great drop-off and far below, soothing and mirror-calm, is the Sea of Galilee.

Even in the twilight I can see that the deep fold of earth we are dropping into is an extraordinary place. The plain gives away, the air warms, the vegetation is no longer the same. Even the smells carried on the soft breeze are different. They are exotic and sensual, as if they've issued from some country richer and gentler than the harsh land surrounding us. Frére Pierre speaks of a *douceur*, a sweetness that makes the Galilee the loveliest place in Israel. And after all these high, hostile hilltops milk and honey seems not far from the truth.

It hasn't rained on the escarpment, and as we head ever downwards I am reminded by the dry tawny grass and dark basalt boulders by the road-side of the lush valleys of East Africa. And in fact this *is* a distant beginning of East Africa. This is the start of the Rift Valley, the tectonic system that splits the earth from here down the Jordan Valley, through the Dead Sea and Red Sea, past the Afar Depression in the Horn of Africa, along the African Great Lakes and on to central Mozambique.

It's not just the rocks and the tall waving grass. As the descent continues and the light wanes we are driving past mango plantations, fields of banana plants, rows of lemon and grapefruit trees. We are well below sea level and it is lush and warm and tropical. As long as there is water – no guarantee, given demands on the Jordan River – anything will grow here.

After half an hour of constant descent we coast into Tiberias on the Galilee lakeshore. Tiberias is ancient, but today it is a sort of Middle Eastern Tahoe, a modern resort-town of hotels, bars and restaurants pushed up against the water. We cruise beneath bright flashing neon lights, past crowds of holiday-makers, waterside promenades and marinas where water-ski boats lie tied up for the night. It is bright, agitated and garish. This is not Frère Pierre's Galilee, nor is it mine, and we are all happy to escape Tiberias and follow the shore road to the Caepurnum Junction and Tabgha. There is still the glimmer of a red sunset behind the high escarpments to the west, and eastwards over the Golan a heavy three-quarter moon is casting a path of light along the surface of the lake.

The House of Living Waters is a secluded, well-protected place. There are high walls and security cameras at the entrance, and Frère Pierre has to buzz an intercom button and talk at length before the automatic gates swing open. Once we are inside the grounds we hardly feel more welcome. Sister Catarina, the squat, middle-aged Italian nun who comes to the door of the two-story building on the lakeshore, has never heard of us. She is reluctant to let us stay.

Frère Pierre protests in his most diplomatic manner. There's been some snarl-up at the booking office handling all Franciscan pilgrim accommodation in the Holy Land, he insists; he's phoned Franciscan Central twice to confirm the reservation. Sister Catarina, standing there in baggy brown robes, her thick-lensed glasses framed by a white wimple, looks more than dubious. She fiddles with the rope-belt that encircles her solid waist, shifts feet encased in short grey socks and sandals. It is only when Sylvia, who speaks several languages, breaks into fluid and sunny Italian, that the nun grudgingly relents. '*Va bene, va bene!*' she says at last as she lets us inside and shuffles off to fetch a register.

Our smiles of triumph are short-lived. For Sister Catarina, Frère Pierre's monkishness does not translate into celestial air miles. She wants to charge us full whack, the tariff foreign tourists pay to stay here on their Holy Land tours. I can see already that the House of Living Waters is a lovely place. The extensive gardens outside are treed, carefully manicured and graced by a clear, burbling spring running down to the lake – the source of the hospice's name. The rooms are airy, the mattresses deep, and the *en suite* bathrooms equipped with modern Italian fittings. It all figures in the price, which is perfectly reasonable, even modest, by tourist standards, but more than two cash-strapped pilgrims and an unbeliever are comfortable with.

Pierre, looking for a solution, says he will sleep in the back of the Jetta. This is obviously unacceptable, and Sylvia tries another tack: could Sister Catarina lower the price if she knocked breakfasts off our stay? The nun's mouth turns down and her jaw juts out. She shakes her head.

'Well, then,' Pierre says, inspired to make savings another way. 'Instead of three singles, what about one single and one double?'

Pierre knows I am too light a sleeper to withstand his snoring. But when Sister Catarina learns he's proposing instead to share a room with Sylvia she can barely keep her outraged sense of propriety under control. A monk, and not even a Catholic but an Orthodox monk, angling to sleep with a hospice matron from the holy city of Lourdes? Her eyebrows shoot up in a high arc.

'But it's perfectly all right, Sister,' Frère Pierre whinges. 'We are old friends. We are like brother and sister.'

Yeah, right, I can see Sister Catarina saying to herself as she looks Pierre up and down. She's heard that one before, but never from a man of the cloth.

But it's not up to Sister Catarina. While the negotiating has been going on Sylvia has taken the trouble to stick her head inside the nearest double room. The two beds are about eighteen inches apart. Now she shakes her head at Pierre. 'No way,' she says firmly. 'It's far too conjugal for me.' Desperate, the monk carries on, trying to persuade Sylvia that this is the only solution available.

Is it Sylvia's remark which finally cracks the nun's granite demeanor?

Morals are more important to her than money. Frére Pierre is obviously a rake and this woman's purity is at risk. Anything she can do to keep her from the clutches of this Don Juan in robes is all for the better. After chewing away at the problem for a moment Sister Caterina relents and adds a face-saving condition. She will give us three single rooms at a reduced rate, provided we don't stay more than three nights.

Pierre beams and seems ready to give Sister Cararina a hug and a kiss, but it hardly seems advisable. Instead we fawn over the nun as she leads us upstairs. The House of Living Water, we coo, is without doubt the most wonderful retreat in the entire Holy Land. By the time she puts Pierre at one end of the hall and Sylvia at the other she is beaming too.

My own room is in the middle, facing inland to the gardens. But after dinner in the communal kitchen and a spot of BBC news on satellite TV, I step outside for a look over the Sea of Galilee before going to bed. Storms of doubt and suspicion have subsided in the heart of Sister Caterina, and in the bright moonlight the lake itself wears a serene face.

The main business of Tabgha is pilgrims, and the next morning the place is crawling with them. Beyond the gates the buses are lined up along the shore road, and if the House of Living Waters is not itself a site of mass-pilgrimage, there are establishments on all sides that are. To our right is the Church of the Multiplication, sited on the lakeside spot where Jesus is said to have performed the miracle of feeding a crowd of 5,000 with five loaves and two fishes. To our left is the Church of the Primacy of Saint Peter, where Jesus was seen by his disciples from their fishing boat after his resurrection. Even in his lifetime he'd made this a famous place – it was near here that he walked on water to calm his disciples in the middle of a raging storm. But the hillside directly behind us is more celebrated than either of these places. It is the Mount of Beatitudes, where Christ preached the famous Sermon on the Mount that begins 'Blessed are the poor in spirit; for theirs is the kingdom of heaven...' If Christians cannot find Jesus here they are unlikely to find him anywhere, and from the beginning to the end of each day they are out there, strolling, singing and praying at the lapping water's edge.

We spend much of the day on the lakeshore ourselves, Frére Pierre and Sylvia in serious contemplation, I in the pure enjoyment of such a beautiful spot. It is warm and sunny, and on the far side of the Sea of Galilee the hills loom a milky blue through the soft and hazy air. Nearer by, around the shores of the lake, palm trees and feathery reeds do their best to make the place look as lushly biblical as possible. And if no shepherds, centurions, apostles or kings heave into view, there are lateen-rigged wooden boats out there on the water that make you think that a vanished age is perhaps not so far away.

Other people find the sun-flooded shore seductive as well, and groups pile up on the pebbly beach one after the other. Lakeside masses take place simultaneously side by side, and there is a great commingling of churches, languages, races and nationalities. Perhaps there are individuals who come here looking for Jesus on a one-to-one basis, but I don't see them. This is a celebration to be shared. There are Filipinos who roll up their trousers and together sing hymns knee-deep in water. There are Goans who stand in circles holding hands and praying. There is a group of Poles conducting a full polyphonic eucharist by the water – donning albs and stoles embroidered with golden thread, they transform themselves from middle-aged men in cheap polyester shirts into a resplendent medieval choir. There are even Canadian pilgrims so encouraged in their Christian identity they are confident enough to set down, if just for a moment, bags and day-packs conspicuously decorated with maple-leaf flags. There is a lot of smiling and generous good cheer. Everyone is having a good time.

Everyone, that is, except Verena. Verena is a lay volunteer and full-time resident at the House of Living Waters. She has been living here ever since taking up the contemplative life two years ago. In exchange for accommodation she helps the Franciscan nuns at the Church of the Beatitudes, selling postcards and Christian trinketry at the souvenir shop there. It doesn't sound contemplative. Coping with the vast numbers of tour buses that labour up the hill every day would be enough to test anyone's faith, but Verena has come through with flying colours.

It's hardly surprising – Verena does her best to out-nun the nuns. In her early forties, she is tall and slim and not unattractive. But she tries to be. She wears dumpy grey dresses with long sleeves, ugly shoes, and a scarf over hair that looks hacked off with garden shears. However demanding a real nun's vows can become, she seems to have doubled the severity of her own vows. She doesn't seem to have a private life at all. She is not interested in discussing the smaller things of existence, but invariably steers the talk towards God and his significance for mankind. If things get in the slightest way personal she'll gear down to tell you of Jesus' intervention in her own transformation; like genuine nuns, she has entered into a spiritual marriage with Christ. It is through the love of Jesus, Verena tells us, that she has rediscovered the miracle of life.

It seems a rather lonely miracle. We don't see much of Verena on our first day in Tabgha. When she's not sleeping or selling rosaries up the hill she spends her time in a little prayer room off the guest dining room. But even nuns have to eat, and late on the second evening, some time after Frére Pierre and Sylvia have retired upstairs, I see the door swing open and Verena appear with a Bible in hand. She's been in there reading and praying for at least three hours, so quiet I wasn't aware of her presence, and has at last emerged.

Is it her intense meditation, a long, silent dialogue with her creator, that has given a flush to Verena's cheeks? She seems to have become warmer and more animated, more willing to be herself. She returns from the next-door kitchen with fruit and yoghurt, but instead of eating she sits at the dining room table and begins to talk.

She tells me how important the Bible is for her. 'It is a blueprint for life,' she says with enthusiasm. 'It turns each day into a new and wonderful blessing.' I'm afraid I'm in for a lengthy inspirational session, but after a few more Christian homilies Verena relaxes even more. Perhaps, after two years of a self-imposed and cloister-like existence the solitude is finally beginning to get to her. She tells me about another life, of her previous existence as a suburban *hausfrau* and all its deceptions.

'When I was young I dreamed it would be perfect,' she tells me, the apple on the plate before her half-peeled and forgotten. 'I would have the perfect, loving man who would share the bad times as well as the good. I would have the perfect child who would grow up in a secure and caring family and love me in return. And when it happened it wasn't like that at all. Everything came apart, and I had to leave.' In detail Verena describes the painful, flaming crash of her marriage. But, she says, it was all part of a process that had at any rate began long before. 'Only now, here in Galilee,' she says, 'do I realise I am on a lifelong path of healing and learning. That is why the Bible is important – everything in my existence, everything in the whole world, is in it. Everything!'

Verena carries on in this vein for some time, becoming more emotional and worked up as she proceeds. Normally I'd try to stay away from this kind of confessional outburst. But pouring it all out seems to be doing Verena some real good, and I start encouraging her instead. The minutes pass, and like clouds gathering over Mount Tabor great declarations of self-knowledge pile up in the air around us. Together, we get profound. From time to time I intervene to insert some specious and high-flown philosophical observation. Increasingly Verena combines talk of Jesus with some sort of syncretic interpretation of the cosmos. It's as if she is shucking off her Christian identity, replacing it with some earlier version of herself. Is there a flower-child buried in this soul seeking so hard for redemption? Eventually we concur that all things are connected in a great web of spiritual causality, that no past action takes place without having knock on-effects in the present, that choices available in the future depend entirely on other choices made today. We become karmic, mystic, New-Age, tantric. Past, present or future, all actions exist for eternity, we both agree, the whole rippling out into space and across time to connect each individual to every other individual. It crosses my mind that this is not Christian thought at all. But whatever it is, it's getting Verena exited.

'*Gott! Gott! Ach, Gott!*' she finally cries out, losing her accent and her vocabulary in her fervour. 'You touch me. Look what you are doing – this talk is giving me *gänsehaut*, what do you say...chicken-skin!' She rises and walks over to the armchair I'm sitting in, pulling back the sleeve of her dress and proffering her bare forearm. I inspect the smooth white flesh, unseen, untouched by sun or any other foreign element, for so long. She is right – she's got goosebumps.

'Feel!' she commands. I run my finger over her arm. Perhaps I shouldn't. 'Ah, *Gott*,' says Verena, 'You touch me in my body.' Her eyes are wide open and liquid, her voice has gone husky. I am not sure whether at this moment Verena remains married to Jesus or not. Perhaps she's taking a short break. Certainly Bible-learning is not at the front-and-centre of her mind right now.

But even if I wanted to I'm not taking any chances with Verena – I've seen the gleam of righteousness in Sister Caterina's eye and heard the pad of her feet as she patrols the halls of the House of Living Waters late at night. The idea of hawk-eyed Sister Catarina on the prowl is enough to scare the daylights out of any potential sinner. Unquestioningly the nun is hostile to all non-Christian varieties of cosmic union – if she even suspected such a thing it wouldn't surprise me if she gave her lay volunteer, like her paying guest, just three days to clear out too. I leave Verena, open-mouthed and silent and no doubt a little surprised at herself, to follow Pierre and Sylvia upstairs to the sleep of the just.

We are up on the Golan plateau before nine o'clock the following morning. Syrian leaders no doubt have their own reasons for so long refusing to negotiate the surrender of even the smallest patch of this high, rugged land. And if I were a Syrian farmer I'd have my own reasons. It is stark and beautiful, a fertile plain that rolls on in field after field of black soil. I've never seen earth so dark and rich-looking – no ploughman in this flint-strewn part of the world would ever want to give it up.

I can also see why an Israeli military tactician might be loathe to hand it back to an enemy. Rolling westward, the elevated plain of the Golan abruptly drops 1,700 feet into the Sea of Galilee. It's not just the view that's spectacular, it's the strategic siting. Before 1967 Syria could lob how-itzer shells onto the towns, farms and settlements below with the greatest of ease. There'd be no guessing about targets from these heights – in the morning light streaming across the lake I can see individual buildings even in far-away Tiberias.

We drive eastwards into the sun, seeing signs of unresolved conflict everywhere. Here and there lie old Syrian forward positions, their con-crete bunkers and block houses now cracked and sprouting weeds. In ruined Arab villages uninhabited for over forty years there are still coils of barbed wire running along the roadside and bright red signs reading 'Danger – Mines'. There are older Israeli defensive positions, they too now also abandoned and covered with the graffiti of long-departed units of the Israeli Defense Force. As the decades pass, as efforts at political resolution fail one after the other, open conflict has bogged down into unchanging stalemate on the ground. Twice we pass armoured patrols of the UN's Disengagement Observer Force. But disengagement is hardly the right word. Apart from more recent military bases fronted by long rows of American-built tanks and Humvees, there is a large and growing Israeli civilian presence on the Golan Heights as well – entire towns of settlers, lush farms of citrus trees and grape vines, and even here those ubiquitous US-style shopping malls. Israelis love shopping malls.

Frére Pierre is not satisfied with any of this. Braced determinedly behind the wheel, he wants to get as close to the Israeli-Syrian demarca-tion line as possible. I can't really figure it out – so ethereally detached, so oblivious of daily realities in his own environment, he seems here to want to come face to face with the gritty truths of physical existence. Perhaps he's simply like the rest of us on holiday. Away from the routine spiritual grind, he's looking for a little diversion.

Le Petit Guide de la Terre Sainte being of no help here, Frére Pierre takes pathfinding duties upon himself. Running parallel to the Syrian line, he strikes off on a tertiary road, narrow, unpaved and muddy, which veers eastwards. We bump along for a few kilometers, Pierre praising the Jetta lavishly for it's off-road worthiness. Along the way we cross a pack of five large and very dirty feral dogs heading in the other direction. There is no sign of whether they are Israeli dogs or Syrian dogs, but they turn and follow, loping close behind the bouncing car until the frontier is very near. Less than a kilometre away now, across a couple of field-lengths of black soil, we can see Israeli flags fluttering from observation towers. The Jetta, though, is not as roadworthy as the monk likes to imagine. The track becomes ever muddier until our tyres are spinning without traction and throwing spatters of mud at the dogs behind us. It makes them not just dirtier still; it offends them. Frére Pierre can go no further. As he reverses back down the road the dogs abandon us and carry on alone towards Syrian territory.

They're not as offended, though, as Sylvia. She finds the whole enterprise childish and foolhardy. Protesting loudly and frequently until now, she presently falls silent, her jaw clenched, as Frére Pierre finds a second, smaller track leading eastwards. Even patient hospice matrons have their limits. When we top a small rise and see, not far in front of us, an Arab village with Syrian flags flying from a minaret, Sylvia finally looses her cool.

'That's it!' she shouts at Frére Pierre, opening the car door as we continue to roll along. 'I've had enough. Do you think I want to spend the next twenty-four hours in an Israeli military lock-up so you can enjoy the thrill of playing James Bond in drag?'

She is right, of course. 'What do you imagine the IDF will think,' she berates him, 'when they pick up a foreigner in a pony-tail and robes on the Syrian frontier? Do you think they'll accept you without question, take you on a tour of the installations, maybe ask for your Christian blessing?'

At this point Sylvia is preparing to throw herself out of the still-moving car. 'Are you mad?' she shrills at him. 'I don't care what the hell the two of you do – for all I care you can try crossing the border on bicycles or ultralight aircraft. But leave me out of it!'

What else can Frére Pierre do but give up, stop the car and turn around? I for one am glad. Touring the Holy Land sites with a devoted monk is one thing. Fooling around on a disputed Middle East border with a guy in a gown and a high hat is another. Sheepishly, without anyone saying much to anyone else, we drive back across the high plain, down the steep escarpment to the Sea of Galilee, and around the northern end of the lake to Tabgha. But I think Frére Pierre is satisfied. He's wearing a little smile all the way.

Sylvia has stayed as long as she possibly can – the next morning her childhood friend loads the Jetta with their baggage and prepares to drive her directly to Ben Gurion airport on the edge of Tel Aviv. Lourdes awaits her return. I will stay on for one more day in Galilee. There is nowhere more relaxing this end of the Mediterranean.

We say goodbye and I walk up into the hills behind Tabgha. A light breeze, soothing and balmy, is blowing in off the lake. The views are superb. I stop often for the sheer pleasure of it all, sitting beneath thick foliage to look up at bright green mangoes or avocados ripening in the dark shade. There are also acres of banana plants, their bunched fruit growing on thick, down-hanging stems that end in sinister-looking banana hearts of deep purple. By mid-morning I have reached the domed building that crowns the top of the hill.

The Church of the Beatitudes may be built with the distant past in mind, but its faux-Byzantine arches and columns don't do much for me. A twentieth-century structure that replaces a more modest site commemorating Jesus' Sermon on the Mount, the whole modern complex lacks authenticity. To me it seems to aim at funneling as many worshippers through the place in the most efficient way possible. And to be honest, by this point I'm beginning to feel I've had enough of the pilgrim-trade to last me a long time. Already the place is packed, but for every bus that leaves the parking lot another couple of buses arrive. There's too much sancity in the air, and it makes me claustrophobic. It's not long before I'm striding off down the hill again.

I am very nearly at the bottom when I stumble into yet one more group of pilgrims. They are Korean Christians, and the women among them, graceful in silk *hanbok* gowns, are holding coloured parasols over their heads for protection against the sun. Emerging from high, tawny grass rippling in the breeze, they are a striking sight, and I stop not far away to watch. Only gradually do I realise where I am – this is the first, the original location associated with the Sermon on the Mount

It is a very simple and attractive site, a small, flattish hillside niche lying directly above the House of Living Waters. The Koreans are gathered around a squarish boulder that looks like it's been sitting there forever. On its sides, chiseled in rough characters, are the eight Beatitudes. Around the stone, arranged in a circle, are other smaller stones. They mark the place, I imagine, where Jesus' disciples and other followers are believed to have sat and listened.

I listen to a brief sermon myself, but understand no more in Korean than I might have in the original Aramaic. When the service is over I move to the lip of the little hillside niche to watch the pilgrims descending the remaining 200 metres of steep slope. Below on the highway that skirts the lake a dozen tour buses are waiting to take Tabgha pilgrims away.

Looking down at the line of descending parasols, I raise both hands, holding my open palms high above my head to keep the mid-morning sun out of my eyes. And as I do I am spotted by a man in the crowd of tourists milling beside the buses below.

'JESUS? ARE YOU JESUS?' he bellows up to me through cupped hands.

It's the kind of question that would attract attention anywhere, and in an instant everyone is looking my way. I suppose I might appear a little peculiar standing on a hill, facing a crowd with my hands raised above me. But only on the Mount of Beatitudes would I get the reaction I do. Laughing at his own humour, the man who shouted now starts cheering and clapping, and within a few seconds everyone is clapping and cheering.

It's not the kind of question I'm usually asked, and it's just too silly and embarrassing to shout back, 'No, of course I'm not Jesus.' So I just stand there, looming over the crowd like the statue that looms over Rio de Janeiro, until I hear a sturdy, familar voice coming up to me from the edge of the crowd.

'Wonderful! Such a wonderful, living picture! It's just like the Bible!' It's Verena, emerging from the garden of the House of Living Waters to see what the commotion is. 'Thank you! Thank you!' she shouts, and begins clapping like the others.

This is getting more ridiculous by the second. All I can do is lower my hands, bow my head, and adopt a dignified silence. I'm glad Verena is loosening up, but it's time to leave the Holy Land. I've had enough of Jesus for a while.

Twelve

Jerusalem lives through cycles, states of mind that are capricious and unpredictable perhaps, but cyclical nonetheless. A certain atmosphere will reign for weeks or months over the city, working its way into every nook and cranny, every outlook, opinion and attitude in the place. Jerusalem's inhabitants will seem never to have perceived each other and the world in any other way. And then without warning, triggered by some incident in a dark Old City alley or a conference-room in a capital halfway around the world, Jerusalem's entire mind-set will flip over on itself. Everyone is taken by surprise. Calm will give way to tension, openness to hostility, optimism to bleakness. Or it might be the other way around. In either case outcomes which looked utterly improbable yesterday seem entirely likely today.

My return to Jerusalem coincides with one such flip-over and a sudden spate of open conflict – shootings in Hebron, skirmishes in Gaza and demonstrations in the Old City itself. As with Jerusalem, so with the Maison d'Abraham – the changed atmosphere in the city seems to have infected everything in its proximity. Before I left on my Holy Land road trip, the Maison d'Abraham had been humming along with ease and affability. Each group of visitors brought something new and different to the hospice on the hill – nuns and pilgrims did their best to help each other, the long hall corridors echoed with eager conversation, and dinners in the old refectory were a delight. But now a new mood seems to have set in. It is fractious and dispiriting.

In the refectory Ashraf Noor and I see the change reflected at the table reserved for guests who come as individuals rather than part of large groups. Up until now our fellow-diners have been entertaining company. Each evening a multicultural gathering over the dinner table produces exchanges on any number of topics – not just religion in Jerusalem, but theatre in Milan, perhaps, the wine harvest in Bordeaux, or adventures in New York real estate.

But on my first night back from Tabgha I find myself seated between Ashraf and a new arrival, a Swedish academic who has been contracted by an international NGO to do research in Jerusalem. It's short-term work, not long enough to rent a house, but too long for the man's organization to pay for one of Jerusalem's pricy hotels. The Maison d'Abraham has proved a convenient expedient; having prevailed upon Father Michael's kindness and found some of the cheapest accommodation in the city, the researcher can keep the better part of his *per diem* allowance in his pocket.

I have nothing against non-religious guests at the Maison d'Abraham. I'm one of them. But not even this man's lucky break is enough to induce him on his first night in the stone-columned refectory to enter into its spirit of generosity and goodwill. A dumpy, balding man with a tooth-brush mustache and unexpressive features, he shows no desire to take part in dinner-time conversation – he chews monotonously, keeping his downcast eyes on the plate in front of him. Ashraf, thinking stiff Nordic reserve might be softened with a little encouragement, tries repeatedly to draw him into the talk, but there's nothing doing – the man's answers to him are so brief and blunt as to border on rudeness.

But his unsociable manner is nothing compared to his wife's boorish-ness. She sits opposite me, unkempt and carelessly dressed, a large woman who overflows her chair. Her eyes, deep-set in a pale, pasty face, are beady and greedy-looking, and there's a permanently sour, dissatisfied look about her.

Unlike her husband, she has no reticence at all in expressing herself. When Soeur Anna brings soup from the kitchen she demands to know what kind it is, and before the tureen has even touched the table informs her that, no, she doesn't like that soup. 'Isn't there another kind?' she blurts out. Refusing this first course, she reaches over the bowl of the diner beside her to grab the bread, knocking his spoon-laden hand in the process. Waving her pudgy arm and calling to Soeur Anna after the main course arrives, she complains loudly and bitterly that she's missing a fork. 'Someone has taken it,' she says, looking accusingly around the table. Once equipped, she eats quickly and noisily, shoveling her food and helping herself to a second portion from the platter on the table before anyone else has finished the first. Over desert, oblivious to eyes turned away in distaste, she spits fruit-skins directly from her masticating mouth onto her plate. I've never seen anyone quite so piggish, slovenly and generally unhappy in life.

The rest of us are in a state of alarm. The nuns, entirely unused to this sort of behaviour, can only giggle. Even Ashraf is left nonplussed, his eyebrows permanently raised in consternation. The conversation, usually so buoyant, inevitably bogs down into intermittent and self-conscious banalities.

Why, I wonder in the long gaps of silence that hang over the table, has this man brought this appalling harpy with him to Jerusalem? In his situation I'd do anything I possibly could to leave her behind in Stockholm. What I would like to do now, despite his presence, is to lean over and ask his wife to behave. This is not a restaurant, I want to say. These people helping you are nuns, not servants you are paying to kick around. But I don't. So awful is this woman that the only plausible scenario that might explain her presence requires my forbearance. She must be so mentally unbalanced and dependent on her poor husband, I reason, that he's obliged to look after her; he's *got* to haul her around, no matter how much of an embarrassment she is. Little wonder he stares at his plate and hustles his wife out as soon as she has finished.

These dinners continue, everyone pretending things are as they've always been, for another two nights. Then finally, the nuns, typically more concerned for our welfare than theirs, take action. At the end of the evening meal, Soeur Nirmala waits until the Swedish guests have departed and apologises for their behavior. 'They won't be bothering you anymore,' she smiles. 'We are moving them. It will be better for everyone.'

But it isn't better for everyone. It's worse. The next evening the couple are sitting at their own table. Rather than looking like a banished exile, the woman seems triumphant, as if she's finally got what she wanted. And she has – they have more space and the table's soup tureens and meat platters all to themselves.

But the triumphalism doesn't last long. Halfway through the meal Sister Anna is once again called up in front of the woman. 'There isn't enough,' we hear her complain from yards away. She glares in our direction. 'The other table has more.'

'But there are more people at that table,' Sister Anna reasons.

'It is NOT enough!' the woman says, her harsh voice rising as she lifts the platter to Sister Anna for return to the kitchen. Her husband merely sits there, his bland face passive. All around the dining room heads are turned towards the commotion.

Rising, I take the platter from our own table and carry it over to the Swedes. There is still food on it. 'Please, take ours,' I say. I am not seeking to defuse the situation; I am fed up, and trying to shame the couple into behaving decently. Without a word the woman takes the platter, serves herself, serves her husband, and puts the now-empty platter on the table in front of her. I grab it and walk back, smoldering. My lesson has gone over their heads.

The situation is finally resolved on the following Saturday, when the Swedes attempt a lightning coup in the laundry-block behind the main building. The little concrete building contains three large washing-machines, semi-industrial models used to launder the bed-linen that is constantly being changed in the Maison d'Abraham. The machines are also used by the nuns and the Maison's half-dozen volunteer ladies for their own personal effects. And finally, they are used by Ashraf and me, who, as long-term residents, have won house laundry privileges. We are happy to have earned them, or otherwise we'd be hauling dirty socks and underwear to distant laundromats in town. But it hasn't been easy.

In a co-ordinated, weeks-long campaign we've had to sweet-talk our way into the confidence and affections of our most vigorous opponents. It's astonishing how reluctant the lady volunteers, normally demure and self-effacing elderly Frenchwomen, can be when it comes to laundry.

So even now, as we stand in the sunshine outside the block door with some of them, I hanging socks and Ashraf gossiping away in his best housewife-on-the-back-porch manner, we are on our best behavior. Consequently we are as startled as the lady volunteers when the Swedes, whose infamy has grown as the days go by, hustle past us into the laundry-block carrying large bags of laundry. Twice they have demanded the right from Soeur Marta to use the washing machines and twice they have been refused – a few weeks' stay does not justify putting even more pressure on heavily-used machines. So now the Swedes are launching a laundry-block *putsch*, determined to obtain by force what they cannot get by negotiation.

Predictably, the ladies who follow the couple in through the door are outraged. '*Mon Dieu!*' they squeal as the Swedes dump the laundry from their bags into a pile on the floor. Some of the items are none too appetizing, and the ladies protest all the louder when they see what's going into the machines on their washday. But there's no stopping the Swedes, whose plan depends on surprise, daring and speed. Not only do they commandeer a washing-machine; they dump its contents, barely through a final spin-cycle, on top of another machine.

But by the time they have located the soap powder there is not a volunteer in sight. Realising that resistance is useless, these good Christian ladies, incensed, march off to seek assistance from the highest authority.

It isn't *Dieu*. It is Father Michael, whose retribution is far swifter and more exacting, who soon appears in the doorway. No one messes with *his* volunteer ladies. Although Ashraf and I don't hang around – guilt through association strikes us as a potential risk here – we later learn that the Swedes' laundry is ejected before it ever reaches the spin cycle. Not only that; the Swedes themselves are ejected, having been asked to make their own further arrangements for accommodation. I am sure Father Michael dispatched them as diplomatically as possible. They are last seen climbing into a taxi at the front door of the main building, the man silent and po-faced, the woman complaining that the taxi-driver is too slow in relieving her of her bags. It is not one of the Maison d'Abraham's more sublime moments.

At the same time that the Swedes are upsetting the old monastery's naturally serene rhythms, the nuns find themselves playing host to yet another problematic character, one Anne-Laure. The latest in a long line of Breton Christians who've found their way to the Maison d'Abraham, Anne-Laure is tall, big-boned and shortsighted. Her physique accentuates her natural awkwardness, making her look as if she's still growing and hasn't quite got used to her own size. And at 28 she still has no idea of where she's headed. Her reasons for coming to the Maison d'Abraham are unclear, even to herself.

Her usual fallback is Christian charity. She has come to Jerusalem, she explains, with a desire to help children in difficulty. But although she is assisted by Monique, a helpful and experienced West Bank aid-worker who occasionally stays at the Maison d'Abraham, Anne-Laure consistently balks when the opportunity to help Palestinian kids actually presents itself. Monique gives her hours of patient advice which she barely seems to take in. Interviews with various aid organisations are arranged for her but she fails to show up. Despite numerous possibilities for involvement, she finally claims that she needs to first acclimatise to life in Arab East Jerusalem.

Mostly this takes the form of accepting dinner invitations from men Anne-Laure meets in the Arab Old City markets. They are very friendly, she says, and willing to teach her about real Arab life. In Anne-Laure's mind there is no question of romantic involvement with these men. Deeply Christian in her upbringing, she is far too chaste for any such thing – she'll readily quote you the biblical injunctions which rule such relationships. But she doesn't seem to realise how she is provoking certain expectations in these men. Nor does she understand why, sooner rather than later, they angrily lose patience with her. She's playing a risky game, constantly moving from one iffy encounter to another. Whenever Anne-Laure fails to show up for dinner at the Maison d'Abraham, there's a concerned look on the nuns' faces, and relief when she finally arrives back late. It's hard looking after a grown-up woman with an adolescent's mind.

No one is quite certain what Anne-Laure's past is. At times she tells us she comes from a large and distinguished family of university academics. At others she implies she is an only child who's struggled hard to escape desperately straitened circumstances. But after a few evenings out she herself has few doubts about her life now. She's discovered, she declares, that she has a natural, innate feeling for Jerusalem, and decided she needs no advice or organisational structure in order to fit right in. It is we, her fellow pilgrims, who have no clue about engaging with life here. 'Do you have any idea,' she asks us in morning-after debriefings at the breakfast table, 'what it's like to sit cross-legged on a carpet? To eat mutton, without knife or fork, from the same bowl as your dining companion?' With derision she indicates the slice of baguette on which Ashraf is spreading strawberry jam. 'You're a teacher, and you think *that's* the way to absorb local culture?'

Anne-Laure's own absorption of Arab culture is hardly profound. Her new friends are teaching her how to sell carpets in their shops. They've shown her how to make Turkish coffee with cardamum. They encourage her to wear the Bedouin embroidered dresses they hang on their shop walls. She's even learned a few market phrases in Arabic. '*Ahlan sadiqi! Min ayna anta?*' she recites. 'Hello, friend! Where are you from?' But in Anne-Laure's view of things you'd think she'd just earned a PhD in Arab studies from SOAS or negotiated the Arabian peninsula on foot without compass or water. In less than two weeks our confused Breton pilgrim has become an accomplished Middle East expert.

Anne-Laure, in short, is a bit of a case, and the nuns are doubtful she can go another week without running into serious trouble – one night, they fear, she'll end up raped or with her throat cut. That might be a little pessimistic, but naive, immature Anne-Laure certainly appears to be heading into deep water. It is with some relief then, that the nuns notice that in no time Anne-Laure has attached herself emotionally to a newly arrived visitor at the Maison d'Abraham.

If Michael is about the same age as Anne-Laure, he is her physical opposite. He is short, stocky, thick-necked and solidly built, a man who moves with easy assurance on the balls of his feet. His head is shaved, his voice somewhat rough and abrupt, and his face set with a certain cocky self-assurance. Unlike Anne-Laure, his whole manner suggests he is a person of strong character who knows what he wants and is used to getting it.

But the more time we spend with Michael the more we understand why he and Anne-Laure gravitate so naturally together – he is as child-ish as she is, and his physical presence only gives him a child's bullying menace.

Michael is a Sydneysider, the product of two immigrant families, one Lebanese Christian, the other Maltese. This is Michael's first time away from Australia and he has come to the eastern Mediterranean, he explains, to discover himself through his roots. Self-discovery, he says, is important to him. It sounds reasonable, and even Michael's earlier exercises in self-discovery, if a little bizarre, at least speak of a genuine search. In the last few years, he tells us, he has spent many profitable hours encased in a stainless steel vat containing a saline solution whose specific gravity and tempera-ture is exactly that of the human body's. 'They're called isolation tanks,' he tells me enthusiastically. 'There's a lid. There is no sound in there, no light, no tactile feeling, no gravity, no sensory stimulation at all. It's like floating in space. It's inner space – you can concentrate on your mind because you feel like you've lost your body. It's perfect for meditation.'

It sounds all very Zen-like, but I sometimes wonder if Michael wasn't introduced to isolation tanks as a form of psychiatric therapy. For the problem is that when Michael's body is not isolated it seems to come into contact with other bodies with a resounding thump. Michael has a talent for discord and contentious relations.

The Australian pitches up at the Maison d'Abraham on the same day he leaves the Old City's Armenian Catholic Hostel in a rage of indignation. In his version of events his original plan was to spend two months in Jerusalem. As a Christian with origins in the eastern Church he believed the holy city was worth that amount of time, and he paid the custodian of the hostel the full amount in advance. He quickly realised, however, that he was far more Australian than he was Middle-Eastern – a few days would be ample. But on approaching the custodian for a refund, the man refused to hand over his money.

'The wrath of God will fall on him.' Michael tells us at the dinner table, his jaw-muscle flexing in anger. Old Testament language is not his forté, and he quickly runs out of it. 'That old bastard's a cheat and a crook, and I'm going to have his arse thrown into jail.'

I have no idea what really happened at the Armenian Hostel, although I somehow doubt it's quite the way Michael describes it. But Michael wants vengeance. In the following days he makes numerous visits to the police, to lawyers, to the Australian Consulate, to the Ministry of Justice and to church officials. Unsuccessfully, he demands an audience with the Armenian Archbishop of Jerusalem himself. None of these refusals surprise me – Michael is out of control, swearing, sweating, shouting, hurling insults and wild accusations at anyone who questions the details of his story. Every day he returns to the Maison d'Abraham defeated, for no one wants to pursue the matter any further. No one, that is, except Anne-Laure.

It is doubtful that in ordinary circumstances they would see each other as allies. But perhaps in Michael Anne-Laure recognises the determination she lacks. Perhaps in Anne-Laure Michael senses a fellow-fantasist. And in addition to following him into taxis and zooming off on the next stage of his doomed mission, Anne-Laure offers Michael consolation. Each day they become closer and more hush-hush, until Anne-Laure finally stops accepting dinner invitations from strange men in the market. Among the pilgrims at the Maison d'Abraham the pair are considered an item. The nuns heave a sigh of relief.

The nuns heave too early. Inevitably, sparks start flying within days. There is bickering at the dinner table. When Anne-Laure drops her halting English for French, a language Michael doesn't understand, he resents being excluded; he resorts to the childish tactic of repeating in garbled form everything she says. When Michael dominates the conversation with his on-going story of cheating priests, corrupt lawyers and wanker consuls, Anne-Laure is unhappy about being forced off centre-stage, a place she thoroughly enjoys. She tells him to shut up and stop boring her. It's like having dinner with six-year-olds, and everyone is soon thoroughly tired of them.

Although Michael and Anne-Laure at last give up on attempting to obtain justice, their isolation only pushes them further together. One day they turn up in a car, complete with a GPS spoken-direction navigational system, that they have jointly rented. It's a disaster. Off they go to the surrounding sites, and each evening we get a blow-by-blow replay of their tussles. There are arguments about what time they need to get up to see the sun rise over Masada, disagreements over whether to pay for shower facilities at the Dead Sea, disputes regarding a planned snorkeling trip to Eilat. They even fight over the GPS. Michael wants to keep the English-speaking model; Anne-Laure, claiming unfair advantage, wants to trade it in for a French one.

It all ends quickly enough. One evening Anne-Laure comes in to dinner alone, while Michael sits in the car outside, refusing to budge. 'He called me an awkward cow,' splutters Anne-Laure, the tears wet on her cheeks. Eventually Michael is persuaded to come inside, although he refuses to sit at the same table as Anne-Laure.

'She crazy,' he says, glowering at her across the dining room and at the same time delicately fingering a lower front incisor with his forefinger. 'She hit me over the head with a Bible. She chipped my tooth. I'm going to sue her for grievous bodily harm.'

But his voice lacks its usual aggressive conviction, and Michael does not proceed with his threat. In fact he retreats altogether, leaving the Maison d'Abraham the next day, never to be seen again. It wouldn't surprise me to learn that he's returned directly to his stainles-steel sensory deprivation tank in Sydney.

Anne-Laure, too, disappears shortly after, destination unknown. Perhaps she's gone back to Brittany. If you can't make it at home you certainly can't make it in this city. Jerusalem has defeated them both, once and for all.

If Anne-Laure and Michael are two of life's hapless bumblers, they're bumblers in the comic vein, and too self-centred to be worthy of endless sympathy. But there are other visitors here for whom it is never possible to heave a sigh of relief. They are truly troubled spirits, and their passage through the halls of the Maison d'Abraham leaves behind them an air of genuine sadness and regret.

Until now I have been alone on my rooftop. Although there is one more room there at the top of the stairs, it has never been occupied. But one wet afternoon I notice a light on under the door. If a new guest has moved in the light is not so surprising – it's a dark, gloomy day. It is more surprising, though, that the light remains permanently switched on. There is a bright strip of illumination under the door when I turn in late that evening, and it's still there when I wake up the next morning. In fact it burns continuously for three days. I'm curious enough that I begin checking the door several times each night to see if the light is finally extinguished.

I become so mystified that I ask the nuns about the new mystery guest. I've seen no one going into or coming out of the room, and there are no new faces at the dining table. The nuns, usually cheerful and good-natured, grow solemn. It's a young woman, Soeur Nirmala tells me, with problems at home. She wanted a quiet room and has asked not to be disturbed.

'She's working things out,' says the Indian nun. 'We must respect that.'

'But is she all right?' I ask. I can't imagine anyone working things out for seventy-two sleepless hours at a stretch.

Sister Nirmala tells me she that she comes down from the roof at least once a day to the glass-doored telephone booth near Soeur Marta's office. And that is where, walking down the hall a few hours later, I finally see her.

Julia is young and pretty. As she sits in the booth with the receiver to her ear she is wearing a bright Indian print dress decorated with little round mirrors and sequins. Her face is partly obscured by a mass of curly black hair. I see her only for a moment in the dim light beneath the stairwell, but she looks OK to me.

The next time I see Julia she is not OK at all. The light is still on in her room when I go to bed that evening, and when I get up Julia's door is ajar. Inside, the room is a mess. It stinks with the sweet aniseed smell of arak. There are dresses, jeans, cosmetics, underwear, a hairdryer and other items tumbled across one of the twin beds, and beside it an upturned suitcase. There are wet towels on the floor, and more scatted clothing. Beneath the second bed – the one that's been used – two arak bottles lie empty on their sides. On top of the bed, sprawled across sheets bunched in the middle of the mattress, half on the bed and half off, lies Julia herself in bra and panties. Beside her is an open medicine bottle, empty.

Julia's head is hanging towards the floor, her hair touching it, but I can see she is breathing. Taking two stairs at a time, I am down to the ground three stories below in seconds, and struggling to catch my breath in front of Soeurs Marta and Ana. I have never seen a middle-aged woman move so quickly. In almost the same time that I take to get down from the rooftop Soeur Marta is back up there again.

Julia's door is closed when I arrive a moment later. But I can hear the nun speaking slowly and loudly, as one might to a deaf person, repeatedly asking questions. The answers are too low and slurred to be intelligible, but I can image what Soeur Marta wants to know. What has the girl taken, and how much?

When she emerges ten minutes later Soeur Marta looks calmer. Through the doorway I can see Julia's been tidied up and put into bed. At the same time a doctor, summoned by Soeur Ana, is coming up the stairs. Half an hour later he heads down again, the crisis over. Julia has swallowed sleeping pills, but not enough to kill her. At the same time she has also drunk a great deal of arak, and is now sleeping it off.

What's worse than attempted suicide? The answer, I think as the sound

of the departing doctor's heels reverberate up the stone stairs, is not difficult: attempted suicide surrounded by strangers in rented accommodation
far from home. The only thing missing in Julia's room for true awfulness
is an on-again, off-again flashing of neon from a hotel sign outside her
window.

The following day an official from the French Consulate arrives
to discuss Julia's departure and repatriation with Soeur Marta. Soeur
Nirmala tells me the nuns have been in touch with Julia's parents – they've
telephoned to tell them of her attempt to end her life. Nirmala is holding
back tears. The parents' response is brief and to the point. They don't want
to hear any further news of Julia unless it's news of her death.

Soeur Nirmala isn't saying it aloud, but I can hear her question nonetheless. How is it that such a pain-filled creature should end up here, in
Jerusalem, a place where there is so much pain already?

I have no answers, but at that moment decide this might be the time
to get away. I'm thinking of leaving the city again, heading not north this
time, but eastwards. By all reports things are no less painful out on the
West Bank. But a change, they say, is as almost as good as a holiday.

Thirteen

From the Green Line bus terminal on the Nablus Road in Jerusalem the Arab city of Ramallah, *de facto* capital of the West Bank, lies just thirty-five minutes away. It's an easy ride. If you ignore the high concrete wall snaking away over the hills in either direction, the Qalandya crossing looks like any border-crossing in the European Union. It seems just as superfluous too, at least if you're travelling eastwards; filled with Palestinians and the occasional foreigner like me, the No. 18 bus barely comes to a halt as it's waved on through by Israeli soldiers. The difficulty lies in heading the other way. For most people in the West Bank the diesel-belching No. 18 Green Line bus might as well be an Apollo spacecraft, Qalandya the edge of the upper stratosphere, and Jerusalem the moon.

Before the creation of Israel, Ramallah was a hill resort for well-to-do Palestinians. They came up from the coastal plains for months at a time to escape the oppressive heat of summer, and lived comfortably in large, airy villas. Some of those villas, most of them now the worse for wear, can still be found sitting high on the city's hill-crests and ridges. But the life that went with them no longer exists. If Ramallah is still the most prosperous town on the West Bank, most of the money that flows into it arrives in the form of foreign aid. Voted by the US, the EU, the UN and dozens of non-governmental organisations, these are the funds that keep Ramallah solvent.

In a city which concentrates most of the West Bank's political power, such as it is, much of this aid remains invisible. It goes into 'state-building', the reinforcing of the fragile civic and political institutions of the Palestinian Authority – the body upon which western hopes for the future rest. There are some results of foreign funding you can actually see. Its facade plastered with posters advertising an international film festival, I spot a wonderful new cinematheque any municipality would be proud of. But through the oily, forehead-smudged bus window, most of Ramallah appears run-down. In hastily assembled suburbs on the edge of town public amenities like sidewalks are in short supply. Instead there are flooded drains, festoons of improvised aerial wiring, and empty, overgrown lots. Everywhere there, strewn around with liberal abundance and varying in size from the conveniently throwable to the too hefty to bother moving, are chunks of rubble. Where does it come from, all the concrete detritus lying around all the towns of the West Bank? It's as if the place is falling apart even before new investment has finished putting it together.

What's not lacking in Ramallah are inhabitants. They are no longer a select group of wealthy summer-people. In a way they, too, are accumulated rubble – they are the children, grandchildren and great-grandchildren of refugees who flooded into the West Bank after the *Nakba*, 'the disaster', of 1948. Today Ramallah is hardly big enough to hold them all. As the bus approaches its final destination near Al-Manara Square, the crowds grow denser until there is hardly room enough for them in the streets. Jostling shoulder to shoulder, they form a mass so thick and impenetrable I have trouble spotting Jesse at our street-corner rendezvous.

Jesse, for all that, is easy enough to pick out in this ocean of olive complexions and jet-black hair. His blue eyes and stubbly, rust-coloured beard instantly mark him as a foreigner. So does the working man's flat-cap he habitually wears. And so, finally, does his name. Jesse Rosenfeld, a rare and exotic species on the West Bank, is a Jew who has chosen to live among Arabs.

Jesse, though, would stand out pretty much anywhere, either in Toronto, where he was born and raised, or in Haifa, where a large clan of uncles, aunts and cousins live. He is a left-wing activist, a militant who has put his radical ideas into daily practice. An aspiring journalist even before his recent graduation from McGill University, he now lives in Ramallah and writes for the Palestine Monitor. There are other young foreign journalists who write for the Monitor, an online publication whose main business is exposing Israeli human rights violations on the West Bank. But Jesse's stand is a singular one. As a Jew he is regarded as a traitor by most other Jews. On the Internet he is listed on a right-wing Israeli website of 'self-hating' Jews whose activities are a threat to national interests. In Haifa his relatives, who include a number of high-ranking military officers, are not at all amused. And even among the Palestinian political establishment of Ramallah there are those who do not approve.

I haven't seen Jesse for quite a while, and am familiar with him only as a student and the former boyfriend of my niece. When they were at McGill both of them lived on the edge of student anarchist and anti-globalisation circles – one of the high points of their relationship was being arrested together at a demonstration that got out of control. As for everyone else in those groups, for Jesse radical politics was very much a lifestyle, part of a Montreal scene that also included music, drugs, partying, squats, food co-ops, feminism, street pamphleting and other anti-establishment endevours. But even then Jesse was unusual – he took a double major in political science and women's studies, provoked storms in the student newspaper, and loudly and publicly renounced a Jewish heritage he felt compromised him morally and politically. A year or so has passed since I've last seen him and he's obviously moved on. Jesse no longer wants to change the world – the Middle East alone will do. Out on the street it doesn't take more than a couple of minutes for me to see that he's lost little of his appetite for change. He wants Palestinian independence wholesale, and he wants it now.

Negotiating the heavy crowds on Al-Manara Square, a place where half a dozen roads meet in the heart of town, I am impressed by the Palestinian Authority's newly-trained force of traffic policemen. They're as sharp as the rest of town is shoddy. Their uniforms are spotless, their trouser creases ruler-straight, their street-work spectacular. There's a man out there making moves like Michael Jackson. They whirl and twirl, they whistle and wave as if street direction were stage drama. I've never seen policemen pirouette before. Is this where the foreign funding is going?

Jesse watches, amused and sarcastic. 'If you think the P.A.'s good at traffic,' he says, 'you should see them at crowd control.'

He's angry with the Authority's police force because of an incident that has taken place recently in Hebron at the southern end of the West Bank. Not only are Israeli settlers shooting Arabs down there, he says. Arabs are now shooting Arabs.

Jesse points to the far side of the square, indicating a large hoarding rising from the roof of a building. Once Al-Manara's central stone pillar and carved lions dominated the prospect here. Now two smiling faces on the hoarding have taken pride of place. They are those of Mahmoud Abbas, the current head of Fatah, and Yassir Arafat, its founder. Despite Abbas's vigorous claims to Arafat's mantle and his stance as the only legitimate leader of the Palestinian people, says Jesse, he has lost the popular confidence garnered by his predecessor.

The Hebron demonstration was an angry message intended to protest Fatah's failure to bring independence any closer. But the Authority, unwilling to allow public criticism by its own people, refused to authorise the demonstration. 'The march went ahead anyway,' said Jesse. 'The P.A. police fired live rounds into the crowd, and a young boy was killed. What kind of leadership is that?'

I have arrived in Ramallah on a day when another demonstration is scheduled, this one organised by the leadership itself. It will take place shortly and Jesse will cover it for the Monitor. But meanwhile, we have time for coffee.

Jesse leads me up a steep flight of stairs to a large, airy room overlooking Al-Manara Square. This is Stars and Bucks, one of young Ramallah's favourite meeting places. Everything in the café, from the double lattes to Wifi, is a faithfully reproduced knock-off – only the logo on the throwaway cups differs slightly from that of the genuine Starbucks brand.

It is a reminder of how sophisticated Palestinians, the best-educated, most-travelled Arabs in the Middle East, can be. This café has nothing of the *keffiya*-and-mustache ambiance of an older, traditional male society. The clientele here, the children of Ramallah's elite, are no differently dressed than any group of twenty-something westerners – the girls wear jeans, boots and make-up, and leave their hair long and uncovered. And they're happy to partake of the one item a genuine Starbucks in the West does not offer – they puff away on nargiles, the tall brass water-pipes of the orient, as enthusiastically as their boyfriends do. In most Middle Eastern places it's something no self-respecting Arab woman would dream of. Ramallah is distinctly secular and liberal, and it's refreshing – as I settle down in a deep armchair with a cappuccino I can feel the religious tensions of Jerusalem draining away.

Just as quickly, however, they are replaced by other, equally-present tensions – the stresses produced by Ramallah politics. Whatever Jesse talks about, he never strays far from two constant, twinned *leitmotifs*. If he is scathing about Israel's bad faith in negotiating the establishment of a Palestinian state, he is equally critical of the Palestinian Authority in that same process. Morally, politically and journalistically, he's gunning for them both.

Palestinian politics are labyrinthine, but as we sit above the milling crowds on the square, Jesse's basic message comes through clearly enough. The Israelis are not serious about peace. Obsessed by the power of their own state after 2,000 years of persecution and victimhood, they are pathologically incapable of seeking accommodation with their neighbours.

'It's all talk,' says Jesse as he blows on espresso to cool it – his young man's impatience with life's slow pace of change extends even to his coffee. 'Do you really think Israel has the slightest intention of allowing the establishment of a truly independent and economically viable Palestine?'

For Jesse it's clear. Behind the eternal diplomatic dallying over an end to settlement-building in the West Bank and East Jerusalem lies a long-term strategy – Israel's retention of strategic settlement blocks as an aid to maintaining a stranglehold over its Palestinian neighbour. Pleading defence considerations, Israeli control of these areas will make the geographical integrity of a new Palestinian state impossible. The result? A severe hampering of the development of an internal economy, and its inevitable absorption into the larger Israeli economy. Territorial and economic compromise will only reflect political fragility – state autonomy and government authority will be fragmented as well. If a new Palestine is established on the West Bank, Jesse affirms, it will be a Palestine built on Israeli conditions for Israeli benefit.

In the meantime, Jesse hammers on, Israeli settlers and an army of occupation are doing what they can to make those future tasks easier. They are driving Palestinians out by creating unemployment; deliberately eroding infrastructure, health and education facilities; hampering the growth of civil institutions; restricting transport and communications through checkpoints and restricted-access highway programmes. Many of Ramallah's suburbs, Jesse tells me, are former refugee camps now incorporated into the city's fabric – there is barely a resident in them, he says, whose extended family has not had someone arrested, land confiscated, a house bulldozed or an olive orchard burned.

But Jesse reserves nearly equal scorn for the Palestinian leadership. Protests in Hebron, he says, do not begin to show the depth of dissatisfaction. Mahmoud Abbas has become unpopular all over the West Bank. It's not just that Palestinians see his administration as corrupt; many have lost faith in his will to advance their cause. The leadership is content to mouth nationalist platitudes, its detractors say, but its real concerns lie in maintaining its own power and privilege. Only half-jokingly, Jesse refers to Abbas as 'the Wall Guy' – some Palestinians believe Abbas has personal financial interests in the cement companies that provide the materials for the construction of Israel's separation barrier. Desperate for improvement in their lives, many West Bankers are fast losing patience. Is it surprising, Jesse asks, that they're looking for radical change? What's evident to me is that in the forefront of those looking for radical change is Jesse Rosenfeld himself.

Jesse becomes so wrapped up in his discourse that we miss the beginning of the Palestinian Authority demonstration. He doesn't seem to be in any hurry to get there, and when we arrive at Clock Square five minutes later I understand why. From the beginning, the demonstration is destined to flop. An attempt to rally mass P.A. support, the event takes the form of a ceremonial unveiling – carved into a large rock prominently placed beneath a colonial-era clock tower are the words of the Palestinian constitution, a document drafted more than twenty years ago. But when, after much speechifying, a sheet is finally lifted and the rock revealed there is only a smattering of applause – there are not more than fifty people present, and most of them are Administration officials in suits and ties.

Jesse only shrugs. 'What do you expect?' he says. 'That young boy was killed just two days ago. This is Ramallah's way of showing its anger.'

But if city residents have stayed away in droves, the event is attended by a handful of foreign stalwarts. These are Ramalla's 'Internationals', members of the International Solidarity Movement, an organisation founded a quarter of a century ago to rally support for the Palestinian cause. Young militants protected by their foreign passports and a watching world media, the Internationals began as a defiant multinational movement. They acted as human shields, preventing Arab street demonstrators from being shot at. They stood in the way of bulldozers, obstructing Palestinian house demolitions. They served as volunteers in refugee camps and assisted in Arab village olive harvests. They were frequently in the headlines.

I watch as a Briton steps up to the microphone beside the commemoration stone to pledge the world's support for the Palestinian constitution. He is young – there is virtually no one over twenty-five among the Internationals – and wears a bright blue design inked beneath his right eye. *Keffiyehs*, tattoos and piercings are all part of the International look.

Jesse, though, is less than impressed. The movement's heyday, he tells me as we stand on the edge of the little crowd, has passed. Once it was serious and dedicated. But as the Middle East stalemate grinds on, fresher fields of contest, better covered by a fickle world media, have dimmed the movement's allure and bled potential recruits. Political *fashionistas*, the Internationals are no less susceptible to fast-changing trends than the rest of the world's digitised youth culture. G8 summits, global warming, same-sex controversies, world economic meltdown – all contend with Palestine as attractive protest issues. Jesse dismisses most of the remaining Internationals as 'Palestine groupies'. They're often less interested in enhancing the lives of Palestinians, he says, than they are in enhancing their own self-image.

After the unveiling ceremony I meet a few Internationals. Some are sincere, some too hip by half. Overall I am given a tepid reception. Perhaps it's because I can't bring myself to talk like Franz Fanon. They may be cutting edge, but the Ramallah radicals use a vocabulary appropriated from the politics of oppression *circa* 1968. Here the noun 'struggle' is pronounced with a capital S. Or perhaps it's simply that I'm too ancient and too low in the radical-chic pecking-order to bother with. I wasn't at Seattle, I wasn't at Rome, and I haven't been tear-gassed. I've got no street-cred and no Twitter address. No one enquires about my Facebook details. I am *persona non grata*.

But there's one piece of advice they're happy to give a rank newcomer to the Struggle. If I haven't made the pilgrimage to Arafat's final resting place yet, I should. So as Jesse heads off to the Monitor offices to file his piece, I walk the couple of kilometres to the *Mukataa*, the Fatah compound once besieged and destroyed by the Israeli army. As a site closely tied to the beginnings of Palestinian nationhood it now serves a ceremonial function. Lying at the end of an oblong reflecting pool, its central piece is a grand mausoleum, cube-shaped and clad in white Jerusalem stone. Outside, a uniformed honour-guard, eyes fixed and arms presented, stands to attention, ramrod-stiff. Inside, inscribed in Arabic and buried beneath bunches of red flowers, is the great man's tomb itself. An atmosphere of grand purpose lies heavy over the place – as surely as Americans see the Lincoln Memorial as a repository of their nationhood, so here are Palestinians in the midst of making their own national myth.

What impresses me most, though, is not the formal state grandeur of the burial sight. It is the deep and humble reverence shown by Palestinian visitors. They stand before the tomb, palms spread wide by their sides, lips moving silently, precisely as they stand during Friday prayers. The Internationals are right – this *is* a pilgrimage. Ramallah may be secular and Arafat a nationalist hero, but from this vantage-point one thing is clear. Slowly, ineluctably, a major figure in the birth of modern Palestine is being transformed into a *marabout*, a revered and holy Muslim saint.

Jesse has not left his old life entirely behind. If he works like a serious journalist he lives like a frat-boy looking to be expelled. To keep up with him, I can see, I'm going to have to behave not just like a tireless worker for social and economic justice; I'll have to try a little dissolute and excessive living, too. In Ramallah, updated and globalised, the gonzo way of life still flourishes.

His piece safely filed, Jesse and I walk from the town centre, through the day's failing light, to the apartment he shares with three other foreigners. One good thing about poor street-lighting is that it softens the edges of the harsh and the ugly. The Ramallah suburb we walk through, recently a refugee camp, looks far better by night than by day. But then suddenly, on its far side, things really are better. Rearing up out of the dark is an modern pediatric hospital built with funding from Bahrain. The further we walk, the more impressive things become. Much of the development, including office space barely risen from the soil and apartment blocks still looking for tenants, has been put up by expatriate Palestinian investors. Having made money in the Gulf and a newly revived Beirut, they've come in on the ground floor here – in Ramallah they believe they've smelled the same kind of business returns waiting not far ahead in the future.

Such is the case with Jesse's apartment building, a new block on a street where the grass verges have barely had a chance to sprout. The owner of Jesse's fourth-floor apartment has been an expatriate Palestinian for much of his professional life, too, but not in Beirut and not as a businessman. The cousin of the notorious Marwan Barghouti, now serving five life sentences in Israel for terrorist bombings, Mustafa Barghouti is also a political activist. He too, has done stints in Israeli jails. But unlike his cousin, he is a democracy activist who preaches non-violent protest and Palestinian independence through negotiated settlement. Along with Edward Said, he was a founder of the Palestinian National Initiative, a political body that offers an alternative to the corruption of Fatah and the fundamentalism of Hamas. He is also the major force behind the Palestine Monitor, and Jesse's employer.

The apartment has been laid on free-of-charge for the Monitor's expatriate staff. Its four bedrooms are large, its stone floors polished to a high gloss, its marble-topped kitchen well equipped with blender, microwave oven and other conveniences. The furniture, stiff and formal in the Middle Eastern way, is brand new. It is the apartment of a prosperous, bourgeois family from the tidy middle-classes. The family currently living in it, though, is a journalistic one, and if they issue from the middle classes they've done their level best to challenge its bourgeois tidiness. In fact, they've defeated it entirely.

I've never seen a place paid so little attention. Although four adults, two men and two women, live here of their own free will, you might think yourself in a maximum-security penitentiary. The apartment is bare, sterile and wholly impersonal. Along one wall books and pamphlets, all political in subject, are stacked. Piled on surfaces in the living and dining room are computers, still cameras, video cameras, audio recording equipment, slews of CDs and other digital paraphernalia. But apart from these things there are there no personal effects anywhere – no pictures on the walls, no decoration, no small sign that anyone has tried to make this home. Jesse's bedroom, where he stops briefly to toss his hat, is nothing but two beds stranded in a sea of floor-strewn clothing. The commonly shared rooms receive even less care. In the living room there is plastic wrapping still on the seats of the upholstered chairs. In the kitchen fridge there is precisely one bottle of ketchup, one empty carton of orange juice, and one jar half-full of pickle juice but no pickles. There is nothing cosy about the apartment – it's a place to sleep and nothing else.

The explanation? Single-minded dedication. There's no time for such matters as mere domestic comfort. Politics calls, and so does partying. Ramallah is a great place to get wrecked.

When we arrive there's a largish chunk of Lebanese hashish sitting on the kitchen table, but it doesn't stay large for long. It's being constantly whittled away at by Toon, a slow-talking, pony-tailed Dutchman in Doc Martin boots. One of Jesse's flatmates, Toon – short for Anton, I think – talks slowly and with searching deliberation. Whether his aptitudes are non-verbal by nature I cannot say. On the one hand he is in Ramallah as a news photographer, not a writer, and a bulky, long-lensed Canon camera is never far from his reach. On the other he is ingesting massive amounts of cannabis resin, and this may be slowing him up somewhat. Certainly his visual and mechanical skills are unaffected – he shows a marvelous proficiency in constructing perfectly even, cone-shaped spliffs from multiple leaves of glued cigarette paper. There is already a heavy fug of hashish smoke in the room when we arrive, and these works of art continue to pass around.

They do nothing at all to slow the verbal exchange between Jesse and the other flatmate present at the table – things only get more animated and garrulous as the evening progresses. A journalist who has recently written a book on the aftermath of the war in Kosovo, Francesca has moved on to inter-ethnic violence in the Middle East. Today she's happy with news from home. Not long ago she interviewed a well-known leader of the Al-Aqsa Martyr's Brigade. Widely published in Italy, the interview has led today, she's learnt, to the man's name being removed from the international list of wanted terrorists. It may be all in a day's work, but Jesse's congratulations on her journalistic coup are effusive. Perhaps they're not solely limited, though, to journalistic concerns. From occasional remarks by Francesca I sense a certain undercurrent of international tension right here in the apartment. Women's studies aside, Jesse and Toon are slobs, and Francesca is tired of picking up after them. This is an opportunity for Jesse to do his part in peacemaking.

There's a short lull in the conversation when Jesse, a few minutes before the Al Jazeera nine o'clock news, rushes out to pick up a couple of pizzas down the street. No one, as far as I can make out, does the slightest bit of cooking at home. When he returns, throwing the cardboard pizza boxes onto a tall pile of empty pizza boxes accumulating in the corner, the news has already started. The pizzas, sitting naked on the kitchen counter, are momentarily forgotten. Stoned or not, these people would rather consume hot news than pizza. When eventually I ask Jesse if I can reheat it in the microwave, he tells me to go ahead – he doesn't know how it works. Neither do I. I can't get the machine going until I look at the wall behind it. In all the months they've been here, not one of the Palestine Monitor's journalists, a team up to their ears in sophisticated gadgetry, has bothered to plug it in.

I do, and with the news over the conversation warms up again with the pizza. A bottle of Arak appears, and after the food there are more of those intricately-assembled constructions of paper, tobacco and hashish. The chunk on the table has almost disappeared. When I ask Toon if it's easy to get hold of, he only laughs – the stuff is all over the West Bank, and Israel too. When soldiers of the Israeli army pulled out of Lebanon they didn't sever their connections with their Beka'a Valley suppliers. The relation continues. How else, Toon asks, do I think IDF recruits while away those endless hours at the checkpoints on West Bank roads?

At this rate of consumption most people would soon be zoned-out on the couch ear-budded to their MP3 players. What strikes me instead is the evening's continuing energy, its unrelenting, almost obsessive preoccupation with Arab-Israeli politics. Not for a moment does anyone drift away into the usual social babble about relationships or entertainment plans for the coming weekend. There's lots of joking and dope-fuelled humour, but the talk remains intense, focused and essentially serious – Mahmoud Abbas, the Byzantine maneuverings of opposition groups inside the PLO, the latest Israeli detentions and house demolitions, the coverage of the Monitor's human-rights-watch competitors, tomorrow's interview at the Dheisheh refugee camp…it's endless. The hashish is ancillary – the fix this bunch needs is ideological. These people are wired.

Jesse, particularly, has a mind that will not let go. It is constantly digging around, dealing not just with the daily practicalities of a military occupation, but with its long-term theoretical abstractions. What interests me in

Jesse is the attitude, the mental make-up of the political militant. When Jesse's father was young he was active in campaigns supporting César Chávez and the unionisation of Hispanic California grape-pickers. Today he is an academic representing other academics in a Toronto university employees union. Jesse's generation of radicals has gone much farther. His visions of an alternate globalised world are infinitely more far-reaching than anything his father dreamed off. But Jesse's not interested in talking about dreams of the past. What fills his mind are visions of a fast-developing future.

A joint makes another round, the arak bottle sinks ever lower, and Jesse warms to his theme. Given the Palestine policies of Israel's current leadership, he believes the two-state solution cannot work. The international community might support the idea of a Palestinian state co-existing alongside an Israeli one, but Palestinians won't. Not once they see the built-in constraints to genuine independence, says Jesse. Irrevocable differences over the future of the West Bank settlements, the Palestinian right of return and the status of Jerusalem as a Palestinian capital have already made the concept unacceptable to many Palestinians. And while some of them have chosen the road of Islamic extremism, others are calling for a third way – the one-state solution.

If Jesse's face isn't already flushed, it becomes so now as he sketches out the shape of a secular, democratic, multi-racial Palestine stretching from the Mediterranean Sea to the Jordan River. Jesse is a great admirer of Steve Biko, the black South African activist who died brutally in a Pretoria prison before his country shook off apartheid. In keeping with the tenets of Biko's black consciousness philosophy, Jesse believes the transformation of South Africa was not radical enough, that economic control and the power that comes with it remain firmly in the hands of the white minority. There are lesson there, though, for the current conflict; Israelis, he maintains, can be pushed into granting Palestinians full political rights in a single state if they believe they can continue to control the economy.

'But Jesse,' I say, 'seen from Jerusalem things look awfully different. How could Israel possibly accept a one-state solution? Most Israelis are screaming that far too many concessions are already on the table for the two-state solution.'

At the current moment, I point out, ruling-party politicians in Jerusalem are calling on Palestinians to officially accept Israel as a Jewish state. It's an enormous demand, one that would formalize the position of Arab Israelis, a full fifth of the population, as second-class citizens. How then, at the same time, could anyone expect the same people to scrap the country's Zionist foundation lock, stock and barrel?

Jesse only shrugs off such argument. He's been through it all before. Of course, he agrees, given the present state of play it sounds improbable. But attitudes change when material conditions on the ground change.

'What conditions?' I ask.

Imagine, Jesse says to me, if the Israelis at the bottom of the ladder, the Yemenis and Ethiopians, the disadvantaged immigrants, the twenty per cent of Israelis living below the poverty line, began wondering if it was worth their while to continue supporting a regime that brought them few benefits. Imagine if disruptions to the economy pushed even better-off, middle-class Israelis into questioning the basis of their prosperity. Imagine if Israeli stability was threatened internally. An atmosphere of uncertainty could be enough to drive the country to elections; enough anxiety about the future could cause right-wing governments to be be thrown out and a new leadership to take a wholly new look at Israel's prospects.

It still sounds like pie in the sky to me, but hardly as pleasant. The approach appears highly theoretical and entirely likely to lead to unforeseen consequences. So emotionally charged are views on resolution to the conflict that large-scale violence between Jews sometimes seems only a step or two behind violence between Jews and Palestinians.

Jesse argues, I counter-argue. In the struggle for a single, unified state Jesse sees justice. I see bloodshed. Is justice not possible without bloodshed? Can justice with bloodshed be called justice at all? But before we are able to put the world to rights Toon intervenes. Has Jesse remembered they have a rendezvous at Sangria's?

It's past midnight, and I've had enough – no matter how good the

Taybeh beer at Sangria's Bar is, it's not going to help the hangover I feel slowly gathering force. The others are undeterred; while they get ready to leave I am shown the bedroom belonging to Julia. Julia is out of town for the next few days, trying to arrange hard-to-obtain press accreditation. Not content with covering the Struggle from the West Bank, she wants to get to its heart, in Gaza.

Julia's room is full of the whine of mosquitoes, and for much of the night I'm engaged in my own struggle, slapping, scratching and cursing. At around three o'clock I hear a key turn in the lock and the sound of voices – Jesse, Toon, and the soft brogue of what can only be a couple of well-oiled Irishmen. It's music and laughter and clinking bottles for a couple of more hours, and then finally there's silence. When I get up for a drink of water just before dawn the lights in the kitchen are on, and there's an Irishman sitting on the floor in the kitchen. His legs are splayed out, his mouth is wide open, and his head is leaning on the side of the refrigerator. He doesn't look too comfortable, but he's feeling no pain at all. He's fast asleep, which is what I'd like to be.

Jesse is long gone when I get up. He's caught the bus to Jerusalem to meet a friend who's arriving on an overnight flight from Prague. I'm bleary-eyed and mosquito-ravaged, and can only wonder how Jesse is feeling. He hasn't had more than a couple of hours sleep.

But he's bubbly and energetic when he returns in mid-morning. So, too, is Colin, who hasn't slept at all. Colin is an old anarchist buddy from Montreal who's come to work as the Monitor's sound-man, recording interviews for its on-line edition. He's skinny and wears a knitted woolen hat from beneath which a braided blond pigtail protrudes. Although he's only twenty-one, he's packed a lot into his anarcho-communal life. He's taken part in more demonstrations, marches and protests than he can remember. He's worked in free food cooperatives, lived with sixteen other militants in a Montreal loft, squatted in Berlin, and spent four months living with a family of *campesinos* in the Santa Clara mountains of central Cuba. He's never been to the Middle East before, but is determined to take it on in his best collectivist style. When he discovers that the apartment's hot water tank is playing up he positively rejoices.

'*Ningún problema*,' he smiles at us. 'Up in the Santa Clara we lived, the whole family, from a barrel of water in the back yard. I *love* cold bucketbaths. And it's a good way to check your resource consumption. From a barrel you get a better idea of, like, demographics and per family-member unit use. Plus it's really cool to stand outside naked under a banana tree to get clean.'

There are no banana trees up on the fourth floor in central Ramallah, but Colin promises us the next best thing. When he opens the fridge door and sees it empty but for pickle jars he raises his eyes and shrugs. When there is time, he promises us, he will show us another invaluable skill learned in the Santa Clara mountains. He makes one mean mother of a banana cake.

But there is no time now – duty calls. Off we slope to the station behind the central market and there catch a *servise*, a collective taxi, to Bethlehem. Unable to take the more direct route through Jerusalem – a drive that without borders and the wall would last about forty-five minutes – we make a wide, sweeping circle across the hilly roads and checkpoints of the West Bank. Two and a half hours later we are at the Dheisheh refugee camp in the suburbs of Bethlehem.

There's not much left of the original tented camp, apart from a turnstyle entrance barrier, left in commemoration of the Israeli army's administration of the camp following the 1967 war. After more than forty years of residence Dheisheh's inhabitants have turned the camp into a warren of narrow lanes and tall brick-and-concrete buildings. Still crowded into the camp's one and a half square kilometres, three generations of refugees now number more than 12,000 individuals.

There are strings of Palestinian flags fluttering over the alleys, and here and there on whitewashed walls rough paintings of Che Guevara or crossed Kalashnikovs. But there is not much fight left in the residents of

Dheisheh – just getting an adequate supply of water in the camp is already a tough proposition. We are led to one of the camp's youth centres. As Jesse asks the questions and Colin, a headset over his ears, records the answers, I listen. Jesse, with his own radical agenda, would like to hear his interviewees condemning the Palestinian Administration as Quislings, collaborators who've sold out to the Israelis. Few of the kids want to go that far, but there's lots of emotion. If they are bitter about the Israeli occupation, it's clear they also feel abandoned and forgotten by the entire world. Normal schooling, jobs, homes of their own – they've never had these things, and they've lost hope that the PA will ever provide them.

But there's another loss they feel far more keenly. None of these boys have ever lived outside a refugee camp. Yet every one of them, without prompting, expresses an almost visceral feeling for land, for the soil itself. It's land that was lost by parents or grandparents decades ago, but they have inherited its memory. Almost all Palestinians can tell you about the family house-key, the item that remains treasured because it's all that's left of former lives. But these boys go further. Even if they have never seen the land in question they can describe it in detail – fields, wells, fruit trees, houses, things that in all likelihood do not even exist anymore. The land, they say, is something that should live inside them. It has been removed, and they will never feel whole until it is part of them again. By way of answer it's indirect, but Jesse pretty well gets the response he is looking for.

It's late afternoon by the time we are finished, and just about dark when we pitch up at Bethlehem's border-crossing into Israeli territory. This is one of the most heavily used transit-points on the separation barrier, and it bears the scars of Palestinian anger – the wall's high concrete sides are daubed with graffiti and its observation towers are splashed with paint-bombs. But at this time of day there are hardly any Palestinians going into Israel. Those few West Bank residents with the required employment or study documents are heading home the other way, and waiting in long queues to be processed through.

'You are a Jew?' a soldier asks. Now it's Jesse's turn to answer questions. His interviewer, sitting behind a thick glass panel and talking though a microphone, is eighteen or nineteen years old, barely older than the boys at the youth centre.

'Rosenfeld?' he says, reading the name on the passport. 'Rosenfeld?' He is frowning in incomprehension. He doesn't understand why any Jew would want to set foot in the territories. Jesse, secure in his Canadian citizenship, plasters his biggest grin on his face and nods. 'As Jewish as you,' he says triumphantly.

'Go,' says the soldier, tossing the passport down and indicating the exit with a sideways flick of his head. On the other side of it Jesse bursts into laughter.

'That always breaks me up,' he says. 'I just can't help it.' For a moment I think he's talking about the whole procedure – the concrete ramps and steel barriers, the metal detectors, the electronic fingerprint readers, the power-operated turn-styles, the verbal grilling, the buzzers and red and green lights that indicate passage granted or denied. But none of it, really, is very funny at all.

Then Jesse points upwards and I see what amuses him. It is a broad banner strung across the Israeli side of the wall by the Ministry of Information and intended for Christian Christmas pilgrims on their way to Bethlehem's Church of the Nativity. It reads, in large red letters, 'Peace Unto You'.

'And unto you, too, *Compañeros,*' laughs Colin before we run for the last bus to Jerusalem. There's nothing like being thrown in at the deep end.

It is seven o'clock by the time we've had three falafels each – the first meal of the day – at a stand near the bus station in East Jerusalem. It is eight o'clock by the time we are onto another bus, over the Qalandiya crossing and back into the West Bank, and nine o'clock before we are sitting at the kitchen table in the Monitor apartment in Ramallah again. Colin breaks out the bottle of duty-free Bushmill's he has brought Jesse as a present, and Toon, who doesn't appear to have been doing much else all day, has at last perfected a preferred model; he is gluing and rolling giant rocket-shaped spliffs, complete with little paper nose-cones.

It's been a long and tiring day, and an hour later I am about ready to turn in. But I've failed to reckon either with Jesse and Colin's inexhaustible energy or with the busy Ramallah social calendar. It's time to become party animals, and it's no use my protesting.

Jesse roots around the wreckage on the floor of his room until he finds something clean to wear. Then we stumble out of the apartment building and down quiet and empty night streets. Some way past Sangria's, floating out from the balcony of another, similar apartment building, we can hear loud voices and the bass beat of music.

'We can't have parties at our place anymore,' says Jesse enviously as we enter the downstairs lobby. 'We had just one and the neighbours threatened to have us thrown out. It was a good one.'

This one appears to be a good one, too. In a well-appointed apartment upstairs – somebody in radical Ramallah has a sense of domestication or at least a good housekeeper – there are forty or fifty guests gathered. The drinks table is loaded with bottles of wine, and however good Israeli wine is there's not a drop of it to be found here. In Ramallah symbolic political gesture is everything, and the wine is all expensive and imported. After a few glasses of fine Montepulciano I'm ready to become politically symbolic myself.

There are all sorts of people present – journalists, activists, writers, academics, documentary film-makers, NGO executives and professional progressives from around the world. There are even a few of the Palestinians for whose benefit the whole global circus in Ramallah has been organised. Everybody knows everybody else, and there is lots of laughter, excited talk and flirting. Jesse, inveterate rhetorician that he is, is soon the centre of a circle of hard political debate. Colin, his hat off, his short blond hair and little pig-tail prominent, is wowing the ladies with heroic stories of revolutionary Cuba. I drift around, clutching a glass and making small talk with whoever will talk with a not so revolutionary visitor from a Christian hospice in Jerusalem.

I chat with Arthur, a bespectacled British writer who is researching a second book on Palestinian society; his first, *Occupied Minds*, is already out. I talk with Anna, a voluble Dutch researcher pursuing a PhD in anthropology – her work on non-violent protest, she tells me, takes her often to violent clashes in the West Bank. And out on the balcony, where too much Montepulciano has driven me for a little fresh air, I meet Joe Devoir.

Joe is an American from Michigan, and actually looks the part of a heroic revolutionary. Tall and square-chinned and intense, Joe is an organizer for Combatants for Peace, a group that unites former Israeli soldiers and ex-Palestinian fighters. Such men have excellent credentials for peacework, Joe tells me. Having fought and risked their lives, no one on their own side can accuse them of cowardice or the adoption of merely intellectual stands – they have come to their pacific viewpoint through hard experience. And secondly, says Joe, having already faced deadly combat in war, they are not afraid of the considerably lesser risks of demonstrating for peace. It is these seasoned combatants who are often at the head of peace demonstrations – followed by less experienced marchers, they can be relied on to hold steady in the face of physical threat by the police, the Israeli Defence Force or West Bank settlers.

In fact, Joe goes on, there is just such a demonstration planned for tomorrow in the South Hebron hills. There, outside a village called Tuba, Israelis from a nearby agricultural settlement have been preventing Arab farmers from ploughing and seeding their fields. Unless they can do so in the next few days it will be too late and the village harvest will fail. Having fired rifles at Palestinian children walking to school, the settlers have also disrupted education in the village. After an Israeli police contingent failed to give the children adequate protection, the foreign volunteers who escorted them to school were badly beaten up. Tomorrow's action, enthuses Joe, will see a large contingent of Combatants for Peace, followed by Israeli and Palestinian protestors, marching with Arab farmers to their fields. They will act as shields to protect the farmers as they plough.

Why don't I come along, Joe suddenly asks me, gripping my shoulder manfully until it hurts. 'Of course Jesse and his Monitor friends are going,' he says in his deep, granite-like voice. 'But we need every able-bodied volunteer we can get.'

I can hardly say 'Joe, you're hurting my shoulder,' which is what I'm really thinking. In fact, momentarily fired up on more Montepulciano than is good for me, what actually comes out is something very different. 'Well, hell, Joe,' I say. 'Of course I'll march for peace. Where do I sign up?'

It's not long after that I know I'll have to leave or fall asleep behind a sofa. My friends, of course, are made of sterner stuff and want to stay on – it's just two o'clock in the morning. So I leave on my own, and it's only in the cold night air on the walk back to Jesse's that I sober up. We may not be marching peacefully at all, I realise. Not only will we be facing the ire of fanatic Israeli religious zealots; there will be the wrath of the Israeli army to deal with as well.

But it's too late. I am committed already, and the mini-van for the South Hebron hills will be leaving from outside the Friends's School at 7:15. Suddenly a night of fighting mosquitoes seems not so horrible after all.

At a quarter to seven I wake the boys. They've had an hour and a half of sleep in the last twenty-four hours, and four and a half in the last forty-eight. Jesse looks like his eyes have been recently transplanted from someone else's face. Colin can hardly get his open at all. Toon is as quiet as ever. But by 7:30 we have arrived at the waiting van. Inside are part of the Ramallah contingent also heading south: Osama and Mohammed, local veteran peace activists, as well as Anna, the Dutch researcher, and Taki, a diminutive Japanese militant with a big smile and spiky hair. I slide into the last row of seats beside Taki and Osama, and off we head through a sunny new morning.

Taki worries me. He and Osama are full of cheerful banter, but I'm not inspired by the subject matter. Taki is as thin and frail as a stick. He's been on enough West Bank peace marches, however, to have built an honourable track- record.

'You afraid of tear-gas?' asks Osama, by way of making light conversation.

'Afraid? Afraid?' says Taki, hamming it up. In fact Taki is a serious guy, a highly trained technician who's in the West Bank setting up video-conferencing systems for Palestinians unable to communicate because of travel restrictions. 'Not at all. I adore tear-gas. If I don't get a little bit of gas every couple of weeks I start feeling sick.'

This gets Taki riotous laughter from everyone in the bus. Someone starts joking about Taki's eligibility for Aum Shinrikyo, the Japanese political cult that once released deadly sarin gas in the Tokyo subway. There's talk about other demos – who was shouting which slogan, who was marching in the front rank, who ran at the first baton charge. Some of it is pure point-scoring – everyone has their credibility to defend. But in the hilarity there is a detectably nervous edge. All of us are keyed up.

Jesse talks about being repeatedly filmed at marches by the Israeli police – they would love to find a legal pretext for expelling him from the West Bank. Toon, normally so taciturn, tells me of the need to hang on tight to camera equipment; on the last demo he was whacked on the head with his own telephoto lens. Anna goes on at length about her previous arrests – the only reason she's still around, she says, is that the deportation of an academic researching non-violence would make the Israelis look bad.

'Watch out for those whippy little plastic handcuffs they like to use,' she advises me. 'If the crowds are thick and there are lots of arrests you can still get away. But with your hands attached behind your back it's hard to run.'

All this chatter is spooking me. I try not to listen and instead press my forehead against the window and concentrate on the land passing by outside.

It's no more reassuring. The country we're driving through is semi-desert, a stark, arid landscape of steep hills and sudden drop-offs where the view goes on forever. If it has an etherial beauty of its own the human element, just as hard but far less appealing, constantly intervenes. There are Palestinian roadside villages, poor and scattered with refuse. Poorer still are the Bedouin encampments, corrugated iron shacks surrounded by dusty enclosures of goats and camels. Also on the roadside are IDF bases and vehicle depots with Humvees and armoured cars parked side by side in long rows. On the winding tarmac ribbon itself there are the long waits at numerous military checkpoints. The soldiers act with slow and studied boredom and the drivers soothe their frustration with Arab music from car loudspeakers. Nearly five hours after leaving Ramallah we approach Hebron, just 120 kilometres distant.

South-east of Hebron the land gets rougher and starker still. We are close to Tuba. Mohammed makes a wrong turn and we end up very nearly driving into Havot Ma'on, the Israeli settlement whose inhabitants we are shortly to face. Sitting on the flank of a hill, surrounded by a dun-coloured wilderness, the settlement looks like a small bit of agro-industrial Europe dropped into an alien land. On the far side of a high security fence there are red-roofed villas laid out with geometrical precision. Long rows of aluminum-sided, factory-style units for the production of chickens and eggs are laid out behind them. Beyond the batteries, covering the hillside, rises a neatly cultivated plantation of pine trees. The settlers have done here what Israelis have always prided themselves on doing – they have made the desert bloom.

We reverse quickly down the hill and drive on the short remaining distance to Tuba. Like Havot Ma'on, Tuba, too, sits on the flank of the hill. We park on the highway below and walk up a dry wadi to the village. The Arabs of Tuba are trying to make the desert bloom, too, but in older, less spectacularly high-tech fashion – their fields have been painstakingly built into the sides of the seasonally-irrigated wadi in a series of stepped, drywall terraces. Alone they are not enough to feed the village, and we will be heading on to other, higher fields beyond.

My mind is wrenched from all thoughts of traditional Arab farming as we top a small rise. There, waiting for us, is what looks like most of the Israeli police force and half the army. The police are wearing riot gear and carrying batons and perspex shields. The IDF soldiers are in full combat drill. They have nasty snub-nosed automatic rifles slung over their torsos. They are wearing body armour and webbed helmets. Some are carrying field radios with tall, swaying antennas. The stand there silent and watching beside their jeeps and armoured cars, looking down at us.

The fact that some of the soldiers are women with hair falling down their backs offers little comfort at all. I glance around. Where are all those brawny Combatants for Peace Joe Devoir was promising? Counting Mohammed the driver, there are precisely seven of us.

God, I think, we're going to be creamed.

We walk another hundred metres and there, in a shallow dip in the hill, lies our salvation. There have got to be 250 people milling about. If the Combatants for Peace group is not as large as hoped for, it is more than made up for by the marchers provided by the protest's other organizer, the Ta'ayush Arab-Jewish Partnership. Bussed in from Tel Aviv, the Ta'ayush contingent are not ex-soldiers. They provide even better protection than that. They are teenage students and urban housewives, retired people and young professional couples in bright nylon jackets and hiking boots. There are bald heads and wattly chins, natty dreadlocks and nose rings. There are T-shirts that read *Up Against the Wall*, or *Jews for Social and Economic Justice*. Some of the young couples are carrying tiny children. Who is going to do serious damage to an eight-month old baby dandling in an OshKosh baby harness on its mother's stomach? Suddenly I feel a lot braver about being a protestor for peace.

Organisers with megaphones are directing the march, and on their barked instructions we start moving forward, past the village toward the barrier of soldiers ahead of us. There is a brief ceremonial tussle when the first protestors reach them, and then the soldiers give way. Short of clubbing us down there is little else they can do. Their instructions, says the man with the megaphone, are to keep us contained in the wadi up which we continue to walk.

We understand why a little further along. Splayed across the hillside on the edge of their pine plantation are the residents of Havot Ma'on. They are Orthodox Jews, and on this Shabbat noontime they have given up weekday work-clothes. The boys and bearded men, sidecurls hanging to their shoulders, are dressed in fresh, snow white shirts and trousers of rough cotton. The women, their heads covered with scarves, are wearing long dresses of the same material. It's got a homespun look, and for all I know they've made it themselves. These are hardy, independent settlers who live and work by their own rules. Standing silhouetted against the rocky hills and desert sky, they might have emerged straight out of the Old Testament.

They follow beside us as we move up the hillside, the younger men angry and jeering and waving at us to leave. As far as they're concerned we are invading their land, land deeded directly to them by God at the beginning of time. Their outrage at us is exceeded only by their outrage at the villagers of Tuba, who long ago usurped it. They only thing keeping the settlers away from us and the Arab farmers is the intervening column of Israeli soldiers. 'Down from the hills like wolves on the fold,' says the elderly marcher beside me, a cheerful Jewish woman with an English accent. She is wearing dark glasses and a large straw sunhat. You'd think she was quoting poetry at a garden party.

Finally we come to the contested patchwork of fields. They are small, poor, rocky things, irregular little plots of soil few people in any more fertile part of the world would bother looking at twice, much less fight over. Palestinian villagers, who've followed hard on the marcher's heels, move up to the fields leading a couple of mules. Others carry leather harness and iron ploughs. The protesters stand in rows on the edge of the field, soldiers and police move close in front of them, and the Havot Ma'on settlers hector them from the other side. We're like a layer-cake, all lined up within a few metres of each other.

The harnessed mules break the first clods of soil. Protestors applaud as a young Arab boy follows behind, casting seed as he goes. Behind the cordon of soldiers furious voices rise into the air. I watch as the end of the field is reached and the ploughman, throwing his whole body into the effort, turns the horse and the ploughshare for the making of the next furrow. The Israeli settlers may have homespun cotton and modern high-tech as well, but Tuba has never left the biblical age at all.

The protestors stay until all the little fields are ploughed. So do the settlers. A couple of them are dragged away when they try to break through the line of soldiers. A couple of peace-marchers are restrained when scuffling with policemen, then released. A policemen equipped with a video camera films as many protesters as he can. Young Israeli and Palestinian boys, never closer in their lives, stare at each other, more curious than hateful. The Israeli boys, unlike their angry, shouting parents, appear to be enjoying an afternoon's entertainment – shut up behind barbed wire, surrounded by a hostile population, isolated in a community dedicated to God and hard work, they haven't had so much fun in years. They especially enjoy the ragged old Joan Baez songs the protestors sing. Even the Palestinian village women are having a good time – as a gesture of gratitude to their Israeli supporters, they pass among them with tea and the hard, salty goat's cheese called *leban*.

And so the afternoon passes. The whole scene is slightly surreal – God's chosen people in ritual white, the Arab sowers of grain in red-checked *keffiya*, the army in green, the police in blue, the marchers bright in their nylon L.L. Bean wind-cheaters. Out here on the edge of the dun and featureless Negev desert it doesn't make any colour sense. It doesn't make any sense at all.

'You from New York?' says one older protestor to one older settler. The groups are so close they can hear each other without raising their voices. And if they are still hostile to each other, the tension has largely dissipated. It's too late to do anything – the army has kept the two sides apart and the ploughing is nearly finished.

'Yeah,' says the settler. Apart from the empty holster on his hip – the army has disarmed him – he looks like somebody's warm and friendly uncle. 'You?'

'Brooklyn,' the protestor nods. Relaxed, the Israeli soldiers stand beside them, watching and listening. They're not terribly interested. Who are these men, after all? Two Jews from a rich city half-way round the world, squabbling over a plot of poor dirt that belongs to neither of them. To me it's insanity; to the IDF men it's just another day's work in the West Bank.

The New York settler, quoting Abraham and the prophets, tells the New York protester he could do with a few lessons in Jewish patriotism. The New York protester, quoting Freud, tells the New York settler that he could do with a few sessions of Jewish psychiatry. He even offers a few address of well-known Manhattan therapists. The two continue to argue but nobody is listening. Slowly, followed by settler-children flitting like forest-elves from tree to tree on the edge of the pines, the protestors begin to move off down the wadi and back to their buses.

The action is over and I am still in one piece. I start feeling heroic about myself. Other protestors are congratulating each other, too. We have taken part in something significant. It's not often that such a large group of Jews comes so far to rescue a such small group of beleaguered Arabs. The value of such interventions, we admit, is not really practical. It is symbolic. We have shown the world there are Jews and Arabs who care about each other.

For the villagers of Tuba the consequences of our actions are a little more than symbolic. On the road on the way back to Ramallah Jesse receives a call on his mobile phone. Waiting for the departure of their uninvited guests, the boys of Havot Ma'on have taken their revenge on the boys of Tuba – they have knocked one of them off his donkey, beaten him up, and stolen the animal. Perhaps they are not forest-elves after all.

Nor does the world at large seem to care anything about Jews and Arabs looking out for each other. I am expecting, if not banner headlines in the papers the next day, at least an honorable mention of the march. In the event there's a tiny piece on a bottom inside page of *Ha'aretz* under the title 'Palestinians – Settlers stole boy's Donkey'. It is a sort of joke item. But what else can it be, given the other titles in the same section of the day's paper? – 'IDF kills 5 Hamas members in Gaza', or 'Study: US, Israel should start talks on attacking Iranian nuclear facilities'. In the face of events pushing Jews and Arabs apart, symbolic initiatives to bring them together remain, like Arab desert-farming itself, marginal. Protestors, like donkeys, are not enough.

By now the Monitor crew are completing their third sleep-deprived day. Their eyes are bloodshot and their minds less than razor-sharp. But they remain determined – for Ramallah radicals the night has just begun. There's time for a quick shower, and then we're off to the bars. Shortly before midnight, with beer and politics once again flowing full spate, I leave Jesse and Colin and steal back to bed exhausted.

I don't hear my activist friends return, but it must be late. Neither do Jesse and Colin hear me when I get up early to head back to Jerusalem. But I get a glimpse of them as I walk past their open door on my way out. Breathing deeply and evenly, they are flopped on their beds in a room littered with dirty clothing, sound equipment and portable computers. Too tired to have undressed, silent and at peace for the first time, they are still wearing boots powdered white with the dust of the South Hebron hills.

Fourteen

Is reconciliation of any kind possible in Jerusalem? The tenor of public life there, the increasingly deformed shape that religion and politics have imposed on Jerusalemites, make one hesitant to pronounce anything but a resounding 'no'.

But if Jerusalem has any defining trait at all, it lies in a perverse specialty – it offers ever-renewed hope to all comers. The tougher and more murderous their own history, the greater their cause for despair, the more often have Jews offered each other that old formula of promise, 'Next Year in Jerusalem'. Christians have seen their own hopes renewed two thousand times in two thousand Jerusalem Easters, each one them a repeated promise of resurrection and life out of death. There are moments in our own times when the hopes of Palestinians look slimmer and less realistic still. And yet there are those who believe that one day, perhaps even in their own lifetimes, this city will be shared – a capital to both Jews and Arabs. Does such a chance really exist? I for one have no faith in either politics or religion, and wouldn't like to bet one way or another.

But sometimes there are people I'd be willing to put my money on. It is people as thinking, communicating individuals who are the real hope of Jerusalem. On my return from Ramallah I meet three very different characters, one Christian, one Arab, one Jewish. And, in them, three different kinds of reconciliation – in Jerusalem, divided in innumerable ways, there is no single, generalised form of bringing things together. The first has found a way to reconcile the different parts of himself. The second has found an accommodation between himself and his community. And the third has found a bridge between communities. To my surprise each of them, in their own small, unassuming way, is an answer to the question, 'Is reconciliation possible?' And that answer is 'yes'.

The first encounter is initially not inspiring; in fact it takes me a few days and some encouragement by Ashraf to warm to John at all. For John is up to his neck in religion, and by this point I've pretty well had it with people who are up to their neck in anything at all in Jerusalem.

John, to all appearances, has given himself entirely to God. He appears one day at the Maison d'Abraham without warning, a man without money, without possessions, without worries for the future. A blithe spirit apparently without ambition or direction, he seems content to be guided here and there by some inner force he has no control over. He pitches up at our refectory dining table as if he's been blown in by a wind from the desert.

It happens on a cold, blustery winter's day when I'm feeling particularly jaded with Jesus. I've just returned from the far side of the Kidron Valley and a visit to the Coenaculum, a room in an ancient stone building revered by Christians as the site of the Last Supper.

'It's ridiculous,' I complain to Ashraf as Soeur Nirmala places dinner before us. 'I wandered around for a long time, trying to find out exactly where the Last Supper was supposed to have taken place. My guide book said a small room on the far side of the main upstairs hall; the leaders of different tour parties told me the big hall itself. It was chaos in there. There were five or six big groups, Italian, Ukrainian, Polish, all singing hymns in different languages.'

We help ourselves from a platter of lamb *brochettes*. 'I finally went to ask the Israeli security guard at a desk at the top of the stairs,' I continue. 'The Tomb of David is in the same building downstairs, so the Israelis are in charge of the place. What does it matter? Jewish or Christian, you'd think a man who lets in hundreds of tourists every day would have the answers.'

'And?' says Ashraf, pushing grilled tomatoes my way.

'He said it's all bullshit.'

'Excuse me?'

'That's just what *I* said – excuse me. And he said it again. "It's all bullshit." He asked me if I couldn't do the maths any ten-year-old could do. The building as it now stands was Jerusalem's first Franciscan monastery. It was built in the 14th century, and is now 700 years old. "And you're asking me," the guard said, "to identify a room where Jesus ate a meal 1,300 years before the room was ever built? It's crap, I say – choose whichever room you like. The tour-guides like the big one because they can fit more people in."'

Ashraf, spooning sauteed potatoes onto his plate, only smiles – he's prepared to accept that in the interests of spiritual faith hard facts can sometimes come second. But I'm not. 'OK, so the guard was bored and rude and I interrupted his newspaper reading,' I say. 'But the point is, he's essentially right. It *is* all bullshit.'

It's at this point that we are joined at the table by a tall, lanky American, a man in his late twenties who moves languidly and talks slowly. He's come to Jerusalem looking for a girl, he tells us as he sits down – he's spent all day either on the phone or out in the city searching likely spots. And he's going to stay in Jerusalem until he does find her. At first I think he's one more no-hoper on a desperate mission – Jerusalem sees them by the dozen. He seems to have wandered in from southern California. His talk is is peppered with surfing slang, his look is one of perpetual detachment, and he has a slow, lazy way of answering whatever you ask him. He's laid-back and unconcerned and kind of goofy. He's a classic surfer dude, the kind who just shrugs his shoulders and says 'Whatever.'

I'm not that interested, but Ashraf sees something in him I don't – he keeps on asking questions. And John soon turns out to be a very different person. He's not unconcerned at all, but shy and without any presumption. His own sense of self-importance has been effaced by a sense of something larger and more consequential.

I'm right about one thing, though. John is from southern California, and Orange County and his surfer life there haven't left him entirely. But he's come to Jerusalem by a long and roundabout route. He's spent five years as a postulate with the Carthusians, a religious order with a reputation for being morally exacting and intellectually rigorous. Most of his time has been spent studying divinity and philosophy in a Carthusian mother-house in Chalon-sur-Saone, in France. Now at the end of his studies, his teachers have sent him to an isolated monastery in the hill-country outside Jerusalem. Here, living under a vow of silence, he's being given time to decide where he will spend the rest of his life as a monk.

'I've got three choices,' he says. 'In France I can go to a forest monastery near Roanne, or to a mountain monastery in Chartreuse near Grenoble. They both sound gloomy. Not my kind of place.' He leans back in his chair, puts his hands behind his head and tilts his head up, eyes closed, to an imaginary sun. He could be on the beach at Malibu. 'I can also stay here. I like the rays, man.' John makes an unlikely monk.

'And what about the girl?' I say, still not wholly convinced. I can't imagine a dedicated Carthusian taking time off from his vows to chase women in Jerusalem.

'Oh, Lindsay?' he says. 'She's from California, too. She's in child education with a school of Franciscan nuns. I've been looking for her all day in one convent after another.' His face is sincere, his eyes clear and steady and artless. John is what he says he is, a guy who's changed direction. Life's much better now, he tells us. In fact it's totally awesome.

Dinner is over and the other tables have emptied, but Ashraf, hearing John say he used to be a guitarist, keeps us on and now displays a heretofore unknown interest in music.

'Yeah,' says John, amused at Ashraf's questions about the L.A. music scene. 'I used to play bass in a heavy-metal group called Music Box Serenade. I still have T-shirts showing a ballerina twirling on the top of a jewelled music box. Very sweet. There was a lot of rage in that music, a lot of violence and hate and angry shouting.'

'Were you louder than the grunge bands?' asks Ashraf.

'Oh, much louder,' John smiles.

'Goodness,' says Ashraf. 'I'm surprised we didn't hear you from Jerusalem.' How does the august Doktor Ashraf Noor, I wonder, know how loud grunge bands are?

'But I'll tell you something,' John admits with just a hint of nostalgia. 'Sometimes I still hear that music all the way from L.A.. In the middle of the day, in the middle of all that silence in the hills, I'll hear some old riff in my head and for a moment it's almost enough to get me going again.' Ashraf nods his own head as if he knows just what John is talking about. 'But if I've had the call – and I haven't questioned it once in five years – ' John shrugs, 'then I have to go by the rules.'

Later, when John has gone and Ashraf and I are walking down to Maison d'Abraham's long, echoing corridor, I ask him about his interest in grunge and heavy metal.

'Well, actually,' says Ashraf, 'I'm more interested in punk bands. A long time ago I...ah...used to play lead guitar in a band myself. Not professionally, of course. We really weren't very good.' He says it with a self-deprecating air of dismissal that implies that in fact they really were rather good.

'God,' I say. I can't imagine it, a soon-to-be authority on the Jewish phenomenological tradition flailing about on stage like Sid Vicious. 'Did you have safety pins through your eyebrows? What was your band called?'

Ashraf looks distinctly embarrassed, and gazes up and down the long hall as if to make sure Soeur Marta isn't prowling about somewhere.

He finally whispers a name. It is indeed not fit for Soeur Marta's ears. 'Just don't tell anyone,' he warns me.

The days go by and John, although he finally finds Lindsay, remains on. He has never spent any time in Jerusalem and during the short leave he has arranged from his monastery wants to see as much as he can. Each day he returns to the Maison d'Abraham, having visited church or garden or tomb, happy and enthusiastic. But he saves the best for last. On the evening before he is due to return to the hills and monastic silence, John tells us he will be going out and not returning until dawn. He has decided to spend his last night at the once-weekly, all-night services at the church of the Holy Sepulcher. He eats a hearty meal and asks the sisters for coffee. These nights at the Holy Sepulchre are renowned for being long and cold and difficult.

He is sitting in the refectory when we come down to breakfast the next morning, red-eyed but radiant. He is ecstatic about his vigil.

'It was just so cool,' he says, still up in the clouds. 'Emotionally? I was totally maxed out.'

Over boiled eggs he describes the services as if they were some sort of gig at a late-night club or L.A. warehouse rave. 'The doors opened at eleven,' he says, 'and the first set was a bunch of Russians. Orthodox guys, like a choir of maybe 200, chanting a communion, with priests dressed in robes with crowns on their heads sitting on golden chairs. The whole nine yards. I thought *that* was excellent.

'Then there's a break. Everyone walks around to stay warm, 'cause it's freezing in there, and the next guys come on. And they're even better! They're Armenians. Only four singers – one bass guy, one alto, two mezzos. Man, they just rocked! Their four voices filled the church with more sound than the 200 Russians.'

The hardest part after that, says John, was simply staying awake. Most worshippers left after the first service. There were only a handful at the second, and by four o'clock in the morning there were just him and three others left. 'They were all priests, super hardcore. We were, like, the last holdouts, and we walked around and around the Sepulcher in circles just to stay awake.'

But when the time came for the final and most important part of the night – the prayer inside the Sepulcher itself, John says he was never more wide awake. 'All four of us went into the ante-chamber and prayed together. But these guys knew I was in my novitiate, that soon I would have to make an important decision. They wanted to do something special for me. So they told me to go into the inner chamber alone. I didn't dare, at first. Can you imagine, standing over the tomb of Christ, completely alone, in the middle of the night?

'But then I decided to take it as a sign, as a message from God, and I went in. And of course I wasn't alone.' John's voice is thick, his eyes fixed on something none of the rest of us at the table can see. 'It was the grace of a lifetime,' he says after a moment. 'It was just awesome. I was totally blown away.'

And in a fashion I, too, am blown away. John is such a good man

– honest, transparent, willing, wanting to make the best of himself and life around him – that I can't help admiring him. What I especially like is his ability to let his old and new selves live together. In Jerusalem ideologies are always excessive. The believer – and especially the new, reborn believer – approves so vehemently of his own way of life that he allows no room for the possibility of other, different ways of life. John doesn't make that mistake, not even inside himself. He acknowledges both parts of himself, and they rub along together in easy co-existence. He may have given himself absolutely to God, yet there's nothing absolute about him. A dedicated, rigorous Carthusian, Brother John, as he will soon become, remains a genuine surfer dude. And that, I find, is totally cool.

My second encounter after my return from Ramallah also involves a musician. And like John himself, Basel Zayed initially gives little clue to his real nature. When I first meet him he appears to be little more than an accomplished house-husband – he is burping a baby in the kitchen of his East Jerusalem home and wondering what to make his wife for dinner when she gets back from work.

But that in itself tells me right away that Basel is no ordinary Jerusalemite, that there is in fact a good deal more to this clean-shaven, bespectacled young Palestinian. However good they might be as traditional fathers, cooking meals and changing nappies are not everyday skills perfected by most Arab family heads. Straight off the bat you can see that Basel Zayed is an eminently modern man, and unburdened by the weight of cultural traditions. Which, again, is something of a paradox, as he's been identified to me as a master of that iconic instrument of Arab musical tradition, the *oud*. When Jesse, Colin and I caught a *servise* from Ramallah to Bethlehem, it was Basel Zayed's voice and *oud* we heard on the CD player.

I've come to talk to Basil because I want to see what culture – in this case musical culture – can become when it's not being manipulated for divisive purposes. Of course, the idea that music can be put to positive and constructive uses is not a new one – it's been put into practice to great acclaim any number of times. The best-known example, perhaps, is the orchestra of Daniel Barenboim, a multicultural enterprise made up of young Israeli and Palestinian musicians.

But that's a high-profile endevour, a much publicised media effort launched on the international level and seeking global recognition. I'm just as interested in the kind of grass-roots initiative that aims at bringing change to culture through popular and local appeal. Barenboim's Arab-Israeli rendition of Mozart's *Sinfonia Concertante* in E flat-major may appeal to liberal music-lovers around the world. It may even touch the sensibilities of sophisticated intellectuals in East Jerusalem and Ramallah. But what does it do for Arab kids throwing stones in the street? Is there transformation in such music for them? In other kinds of music musicians like Basel Zayed may have other kinds of solutions.

But before Basel talks to me about the clarinets, *ouds, neys* and guitars of his group, Turab, he wants me to know that music is not for him an end in itself. Shorn of context, he says, music has no meaning at all. And the context here is stark and fundamental – it's the survival of identity itself that's at stake.

Few people, he says with the baby dribbling over his shoulder, are as well placed to realise the fragility of cultural identity as the city's Jerusalemites. He's using the term here not as it applies to all the city's inhabitants, but to a more specific, legally-defined group. They number some 250,000 individuals – one third of the city's population – and live in Jerusalem in judicial limbo. The group is overwhelmingly made up of Muslim and Christian Arabs, but also includes tiny populations of Armenian and other ethnic minorities long established in the city. What unites them is their lack of nationality or permanent right of residence. They are people who've been granted a city on a provisional basis, but have no country at all.

'It's an exceptional situation,' says Basel. When a foreign cultural aid grant recently financed Turab on a European tour he had to apply for a 'laissez-passer' and an exit permit from the Israeli authorities. 'Like all Arab Jerusalemites I have a Jerusalem ID card,' he tells me. 'But I have no passport. And not all Jerusalemites who leave the city are allowed to return; if you stay outside the country too long, if you obtain foreign residence documents, or even if you are deemed to have a 'centre of life' elsewhere, your right of residence can be revoked.'

Some Jerusalemites are eligible for Israeli citizenship. But like most of them, Basel tells me, he's turned down an Israeli passport. It's not just a matter of principle, he says, a refusal to become a citizen without a citizen's full rights. There are immediate practical reasons, too: Israeli settlers may be allowed to travel between Israel and the West Bank, but Arab citizens of Israel aren't. Nor can he accept one of the 250,000 Jordanian passports that the king, Abdullah, has offered Jerusalemites as a way out of statelessness: with it comes the risk of expulsion.

'Here, you hold the baby; I'll make the coffee,' says Basel proffering a squirming infant in a yellow pyjama-suit. Soon his son is drooling on my shoulder instead of his, and Basel is zipping around the kitchen, banging cupboards and pulling open drawers. As he assembles a tray of coffee and pastries Basel continues to reflect on identity.

'I've lived all my life without a state,' he says, 'without papers, without the vote, without the same secure status as other people in the same city. But for me it's not the idea of the state that must come first – it's the idea of nation. If a new Palestine is created I myself wouldn't want Jerusalem to be split in two to make separate capitals. Jerusalem shouldn't belong to anyone at all – I'd make it an international city open to everyone.'

That's not a new idea either – at least twice in the last century such a proposal has been floated by the international community. But Basel, of course, knows it's a slim possibility. No one who's ever held Jerusalem, no one who's even claimed a moral right to the city, has been willing to fling open its gates to the whole world.

'But what's got to come before any of that,' he continues, 'is the sense that we Jerusalemites belong to a people – that we Palestinians, Christian like me or Muslim like most Jerusalemites, have a common, shared identity. And the best way I can help foster and preserve that identity is through my music.'

'Do you know that Arab kids in Jerusalem don't listen to Arab music any more?' Basel says, wincing at the thought. 'They listen to Israeli radio, so they sing along to the same songs as Israeli kids do.' Arab culture, he says, is dying in the city. While local authorities lavishly fund Jewish culture, Arab traditions languish. Discouraged, most Palestinian artists, writers and musicians have left the city to live in exile, either in Arab capitals or in the West, where they can make a decent living. Basel himself could be living in America – his wife, who not only works in a health clinic for Palestinians but plays string bass in Turab – is a Bostonian.

Nor, says Basel, is it just Israelis who deliberately seek to weaken the popular, secular traditions he would like to nourish. 'Never mind Jewish extremists,' he sighs. 'There are Muslim extremists who do just as much harm to our people. They say music is sensual, sexual and immoral, that it has no place in a holy city. They'd also like to see us pack our bags and leave Jerusalem.' But Basel and his wife have agreed on two basic principles, he says: Jerusalem will remain a central part of their lives, and they will do whatever they can to revitalise its Palestinian traditions through music.

Basel has spent six year studying classical composition and the traditions of the *oud* at the Magnificat, the Old City's Christian music conservatory. But he knows that music is a living, changing element, that to keep his own culture alive he must transform and adapt the music he loves. The message, he says, is contained in the words of the Palestinian poets he adapts to song; the popular appeal lies in the music he composes for them. The songs produced by Turab – the name means 'soil' – are based on classical Arab *maqamat*, or musical tonal scales. But they are fused with modern rhythms – Latin, jazz and reggae, among others – and played on instruments that vary from the western accordion to the eastern *bazouk*.

The result is a sort of Palestinian pop fusion with classical underpinnings, a form, he says, as adaptable to old instruments as young Palestinians. He picks up a case from behind the sofa where we are drinking coffee. Inside lies an *oud*, a polished, gleaming thing with a short neck and a deep, round back. It settles as comfortably into his arms as his small son did a minute before. He sings a song by Marcel Khalife, the Palestinian singer-poet who has been lamenting the fate of Palestine for forty years. It is haunting, a dirge that makes even the Jerusalem sun streaming through the window seem less cheerful. He then puts on a Turab CD. The voice is as strong, the *oud* as evocative, but the mood is wholly different. Its is celebratory. And it makes him happy, says Basel, because it represents continuity in change.

'Do you know, in the end, why I do this?' Basel says, sliding the *oud* gently back into its case. 'So that he' – he indicates the baby now lying silently on the sofa between us – 'can be as peaceful in Jerusalem in the future as he is right now in his sleep. Is that not too continuity in change?'

Not far from the site of the old Mandelbaum Gate, the only place where you could cross from Israeli- to Jordanian-held parts of the city before 1967, lies an old suburb. There's not a great deal that's old in this part of central Jerusalem any more – where once the dividing 'Green Line' ran, broad, multi-lane highways now slice through the city in a effort to relieve traffic congestion. But Musrara is a little island of peace in the middle of it all, a quiet quarter of solid old Arab houses set back in carefully tended gardens. Here tendrils of fragrant blooming jasmine cling to quarried Jerusalem limestone and houses sit dark in the deep shade of trees.

It is in one of these houses that I meet yet other reconcilers. As heartfelt as John the Carthusian, as internationalist as Zayed the *oud*-player, they are attempting the toughest rapprochement of all, the reconciliation of Jerusalem with itself. That they choose to live smack on top of the Middle East's greatest historical fault-line is perhaps not entirely an accident.

Peter Cole and Adina Hoffman are Jewish; even, by their own admission, 'deeply Jewish'. But their names are not particularly so, and they rather like it that way.

'We prefer to keep people guessing,' smiles Hoffman as we drink Fundador Spanish brandy from snifters around a low, beaten-copper table. It is a brandy-drinking kind of evening, a cold, drizzly night that not even thick oriental rugs and a glowing heater in the corner of the room can entirely ward off.

If the pair do not loudly proclaim their Jewishness it's not because they are ambivalent about their identity; it is because they are confident enough in it that they want to share in what is common in other identities, too. As Americans who've chosen to make their home and professional lives in Israel, Cole and Hoffman have a certain reaction to the quick and convenient pigeonholing by which the region's inhabitants are automatically divided – they like to confound it. In their view religious and cultural diversity is far too complex in this part of the world for simple, arbitrary division. For them even the term 'Middle East' itself implies a type of compartmentalisation, the beginning of false conceptions that ultimately lead to the creation of uncrossable barriers. The pair prefer another term that has fallen out of fashion these days, but which implies a greater, more subtle complexity to the region – the Levant.

Peter Cole stands, walks to a bookcase, and selects a volume. When talking about the Levant he likes to refer to the writings of the Egyptian Jewish essayist Jaqueline Kahanoff.

'*The Levant has a character and history of its own,*' I read in the open page he proffers me. '*It is called the 'Near' or 'Middle' East in relation to Europe, not to itself. Seen from Asia, it could be just as well called the 'Middle West'. Here, indeed, Europe and Asia have encroached on each other, time and again, leaving their marks in crumbling monuments, and in the shadowy memories of the Levant's peoples. Ancient Egypt, ancient Israel, and ancient Greece, Chaldea and Assyria, Ur and Babylon, Tyre, Sidon, and Carthage, Constantinople, Alexandria and Jerusalem are all dimensions of the Levant. So are Judaism, Christianity, and Islam, which clashed in dramatic confrontation, giving rise to world civilizations, fracturing into stubborn local subcultures, and into the multi-layered identity of the Levant's people. It is not exclusively Western or Eastern, Christian, Jewish or Moslem. Because of its diversity, the Levant has been compared to a mosaic – bits of stone of different colors assembled into a flat picture. To me it is more like a prism whose various facets are joined by the sharp edge of differences, but each of which reflects or refracts light.*'

Why should the perception of the region in which they live be so important to this Jerusalem couple? Because Cole and Hoffman believe that in the Levant definitions of diversity are too important to be left to political and religious authorities alone. In everything they do they try to enlarge the shared middle ground which politics and religion by themselves have become incapable of enlarging. In Jerusalem the language of such activity is uncompromising – it is used to defend positions that have become non-negotiable.

At the same time, though, they see another language which is much better suited to surmounting barriers and making the most of diversity – it is the language of poetry and literature, and when it is translated into a common tongue it can do much to aid the discovery of common ground.

Peter Cole and Adina Hoffman did not start out translating and publishing books. Their publishing enterprise, Ibis Editions, came long after they had moved to Jerusalem and become established writers on Jewish and Levantine subjects. Hoffman moved on from film criticism to a book on Musrara, where she and Cole live, and the biography of a Palestinian poet. Cole, a major poet in his own right and a translator from both Hebrew and Arabic, is an authority on the poetry of medieval Spain. His book of translation, *The Dream of the Poem: Hebrew Poetry from Muslim and Christian Spain, 950–1492* has won him worldwide acclaim.

Cole pours us more brandy and puts on some music. 'Ibis began as a very small and unambitious venture,' he tells me over the voice of Leonard Cohen. 'We were a small group of friends who knew that good literature and poetry, if given a platform, could build bridges. There are all sorts of obstacles to cross-border, multi-cultural publishing in the region. One of the biggest is the reluctance of traditional funding sources, invariably nationalist and supportive of a single culture, to become involved. Israeli institutions will not publish Syrian writers, and vice versa. We are still non-profit and still operate with minimal resources. But because of the high quality of the books we publish – works by both contemporary and long-overlooked authors – people from all over the region are now knocking on our door looking for translation.'

From another bookcase Adina Hoffman pulls out Ibis's backlist. It's impressive – it offers everything from essays by Haim Nahman Bialik, the greatest of twentieth century Hebrew poets, to verses by Taha Mohammed Ali, a contemporary Nazarene poet who works in a souvenir shop. 'He's very droll,' says Cole. 'Taha jokes he's spent most of his life selling Christian trinkets made by Arabs to Jews. But,' adds the translator, who has published him in English, 'he is also an extraordinary talent.'

How far can this cross-cultural vision of the Middle East go? In the world of poets, much further than anyone else today can dare believe. I continue flipping through Ibis material until I come across an excerpt by the Palestinian poet Mahmoud Darwish.

The day will come when the Jew will will not be ashamed to find Arab elements inside himself, and the Arab will not be ashamed to declare that he also contains Jewish aspects...I am a product of all the cultures that have passed through this land – Greek, Roman, Persian, Jewish, and Ottoman...Each culture passed on, and left something behind. I am a son to all these fathers, but I belong to a single mother. Does that mean my mother is a whore? My mother is this land, which absorbs us all, and was both a victim and a witness.

Perhaps the day Darwish envisaged will arrive. For the moment it is remote. What, instead, about the here and now, about Jerusalem today? I ask Cole and Hoffman how they see their own lives in the city.

"Ah, yes, Jerusalem, the world's most central backwater,' quips Hoffman. 'It's not always so droll.'

'It can drive you crazy,' says Cole.

'It generates energy and exhausts energy at the same time,' says Hoffman. 'You don't know why until you figure out what the source of all that energy is – it's human and it's produced by friction.'

'No, you don't know why a lot of things are the way they are,' says Cole. 'And sometimes you never manage to figure them out. They only get more complicated.'

'You've got to get out from time to time,' says Hoffman.

'You've got to get away to New York or Paris to regenerate,' says Cole. 'Even Tel Aviv can sometimes seem a long way from Jerusalem.'

This kind of exchange ping-pongs back and forth across the copper table for some time. What the couple are saying in the end, I think, is that they have a deep and abiding love for Jerusalem. But like many such loves it's frustrating because it doesn't always reciprocate – among other failures is its failure to be the cosmopolitan city it could and should be. It has all the human elements, all the intellect, dynamism, and variety a great city requires. And yet the vital synthesis never happens – there is none of the overlapping, the borrowing, the spontaneous cultural osmosis on which real cosmopolitanism depends. The city at the centre of the world remains inanimate, somehow, in its own centre.

And yet against all the odds this pair persist. Phrase by phrase, line by line, they are determined to extend by the written word the boundaries of Jerusalem's common, shared experience. It's only when I've walked halfway back to the Maison d'Abraham, the headlights of cars stabbing through the steady drizzle falling on the Mount of Olives, that a phrase of Peter Cole's comes back to me.

Even Tel Aviv can sometimes seem a long way from Jerusalem, he'd said. Of course Tel Aviv, less that an hour's drive away, is no distance away at all. What did he mean? That the city on the sea, unlike Jerusalem, is a cosmopolitan city? Or that, for all its acclaimed differences, it isn't? And suddenly, arriving in the dark at the gates of the Maison d'Abraham, I decide I will head west, down from the dark hills to the bright lights at the water's edge. It's time to find out.

Fifteen

It doesn't really matter how close Tel Aviv is to Jerusalem. The city itself, thin and stretched out along the coastline, is plagued by road construction and heavy traffic – it takes me much longer to get downtown from the Tel Aviv bus station that it does to travel from one city to the other. But no matter how slowly the Number 17 crawls along Allenby Street the woman in the seat beside me never tires. She is small and pale and dark-haired, and her eyes are as bright as a mynah bird's. They dart everywhere as she gazes out through the bus window, and she never stops talking.

'You see this square?' she says. I can hardly help seeing it. Traffic has slowed to a standstill and the workmen ripping up the square's tarmac are labouring beneath our noses. Further along, they are laying cobblestones. 'Well, this square is exactly the same age I am – eighty. We were born here at the same time,' she says emphatically. 'I wish they could rebuild me, but they can't. They're rebuilding Tel Aviv. They want the square to look the way it was when it was young. We're celebrating a birthday – the city is a century old.'

My companion seems to be talking as much to herself as she is to me. 'Naturally *Papa*' – she puts a Gallic inflection on the word – 'arrived here even earlier, at the beginning. He was very young, yes, and still poor then,' she says, her head turned to the glass beside her. 'But so proud, of course. And so hard-working. He had fifty Turkish lira in his pocket when he landed. He was an Ashkenazi from Salonika. *Maman* was a Ladino from Istanbul, very sophisticated, very *soignée*. She spoke exquisite French. He

237

wanted the best for her. He built her a house in Florentina Street. Do you know Florentina Street?' I shake my head, but she isn't looking.

'It's *chic* now, and too expensive,' she says, with more than a hint of regret in her voice. She has come down in life, perhaps. 'Of course there was nothing here then – only sand-dunes and grapefruit trees and Arabs. The Arabs lived in Jaffa, just down the coast, until '48. Then the Haganah came. The Arabs were drinking coffee in their houses, and the Haganah men sent them out.' Fingers down, palms turned in, she raises her hands from her lap and makes delicate little shooing motions. 'They went away. And we kept building.'

I wonder if my new acquaintance's wandering mind won't wander too far. To bring her back I ask her if she likes Tel Aviv as much now.

It's as if I've made a rude proposition. She sits up with a start and shakes her head violently. 'No, of course not,' she says. 'Before, we were like a big family in Tel Aviv. Everybody knew everybody else. We were Jewish. We behaved like Jews. Tel Aviv is no longer Jewish, it's just another city. There are people from everywhere, Ethiopians, Americans, Yemenis, Russians, I don't know what. They're rude. Some of those Russians don't even pretend to be Jewish. No, the city is not so nice now.'

I shouldn't have interrupted. I've broken the spell of reminiscence, and my fellow bus-rider is just one more elderly person griping about the world's inconstancy. She begins a long story of having to stand in the bus the week before. She, a woman of eighty, with bad knees! While Russian teenage louts sat playing games on those screen-things! But by this point we have reached a place where the crowds outside are dense and growing denser. If ever there were sand-dunes here, they now lie buried beneath teeming pedestrian malls. I'm happy to walk.

The little lady with the bright eyes is right. Tel Aviv is no longer Jewish – at least no longer Jewish in the way Jerusalem is Jewish. There are no dark overcoats in the crowd I step down into, no somber faces encumbered by hats and side-curls and eyeglasses. This place is Magen David Circle, named after the Star of David because half a dozen major streets meet here. They might stretch on outwards forever – every Jewish people from every far-flung place across the globe has followed them in to the heart of this city. But there's no visible sign that they've brought their faith with them. Tel Aviv may be as culturally complex as Jerusalem, but it's not a culture that revolves around religion. There's not a menorah or a mezuzah, a tallit or a tzitzit in sight.

For the time being the Magen David Circle seems to revolve instead around a vast arts-and-crafts market – it starts on the central plaza here and spills down broad streets blocked to traffic. Such things exist in other cities, too, but I can't help being impressed. Either this is an extraordinarily raffish and colourful human gathering or I've been in Jerusalem far too long. It's not just the stall-holders and artists who look bohemian and extravagant. I've seen them elsewhere before, the sellers of paintings and rings and tie-dyed shirts, the hawkers of silk scarves and hand-made soaps and perfumed candles. Nor is it the entertainers, the jugglers, street clowns, mimes, sleight-of-hand artists and ambulating musicians.

No, it's the crowd itself, the ordinary people of Tel Aviv ambling insouciantly along on this Tuesday mid-afternoon. Right away I can see that they live a very long way indeed from Jerusalem and its sober, restrained behavior. Suddenly God is no longer peering over the shoulder of each and every one present. And with his going goes, too, the religious inhibitions and social constraints. The crowd is garrulous, energetic, informal, irreverent, wisecracking and endlessly extroverted. These may be Jews, but they are secular Jews, and they are doing what Jews in Jerusalem seldom do. They are having fun.

With just a little more people-watching I *know* I've been in Jerusalem too long. Not only are these people having fun; they are having sexy, guiltless fun. I don't think I've seen women dressed like this anywhere. Compared even to Jerusalem's most daring females these women are brazen and fearless hussies. So immodestly dressed are they even now, in the plain light of day, that I wouldn't be surprised to see freshly-arrived Jerusalemites gazing skyward, fearful that the inhabitants of Tel Aviv might be struck down right here on the sidewalk by a heavenly hand. Whatever these women have, they flaunt it.

And they have quite a lot. I see women with Louis-Vuitton-style handbags, alarming things with mixed skull-and-crossbone and Star of David motifs. I see leotards worn with leg-warmers and sandals, pierced belly-buttons, acres of midriff, swathes of gold lamé, plunging decolleté, bleached-blond hair, rhinestones and gold chains, stiletto heels, thong underwear and low-riders so low I have no idea how they stay up. There's a definite Tel Aviv style, brassy and provocative, perhaps, when seen from other parts of the world. Seen from the stern heights of Jerusalem, it's a look that ranges from border-line vulgar to outright tarty. For a poor boy straight out of the hills of Judea it's all too much.

I mill with the fair-shoppers for a while, then continue walking up Allenby Street. Fashion aside, the ambience in the city is so different it's difficult to identify. There's an urban buzz on the sidewalks. There are neon signs and rushing crowds, taxi cabs, busy bars, delicatessens and boutiques. Tel Aviv may not be the New York of the East its admirers like to imagine, but it does have a punchy, energetic drive, a vibrant western rhythm not much seen this side of Istanbul.

There's something else in the air, though, another, more forceful identity that asserts itself with every step I take. As Allenby Street curves suddenly westward the atmosphere perceptibly changes. There are outdoor cafés and restaurants with people eating salads on the side-walk. There are kids in shorts doing tricks with skate-boards. There are couples with bags and blankets over their shoulders heading in the same direction I am. Three teenage boys overtake me. Tanned, bare-chested and dressed in baggies and flip-flops, each is carrying a surf-board under his arm. Suddenly the street comes to an abrupt halt and I see where everyone is heading, where everything in Tel Aviv leads – to a palm-fronted beach-promenade and a bright blue Mediterranean Sea rolling away beyond it.

It's all so relaxed and easygoing I spend the rest of the afternoon on the beach. Back in Jerusalem it's cold and rainy, and although Christmas is just three weeks away, the air is gentle here still – the promenade is alive with joggers, cyclists, surfers and café loungers, their heads turned indolently towards the winter sunshine. Further out, there are even a few brave souls splashing in the water.

But if simple physical hedonism is one of the elements wafting in from the Mediterranean, there are others as well. While Jerusalem in its hilltop fastness looks to the heavens for comfort and guidance, Tel Aviv, like maritime cities everywhere, is open to the sea born influences of the outside world. And like all coastal cities in this part of the world it is the Mediterranean itself that has shaped life here. Are the faces turned towards the sun here really any different than the faces turned to the Temple Mount in Jerusalem? In some ways I think they are.

This is another world. From one end of this sea to the other the Mediterranean environment has given a remarkable consistency to the region, dictating everything from the food people eat, to the houses they build, to the way they make their living. And such is the absorptive, homogenizing power of the Mediterranean that Tel Aviv is part of it all. While Jerusalem addresses itself to history, to the laws of tradition and entrenched habit, this city rejects the past and wants little of tradition. Not caring for God's opinion, unattracted to the monotheistic philosophies that over the centuries have sprung from the stark deserts to the east, it seeks its fulfillment elsewhere. It looks not to its spiritual hinterland, but westwards across the water. And so in the end it resembles other places in the Mediterranean, port-cities where sea and sensuality and the keen pleasures of material existence hold sway.

I enjoy my own afternoon of fun in the sun, and as I sit beneath rustling palms I can once again feel Jerusalem's tensions draining from me. Nor does it matter where I look – nowhere do I see any sign of that tension in anyone else, either. If I concentrate on the illusion hard enough, I could be on a beach in Spain or Italy. The whole decades-old, bogged-down, hate-filled mess only an hour to the east might never have existed. There is not an Arab in sight. There's not a single stretch of separation wall, not a soldier or a checkpoint or a gun. On the sun splashed beaches of Tel Aviv denial is not only easy; it's not even required.

It's so comfortable being by the sea that when the sun sinks I can only drag myself a couple of hundred metres away. On the corner of Ben Yehuda and Trumpeldor Streets I find a transient's hotel. It's a dump. It's neither clean nor quiet, but it is cheap and central. I drop my bag on a sagging bed and head out again for an evening stroll through the city.

Not far from the Magen David Circle, wandering aimlessly, I turn up Rothschild Boulevard. The street is as elegant and distinguished as the name. Unbidden, Jesse Rosenfeld comes to mind. It's easy enough for him, gazing towards Tel Aviv from Palestinian Ramallah, to dream of a united Jewish-Arab state. But from this broad boulevard such a vision for the moment looks more than a little improbable.

Everything here militates against it – the grand residential villas, the trim parks, the university students returning home on bicycles, the neighbourhood children walking their dogs, the couples sitting on bar-stools at little street kiosks drinking cappuccino. *Mittel Europa* lies many thousands of miles away, but on Rothschild Boulevard its meticulous recreation in the Middle East begs a question of psychological intent. By cocooning themselves in the trappings of a bourgeois European existence, are Israelis trying to create an illusion of the safety and security that usually comes with it? When the home-furnishing company Ikea first established itself here its presence was hailed by sociologists as a transformative cultural event – wildly popular, it allowed even ordinary Israelis access to the reassurances of conventional European life. How willing would the residents of the boulevard be to let surrounding Arab culture – even moneyed and sophisticated Arab culture – impinge upon this elaborate mental construct?

No more willing, I imagine, than the boutique owners of Sheinken Street, the commercial thoroughfare that runs along the top of Rothschild Boulevard. Most prosperous cities in the world have a Sheinken Street – locales once genuinely bohemian, but now overrun by the fashionable and well-off. It's a designer-street, an expensive, self-consciously arty street lined with small clothing boutiques, skillfully-illuminated galleries, bookshops with large alternative lifestyle sections, and bars jammed with lively night-time crowds. A hip, youthful look is studiously cultivated on Sheinken, as is the cult of *far-niente*. It's good to be seen to be doing nothing here, but better to be seen doing it fashionably.

From the bottom of the thoroughfare I stroll down King George V Street, a funkier, grittier version of Sheinken that's still awaiting its makeover. There's less money here, but scattered among older small-business premises, now grimy and languishing, are music clubs, piercing parlors, and trendy, avant-garde hairdressers. There are vegan eating establishments, minimalist cafés, rare book shops and alternative medicine stores. On one side of the street I look through a plate-glass window at male and female clients sitting on rugs on the floor to have their hair tressed. On the other I gaze into a dark, mysterious garden restaurant, illuminated only by faint strings of fairy lights and frequented by pale Tel Aviv denizens who, I'm sure, come out only at night.

It's all a far cry from the rigid and convention-bound quarters of Jerusalem, and I enjoy just walking around, gawking – I feel like a hayseed tourist come to the big city. Even the Dizengoff Center, a large and lurid multi-story shopping mall, has me enthralled, if only because I've escaped the all-encompassing clutches of religion.

But in the end it's the seaside I find myself craving most of all in Tel Aviv – it's as if the fresh breeze, blowing in over the open Mediterranean, is bringing some kind of relief from far away. An hour later, completing a circle around the center of Tel Aviv, I am back on Allenby Street drinking beer on the sidewalk within sight of the now dark water.

From where I am sitting I can see the seafront Tel Aviv Opera House at the end of Allenby and, waving in the night breeze, the palms that line the beach. Stretching away in either direction along the promenade there are the bright lights of restaurants, music-venues, up-scale bars and luxury hotels. But there's seediness and neglect here, too – the sidewalk behind me is lined with shabby buildings and doubtful businesses. Just past the rundown Metropole Hotel on the nearest corner, couples come and go from an establishment that rents rooms by the hour. On the other side of the street the façade of the Hotel Galim, advertising a strip-show, sports a neon girl sliding up and down a neon pole. Down closer to the water there are ragged men sleeping on benches. Tel Aviv may be the Middle East's high-tech and financial services capital, but in a city now more expensive than Helsinki or Rome not everyone has kept up in the race to riches.

Certainly my sidewalk companions haven't. I'm not sure they were ever registered to compete in the first place. The little sidewalk bar, run by immigrant Russians, is poor enough. It doubles as a corner store, selling noodles, tins of sardines and evaporated milk from shelves behind the bar. Its tables and chairs are made of rickety plastic, its list of bar prices is hand-lettered and stained. But the premises are not nearly as poor as the patrons.

I'm not sure where they come from. My fellow-drinkers are Jewish migrants from somewhere in the Middle East or West Asia, I think. They could be Kurdish, Turkish, Iraqi, Persian, Yemeni or Bhukari. They are as dark as gypsies, and dressed in broken shoes and hand-me-down clothes. They are certainly not European Ashkenazis and they are certainly not speaking Hebrew. Their music, which floats out over the sidewalk from a boom-box placed under a table, is heavy on minor oriental chords, on hand drums and swelling, over-emotional strings. Wherever their origins, my companions form a threadbare little group of their own, a dozen or more drinkers sitting on a dim sidewalk, oblivious of passers-by and a city that is equally oblivious of them.

They're misfits. There is a man who limps between tables with a broken crutch; a girl with her front teeth missing; a palseyed chain-smoker with a shake so severe he can barely bring his hand to his mouth, There's a bent and shriveled old woman who, on opening her mouth to sing with the music, becomes a glorious, sweet-tongued eastern houri. I feel as if I'm sitting with a collection of curiosities from a travelling show.

But no, these are only people who've left one place and never been fully adopted by another. It makes me think once again of Peter Cole and Adina Hoffman, about the question that came to me on a rainy evening spent with two cosmopolitan Jews in an old Arab house in Jerusalem. What does it mean to be cosmopolitan in this part of the world?

Tel Aviv, modern, dynamic, extroverted, motivated by the material rather than the spiritual, *should* be a truly global and cosmopolitan city. It sits on a sea whose history is defined by cultural and commercial exchange and whose common civilization spread long ago to all its ports – two thousand years ago the dark water stretching out before me was known simply as *Mare Nostrum*, Our Sea. Demographically, too, Tel Aviv has had cosmopolitan advantages – thanks to massive inward migration over the last half-century, the city has a population more varied in geographical origin, more diverse in education, skills, and intellectual capacities than most cities on the globe.

But that's not all – in this part of the world the very *idea* of the cosmopolitan city, a multicultural society in which each group finds its place, has always played a special role. Despite a bad press, the history of the Levant is not just one of conflict and separation. The meeting place of different races and religions, the eastern Mediterranean has also shown itself capable of evolving special institutions to accommodate these differences. Here the idea of a cosmopolitan society traditionally involved much more than its simply being 'urbane' or 'sophisticated', as it does in the West today. It implied instead a particular kind of social compact which acknowledged cultural differences and at the same time encouraged peaceful co-existence. What it called for was the offering of mutual advantage to all concerned.

There's not much evidence of that kind of arrangement left on the eastern rim of this sea today. But still I can think of other Mediterranean places, not so far from Tel Aviv, which at one point or another harboured these genuinely cosmopolitan societies. The international trading city of Alexandria in pre-Nasser days was one. Constantinople, capital of a vast and varied empire under the Ottomans, was another.

The multiculturalism that was the distinguishing trait of both cities grew out of an old Ottoman institution known as the *millet*. Originally introduced as an aid to tax collection, the system categorised the empire's subjects not by nationality, but by religion – you could practice your Christianity or Judaism under the Muslim Ottomans if you wished, but it would cost you more. Not only was this good for the Ottoman tax base; as the empire evolved and became more complex it became a way of neutralizing the potentially dangerous and divisive claims of nationalism.

Under the *millet* each subject of the empire belonged not to a national political entity, as was the way in Europe, but to an empire-wide religious community, a supranational body that transcended old borders. But the simple recognition of a religious identity would not in itself have been enough to ensure peaceful relations between different groups. In Constantinople, today's Istanbul, it was the Sultan who personally guaranteed the rights and traditions of each community; in return, community leaders promised the cohesion of the group and the loyalty of each subject in it.

Above and beyond identity, the system provided equality of opportunity; in return for service to a multicultural ideal under a single authority in Constantinople, subjects from the vast imperial mix were all candidates for positions of power, prestige and material reward. At their best, before decline and corruption set in, the Ottomans offered a highly successful multi-racial, multi-religious meritocracy. From Montenegran Christians to Salonika Jews and Damascus Arabs, all participated in the great military, administrative and commercial endeavours of the day.

In Alexandria, reward across a wide ethnic and religious spectrum had reached its peak. Ottoman influence, of course, eventually declined in Egypt as it did elsewhere, and gave way to British hegemony. But the pluralistic model of the *millet* system remained behind and nourished a cohesive, multicultural society in Alexandria even as it embarked on the competitive rigours of 20th-century capitalism. Growing rich on Egypt's cotton trade, Alexandria attracted not only dozens of communities from across the moribund Ottoman empire, but large populations of Greeks, Italians, Britons and other Europeans. The result was a vibrant multiplicity of groups – 'Five races, five languages, a dozen creeds,' as Lawrence Durrell wrote of the city – all participating in the cut- and-thrust of modern international commerce. It was made possible by a financial elite that stood at the top of Alexandrian society – the leaders of the city's family-owned export houses. Composed of members of all the religions and races represented in Alexandria, this was a clique which, in dealing with each other on a daily, personal basis, assured the harmonious functioning of the city as a whole. In the end Alexandria fell victim to nascent Egyptian nationalism, but for almost a century it maintained a society whose economic dividends made multicultural cooperation an attractive proposition.

It may be that Tel Aviv is simply too new a city for that kind of historical influence to filter through. It may also be that Tel Aviv, not being a true port – in Israel Haifa fills that function – has never had the kind of maritime exchange on which such cosmopolitan attitudes were built.

But the real reason for Tel Aviv's failure in this regard is more fundamental. It lies in its exclusive nature – religious and ethnic exchange is simply not on its programme. Whatever the reasons, Israel does not explore contacts with its outside neighbours; it repels them. It's own internal Arab Israeli population live an existence apart. And within Jewish Israeli society itself, life is divisive and contentious.

The exclusion of various cultures from mainstream Israeli society – my fellow beer-drinkers being one example – is just one of any number of internal domestic tensions and imbalances. Ashknazi versus Sepharad, secular versus religious, civil versus military, recent immigrants vs long-time residents, old-style Zionist socialism versus the newer values of the free-market – all these divisions keep Israelis in a state of imbalance and pent-up conflict. Worse, the advantage of vested interests within these conflicts does not lie in the promotion of multicultural cooperation. How better for the country's conservative religious ideologists, for its defence establishment or its right-wing politicians to justify their *raison d'etre* than by encouraging a sense of insecurity? Such are Israel's internal pressures that one wonders what a sudden removal of external pressures might produce. Dramatic implosion might be one result.

Tel Aviv may be hedonistic, sexy and secular, but it is not cosmopolitan.

Peter Cole, I reflect, was right in his pronouncement about Tel Aviv merely seeming to be a long way from Jerusalem. It isn't.

Any further sidewalk contemplation on my part, though, is interrupted by a new arrival. Bundled in scarf and woollen hat against the approaching night cold, a man emerges from the gloom trundling a three-wheeled cart. Behind bagged snacks of chickpeas, olives and hummus sits a large metal chest. Lifting the lid, the vendor plunges a pair of long-handled tongs into billowing clouds of steam and from the boiling water below extracts hot cobs of corn. Money in hand, the sidewalk-drinkers rise from their tables, and so do I. For suddenly I realise I'm hungry – I haven't eaten since leaving Jerusalem. Downing my beer, I amble up the seaside promenade to look for something more substantial than snack food.

Mike's Place is a blues bar, a busy beachfront entertainment venue not far from the American embassy. I haven't been anywhere like it for a long time – all Jerusalem's got the blues, but nobody sings it that way. There are no lines stretching out the door because there are no big names on the bill on Tuesdays – it's Jam Night tonight. And the place serves meals as well, so in I go.

A young crowd fills the space inside – it's popular with Israelis and expats alike. The atmosphere is anonymous, the decor international. At the bar young men are challenging each other to tequila shots, and at tables around it couples are drinking beer and eating nachos dripped with melted cheese. The music hasn't started yet. On three or four large television screens scattered around football fans are watching a loud game – Liverpool versus Marseille. I am reminded of the little mynah-bird lady on the bus. It's just any other night in any other city.

When the man on the bar stool next to mine tells me his burger and chips are good, I order the same. We chat and drink beer as I wait. An Englishman, he's dressed in dark flannel trousers and a white shirt with the sleeves rolled up. He looks like a young corporate employee with time on his hands. But when I ask him if Tel Aviv is a good place to mix business and pleasure, he laughs out loud. He wouldn't know, he says. He's had neither – he's been holed up in the Sheraton Hotel for three days and only comes out to eat.

'It's just as well Mike's burgers are good,' he says ruefully, taking a pull at his beer. 'They're the only satisfaction I'm likely to get out of this trip.'

He works for Nortel, the communications firm, and has flown to Tel Aviv to complete a deal on the sale of an automated voice-recognition system. 'It's nothing new,' he tells me. 'It dispenses with company telephone receptionists. The caller is asked who he wants to speak to, the system recognises a name, and the call is automatically transferred to the required party. Simple.'

But not so simple, apparently, in the eyes of Israeli security. At Ben Gurion Airport his computer, containing the software for the programme as well as the legal documents needed for the handover, was confiscated. The Nortel man has been promised it will be returned after its contents have been examined. He's got to fly home in two days. Even if the computer is returned he doubts he will have time to complete the handover. It's been a wasted trip.

'Actually,' he says with a smile, 'we've had some trouble with it anyway. The voice-recognition system works perfectly well everywhere else, but we were having problems with it here. It doesn't like being barked at.'

'What do you mean?'

'Well, Israelis, and Israeli men especially, are a little too aggressive with the system in the way they talk – our voice algorithms aren't built with the kinds of tolerances needed to handle that kind of talk. The machine can't always recognise who's being asked for. Instead of redesigning the whole system, we're re-recording the voices of the automatic receptionists asking callers who they want to be connected with. We're using younger women. We reason that the younger-sounding the receptionist, the more sympathetic the caller will be and the gentler his voice.'

'Has it worked?' I ask.

'Not entirely. We keep on lowering the age of our receptionist,' the Nortel man says glumly, 'Twenty-three, twenty, seventeen...we still haven't got the right match yet. Too old, and the callers continue barking.

Too young, and the receptionists lose credibility. We find that the voice of a seven-year-old is just a little too immature to be taken seriously.'

Our chat comes to an end when half an hour later a man with long black hair steps up to the stage microphone. There will be a set by Mike's Place's own house-band, he announces, then around midnight the stage will be open to all comers. There's are cheers and whistles from the crowd; they obviously know and like this guy. He straps on a bass guitar. The other band members come on and, as bands are wont to do, fiddle with tuning and sound-levels for a few moments. The loudspeakers on the stage hum, screech and blare. Then the group is off and running.

Now, I don't know if it's the beer I've been drinking all evening, or if, on the other hand, it's the fact that I am once again hearing the music I've heard all my life and then suddenly stopped hearing. Music is a background hum to ordinary existence, a noise that came to an end when I moved into a pilgrims' hostel in an old monastery overlooking Jerusalem. I am not a serious music fan, and the band's not being terribly serious either – they're jumping from the sixties to the nineties, from blues to reggae to rock-and-roll. But it's a good, tight band and they know what they're doing. When they segue into Procol Harum's *Whiter Shade of Pale* – a song I haven't heard for at least a decade – I'm surprised to discover a hard lump in my throat. It's as if life here, the violence, the repressed tensions, the wasted energy, the whole jagged, disconnected existence of Jerusalem, has suddenly become too much. When you find yourself overwrought by a forty-year-old pop song, you know, whatever you've been telling yourself, that somewhere inside you're finding the going tough.

But at the same time I'm enjoying escaping into here-and-now of this place and the easy, non-conflictual nature of it all. It comes as a relief – the rock-and-roll, the pleasure of the crowd, the enjoyment of the musicians for whom this is more than just a job. I'm particularly fascinated by the bass player, the man who introduced the band. An English musician who has moved to Israel, his name is Barry Gilbert, and if he's a good bassist with a decent voice that's not what interests me most. It's not the music but the man himself that's intriguing. He's tall and lean, and his dark, straight hair falls over his shoulders to his chest. The face it surrounds has a hard-lived-in look. Not weak or dissolute, it's lined and world-wise and weary. It's been marked by a lot of life. Barry Gilbert won't see forty again, but he's got the energy of someone half his age. He lives for the pleasure of his music – he's a sybarite, an old rocker who's seen all the sensuality in the world and keeps on coming back for more. Intellect, reason, morality, memory: they're all there, perhaps, but they take second place to the immediacy and enjoyment of physical being. Looking at that face, Jerusalem seems to be further away than ever.

I leave Mike's Place sometime around two in the morning, and spend a sleepless night in my hotel room. There's a harsh, purple spotlight trained on the hotel façade from below, and even with the thin curtains pulled close it lights up the room in a ghastly nightmare brightness. Between two and five o'clock cars occasionally roar down the street. By six a.m. there is a steady stream of vehicles honking and jockeying in the street below. When I pull open the curtains the spotlight has been turned off and in the half-light of early morning I see a large knot of dark figures gathered on the sidewalk below. They are Jewish Ethiopian labourers waiting for employment in some sort of casual street-side daily-labour market. Trucks and vans stop by and pick them up in ones and twos, and by the time I leave the room there are only a few left standing waiting on the corner. Then, giving up and drifting away, they too are gone.

Ashraf Noor has joked that I might find the temptations of Tel Aviv too much and stay on indefinitely for the all-night clubbing. But I find this sight of these dispirited men depressing, and suddenly I want to get back to the Maison d'Abraham. An hour later I'm on a bus, Jerusalem-bound.

On return, there's no mistaking the undercurrent of tension that pulses incessantly through the life of Jerusalem. At the exit of the Central Jerusalem Bus Station two armed IDF women in military fatigues, combat boots and green berets are verifying the identity of arriving travellers. It is a routine exercise – they are checking only Arabs – and their faces remain bored and impassive as they demand ID cards and radio in the details. The Arabs, too, retain faces as impassive as those who detain them. They say nothing, make no complaint, express no emotion, and then depart. It's just another day at the centre of the world's trouble.

But there's something of Tel Aviv that won't let go. All night long and throughout the journey back to Jerusalem the face of Barry Gilbert has kept surfacing. I have no idea why, if not because he is the very antithesis of Jerusalem life, a man strong enough in his life of music that he remains oblivious and untouched by the realities around him. Even in a city in denial that's quite an achievement, and I want to know more about him.

There is, I discover the next morning, another branch of Mike's Place in Jerusalem. By noon I have made way up the Jaffa Road to a gloomy, unlit premises smelling of stale beer and cigarette smoke. It's far to early for the bar to be open to the public, but in a small office in the back I find a man adding up figures on a calculator. He's Barry Gilbert's business partner, and in one brief moment he changes the way I look at Barry Gilbert and Tel Aviv.

'Sure,' says Gilbert's partner, 'Barry loves playing and he's made a life of music in Tel Aviv. He's invested his money and himself in Mike's Place. But don't get the idea that he's isolated from the life of this country. His music came close to turning him into a dead man.'

On an April night in 2003, another Jam Night at Mike's Place in Tel Aviv, Barry Gilbert was playing on stage when two Muslims came off the beachfront outside and detonated a powerful suicide bomb. Although the explosion took place near the club's entrance, it was powerful enough to knock Gilbert off the stage and concuss him. Others were not so lucky. A waitress standing nearby had her arm ripped off at the shoulder – she later died. In all, three Israelis were killed in Mike's Place that night and more than fifty injured.

So Barry Gilbert, rocker, sensualist, partaker of immediate pleasures, does not remain untouched by the violence of the Middle East, any more than the seaside city itself does. It's not just Jerusalem and the West Bank

– conflict, and the responsibility for conflict, surrounds everyone here, whether they are willing to recognise it or not. And I'm ready to bet it continues to surround Barry Gilbert in an especially gripping way, each time, each week he climbs to the stage at Mike's Place to host another Jam Night. It's the price of rock-and-roll in Israel.

Sixteen

From time to time Ashraf Noor and I get a hankering to splurge on sticky sweets dripping with syrup. Sometimes they are layered filo pastries rolled in crushed, bright green pistachio nuts. Sometimes they resemble cylinders of crisply baked shredded wheat. At other times they are diamond-shaped lozenges sprinkled with almond or redolent of fragrant rose-water. But our one unchanging criterion is that always they must be oozing a thick and horribly sweet syrup. Of course we know this goopy stuff is no good for us, but still we can't help it, and afterwards we feel guilty. Is that why we seek out sweet shops in the narrowest, most hidden lanes of the Old City? Ashraf knows a dozen places where we can indulge our weakness in near-complete and anonymous obscurity.

It's not a question that has occurred to me before, but one noontime as we sit smacking our lips after a mixed plateful of sticky delicacies I ask him how he knows of the existence of such places.

From our fortified position behind broad trays of freshly baked semolina cakes he gazes through the window of the little shop where we're sitting. It lies in a stepped ally that descends an incline somewhere at the meeting place of the Muslim and Christian Quarters. On the far side of the street is a blank, whitewashed wall. It is a view that changes now and then as Indian women in blue-bordered, sari-like habits drift by. Their presence tells me we are somewhere near the home of the sisters of the Missionaries Of Charity, an order founded by Mother Teresa. Not in a hundred years, however, could I find this little alley again.

But Ashraf could. 'It's easy,' he says, pointing. 'Look – you see that door?' In the wall on the other side of the street is a low doorway so unremarkable, so much the colour and texture of the surrounding wall, that I haven't noticed it at all. 'I used to live there.'

Ashraf Noor is not a secretive character; he's one of the most candid and forthright persons I've ever met. But so mixed are his origins and experiences, so varied is his past, that he never ceases to surprise me. It's as if he's had not just one life in Jerusalem, but several.

'Well, in all the coming and going one ends up living in a lot of different places,' he reasons. 'In fourteen years it's rare that I've ever taken the same lodgings twice. I know bits of the the Arab, eastern half of the city. But I know other parts of it – the Christian Old City and Jewish West Jerusalem – much better.'

And as if to show me that, when it comes to Jerusalem's three great divides, he cannot and will not pronounce on any one of them to the exclusion of the other two, he now invites me on a walk across the city. He wants me to see another house he once lived in. It sits in Talbiyeh, one of Jewish Jerusalem's leafier, more affluent suburbs. He still thinks of it often, he says. He hasn't seen it for many years.

The winter's day is mild and sunny, and we both have the afternoon off. 'It will do us good,' he says, patting his stomach. But apart from the exercise I'm delighted to take a stroll with Ashraf, for I know that his Jerusalem does not resemble most people's Jerusalem.

Heading for the New Gate and the Jaffa Road, we cut through the heart of the Christian Quarter. In a little square behind the Casa Nova, the looming building that houses many of the city's Franciscan monks, he ducks his head into a barbershop.

'Tony!' he says in greeting to the man standing behind a barber's chair with a straight-blade razor in his hand. Anthony, who has been cutting Ashraf's hair for years, looks up and beams in recognition. But we see he's got his hands full for the moment. He's in the midst shaving a couple of plainclothes Israeli security men – we know they are policemen because they've set squawking two-way radios on the shelf by the wall-mirror

– and he looks a little nervous about the job. Monk's tonsures are more in his line, and a safer bet. When you're holding a honed blade against a policeman's throat you don't need any distractions.

'OK if we visit my old rooms?' says Ashraf, cutting short the visit. 'Fine,' replies Tony as he wipes lather from the blade onto the edge of his palm. 'They're rented out, but go as far as the terrace.'

'Tony cuts hair, but he also dabbles in rentals and real estate,' says Ashraf as we head up a gloomy passageway. We head down another, turn left at a third and in a minute I've lost all sense of direction. 'He knows places not even those policemen would dream existed,' Ashraf adds as, in the midst of a warren of crooked streets, we make our way through an obscure doorway. It looks like the entrance to private quarters to me, but on the far side there are further narrow alleys and more choices to make – stairways leading up and down, courtyards with multiple exits, passages that terminate in dead ends or connect with other passages.

'At night it's sheer murder,' says Ashraf. 'After dark all of these doors are locked – you need a large set of keys to get home, and heaven forbid if you've forgotten your electric torch.' We continue through a maze of passages and tunnels, burrowing our way ever further into the innards of the Old City, until at last we come to a tiny open terrace. There's a bit of blue sky above and on the terrace floor pots of flowers sit posed in early afternoon sunshine. It's the entrance to one of Ashraf's earlier Christian Quarter homes.

'This,' I say, marvelling, 'must be the best-hidden bolt-hole in the entire Middle East.'

'Not at all,' says Ashraf lightly. 'The entire old city is honeycombed from top to bottom. If you knew the way you could probably walk under cover from one end of it to the other without ever seeing the sky. There are aerial walkways, too – there are lots of streets in old Jerusalem, even markets and major thoroughfares, that are roofed over. If you knew the right routes you could probably cross the rooftops of the whole city without ever descending to ground level. The point is, though, that nobody knows the whole city. You can know a certain part of it back to front and inside out, but only if you belong to it. You can't know all of it. It's too complex, too secret, too private.'

What goes for spiritual Jerusalem, it seems, goes for physical Jerusalem as well. We worm our way out of the maze, pass through the New Gate and start up the Jaffa Road. I've walked this route a score of times – it's noisy and traffic-laden, and I don't mind when Ashraf steers me into some quiet lanes a block or two behind the thoroughfare. 'The new city is not so different from the old city,' he says. 'The most direct routes, the most obvious and accessible spots, aren't always the most interesting. It's the hidden ones that can lead you places.' And he's right. In these tangled little streets where visitors to the city rarely come there's another, more intimate life – something other than the anodyne tourist shops, public buildings and fast-food places that occupy the bigger downtown streets.

We pass through a gateway, walk down a high-walled alley, cross a courtyard and climb a set of ringing metal steps. On the balcony at the top of the steps are a few plastic tables and chairs. It doesn't look like anything very special, but through a door waits a wonderfully cosy, bookish café. Packed shelves line the walls, little table lamps illuminate the space with a soft glow, and the air is full of hushed conversation. Tmol Shilshom is as close as anything I've seen to a literary café in the Middle East. A venue where you can drink mid-morning coffee, eat pear-Roquefort ravioli for lunch, listen to an evening book-reading, or peruse the volumes that sit at arm's-length from your table any time you like, it is a meeting place for the city's cultural avant-garde. And like those private places that lie hidden in the complex labyrinth of the Old City, this cafe, too, is for initiates only. Jerusalem, intimate and circumspect always, reserves its inner self for discreet groups.

We emerge from the lanes behind Jaffa Road into King George St, and on the far side of the road, pass by a small office with a sign over the door. I can't understand most of the sign – it's written in romanised Hebrew. It ends in *konzentrationslager*, though, a word which I recognise from visits to the Holocaust museum – it means concentration camps. But without the exit of two elderly men from the office door, it's not a sign I would have noticed at all. These men have something about them, though. It's more than just their advanced age, their old suits and worn faces.

'Camp survivors,' says Ashraf after we've passed by them. 'There are still welfare organisations like this one that look after them. But the survivors are getting older and every year there are fewer of them. When I first came to Jerusalem it was different. You'd be riding in a crowded bus on a hot summer day with a man strap-hanging next to you. Suddenly three inches in front of your face you'd see the tattoo, a string of blue numbers on his raised forearm.' A moment passes and Ashraf shrugs. 'It still leaves me speechless.'

I turn to look at the two men disappearing down the sidewalk. I don't need to see tattoos – their backs alone are enough to open a pit at the bottom of my stomach. What kind of Jerusalem is it, I wonder, that belongs to walking ghosts? What do they see when they stroll these streets? Certainly not what I see, but something special, a Jerusalem that belongs to no one other than themselves. But our walk, as we continue westwards into Jewish Jerusalem, only serves to show me that each person's Jerusalem is special, that it belongs to him alone.

From the bottom of Bezalel Street, we circle around through Nahalaot. Once the most modest of suburbs, its original inhabitants were poor Turkish and Yemenite Jews. Some live here still. Their houses are a mishmash of corrugated iron, patched concrete and wild colour schemes, their little gardens overgrown riots of lemon trees and potted plants. But like the camp survivors, there are fewer and fewer such people. In little time wealthy Israelis and foreign Jews, seeking homes close to the Old City, have bought property here for development. Even a small flat in one of the new residences taking shape can cost half a million dollars. I watch an old Yemeni woman tending dahlias in rusty iron paint-tins, and wonder how she regards the flashy new neighbours driving by in their SUVs. Do they live in the same city at all?

We turn southwards, and Nahalaot gives way to Rehavia. It's entirely different, a place of quiet, well-heeled affluence since its beginnings almost a century ago. We walk through an intimate suburb of leafy streets and well-kept gardens, a showplace of modernist, cube shaped volumes inspired by the German Bauhaus style. It's not just the architecture that's German; in the 1920s Rehavia was settled by German-Jewish immigrants, many of them professionals from the worlds of academia, psychiatry, or architecture itself. The quarter, Ashraf tells me, has maintained its upper-class appeal ever since — David Ben Gurion, Golda Meir and Benjamin Nethanyahu have all lived here.

And as if to punctuate his affirmation, we hear a great wail of sirens break out as we are crossing Aza Street. Looking up the road, I can see a barricade, and beyond it, guards and gates. Suddenly, with a squealing of tyres, a cavalcade pulls out of the gateway onto the street, headed by a police-car blaring a message in Hebrew. The voice on the loudspeaker can only be saying 'Make way! Pull over!', for up and down the street cars are coming to a halt by the curbside. The police car is followed at high speed by half a dozen large four-by-fours, all of them identical and finished in the same metallic gold colour. Identical, too, are the figures behind the windshields, men in dark suits with close-cropped heads and sunglasses.

'It's the Prime Minister on his way to the Knesset,' says Ashraf, looking at the street barricades and gateway. 'That's Agion House, his official residence.' I strain to glimpse the P.M. as the cavalcade rushes by. But the rear windows of the four-by-fours are tinted and impossible to see through.

'How do you know which one he's in?' I ask.

'You don't,' says Ashraf. 'That's the whole point. Right now, for all we know, he could even be headed to the Knesset by another route in a rusty VW van.'

Ashraf doesn't seem impressed by the wily ruses of the secret service. But why should he be, when there are other residents of Rehavia whom he knows well and who do not rush by at 50 miles an hour with their faces hidden? For Ashraf, of course, has lived in Rehavia, too.

The first old acquaintance he meets is going considerably slower than the prime ministerial entourage. One of the original German emigrés, she's a tiny, white-haired woman, ancient and fragile. Pushed by her Filipino nurse, she's rolling along the sidewalk in a wheelchair.

Ashraf greets her with a '*Guten Tag*,' and stops to exchange pleasantries on her health, his health, and the fine winter sunshine. I am introduced, but as we have no common language our own pleasantries are soon curtailed. Perhaps I'm fortunate. Frail she may be, but she's an inexhaustible talker and likes to keep up with neighbourhood gossip on her daily rounds. If you've ever lived in Rehavia, says Ashraf, she's impossible not to talk to.

Our second encounter is even heartier. Hailed from across the street, Ashraf is given a bear-hug and a solid back-thumping. They're administered by Sergei, a jovial journalist who came to the Middle East when eastern Europe was still communist and the Soviet Union still supported the P.L.O. He's still here, a freelance with a video camera. 'We shared a flat in Rehavia one year,' Ashraf muses as we walk on. 'Sergei's a dynamic fellow. He'd go off on a story and disappear for days at a time. Then he'd pop up again, usually early in the morning. He'd be sleepless and dirty and exhausted. But triumphant, too. He was always surprised when I wouldn't join him in a bottle of vodka for breakfast. He'd drink it himself, sleep, then start in on another story.'

Not a minute later, at the exit to an elegant little European-style café, Ashraf spots another neighbourhood character. He's in his sixties, bearded, and wears a long-billed forage cap of grey wool. Ashraf introduces him to me simply as 'the Guardian of Rehavia.' He has a distracted, inquisitive face, as if he's spent much of his life recalling distant acquaintances like Ashraf. Perhaps he has. He's a man, says my companion, who knows absolutely everyone in the neighbourhood. Our sidewalk chat – a pleasant digression into life at the Maison d'Abraham on the far side of the city – takes place in German and English. Had we been Chinese, Ashraf assures me, it would have been just as easily conducted in Mandarin – the man spends his days in cafes talking to anyone and everyone in a dozen languages. There is no one quite as sociable as the Guardian of Rehavia.

'But what does he actually *do*?' I ask. No matter how convivial, the man has to earn a living.

'But that *is* what he does,' says Ashraf. 'He talks and listens. People say he is an agent of the Israeli intelligence services. That's what people may know about him. Of course he knows a good deal more about them. And now he knows about you, too.'

On the southern side of Jabotinsky Street there's a not-so-subtle transition. Where before the houses along the way were modern and European in design, they are now Arab and traditional. We are coming into Talbiyeh, before 1948 a fashionable Palestinian quarter and today one of the most exclusive parts of Jewish Jerusalem. Up and down the streets grand old mansions display the comforts of a life that, for their former owners, has all but disappeared – here I see the delicate arch of an Ottoman window, there the deep blue gleam of glazed ceramic tiles, further on the elegant repetitions of a carved stone colonnade. Some of the most beautiful old homes of old Palestine live on today in Talibiyeh.

'I used to work down there,' says Ashraf, pointing ahead as we are walking along Ha Nassi, one of the broader, busier streets of the suburb. For the moment all I can see in the distance is a man in a dark suit. Why he's standing immobile in the middle of the road is unclear. As we approach I notice something more curious still – he has an Uzi machine-pistol hanging from his shoulder and is talking into the sleeve of his jacket.

'You worked here?' I ask Ashraf incredulously as we walk past the man and the gateway he's standing in front of. I have difficulty imagining Ashraf handling an Uzi.

'No, of course not,' says my fellow stroller. 'Next gate. Shimon Peres lives here.'

The building on the grounds next door might not be quite as prestigious as the Israeli president's official residence, but it is opulent and well-maintained nonetheless. Long and white and low-slung, its smooth lines landscaped into the sloping gardens in which it sits, this is the Van Leer Institute. Founded by a wealthy Jewish Dutch shipping family, the institute sponsors academic research into the nation's contemporary social life. The place seems to be a hothouse of liberal Israeli thought – among the themes pursued by Van Leer academics are the bolstering of Israeli democracy, the development of civil society, the integration of Israel's non-Jewish population and the promotion of discourse and engagement with its Arab neighbours. Israeli society, in this view, is not a fixed and rigid entity, but one that can be encouraged towards a more balanced and equitable future through gradual transition.

Ashraf tours me around the building. It is an architectural symphony in split-level volumes, harmoniously curving surfaces, and subtle, diffuse lighting. There is no room for high emotion or excitement here, no place for the rallying of raw ethnic pride or unthinking patriotic nationalism – this is an environment made for cool, detached contemplation. The Van Leer Institute is quieter and more serene than any of Jerusalem's churches.

On a bottom floor of the building I look into a specialised research library of 27,000 volumes, a place where Ashraf, still an Institute Fellow, comes to work from time to time. On a mid-level I step onto a terrace to look out over the Israeli president's impeccably manicured grounds – I check to see if he might be in his garden, clipping a rose for his lapel perhaps, but there's no sign of anyone. On the top floor I admire an exhibit of black and white photos showing the early history of the country. Not only are there pictures of hearty, sunburned young kibbutzniks in shorts taming a rough and arid land; there are also photos of the Bedouin Arabs who lived there for centuries before them.

It's all very encouraging, but once out of the institute doors and into the streets again I find it difficult to hold on to the Van Leer vision of harmony. Those hushed halls, that sedate and academic view of reasoned transition, only serve to emphasize the existing rupture and discontinuity that divides the city around me. To anyone crossing Jerusalem the city reveals itself in one disparate physical space after another. To negotiate it successfully requires making corresponding leaps in mental space as well. Ashraf Noor might be able to do it, but not many people can. A fractured city makes for fractured minds, and for most of them crossing Jerusalem, either physically or mentally, is impossible.

We continue walking and Ashraf continues bumping into old acquaintances. On the steps outside the bulky monolith of the Jerusalem Theatre we come across an odd little man, unoccupied and looking a little vague. Dark-complexioned, he's wearing a knitted blue woollen cap, a worn pullover, and zip-up plaid bedroom slippers. Ashraf greets him warmly, and behind a wispy little beard and mustache the man's face lights up in recognition. They chat for a moment about mutual friends at the Van Leer Institute, and agree to meet again soon.

The man doesn't seem like an academic type; he has the slightly lost air of someone who's led a vagrant life. As we walk away I ask Ashraf who he is. 'That,' says Ashraf, as if it's the most ordinary thing in the world, 'is the man some people say is the illegitimate son of Haile Selassie.'

It's the kind of thing that leaves you blinking and thinking that no encounter quite as odd can happen again soon. But we've walked no great distance before Ashraf turns into a driveway on a quiet street. He needs just a minute, he says; he wants to say hello to an old friend.

At the end of the drive, Ashraf knocks on the door of the house belonging to a teaching colleague at the Hebrew University. The man's not in, but a face appears at the window beside the door. The jowls are heavy, the teeth long, the forehead bony and massive. The old friend in question is a very large, furry and excited dog.

'Hello, Dalai! Hello, Dalai!' says Ashraf through the window. The dog seems delighted to see him. He wags his tail and stands there barking a greeting so deep and loud it sets the glass in the window vibrating. I'm happy the dog's happy. Angry, Dalai's head is so big, his chest so broad, that he could come charging through the glass at us without thinking twice. But why, I ask, the name?

Shrugging, Ashraf smiles. 'What else would you call a Tibetan Mastiff that used to belong to the Dalai Lama? My teaching colleague is a prominent supporter of Tibet and a friend of the Dalai Lama's. The dog was a gift from him. With a coat like that Dalai finds the Jerusalem summers a bit warm, but otherwise he doesn't miss Lhasa too much. They're both holy cities, after all.'

'Ashraf,' I say, 'this is a setup. You've laid it all on.' Normal people in normal cities, I protest, simply don't run into reputed secret servicemen, possible claimants to the Ethiopian throne and the Dalai Lama's dog in the course of an afternoon's stroll.

But no, Ashraf assures me, laughing. Nothing was set up and this is not a normal city. Such is Jerusalem that not only does it attract unusual, larger-than-life characters from other lives; so relentless are its themes, so compelling is its own political, religious and historical life, that it takes perfectly ordinary people and *makes* them larger than life.

By this point we have walked into a quiet residential street of Talbiyeh and come to a halt in front of a large, old house. It's undergoing renovation; the facade is covered in scaffolding and through open windows above I can see men in construction hats bashing away at walls.

'Here's the house of a man,' indicates Ashraf, 'who was larger than life before he ever came to Jerusalem. This is where Martin Buber lived.'

I know little about one of the great figures of 20th-century philosophy. But I know that the Viennese-born thinker, a Zionist whose own brand of Zionism led to an early call for the establishment of a united Jewish-Arab state in Palestine, is important to Ashraf. The guiding principle that is central to Ashraf's personal life is the same principle on which Buber built an entire philosophy of religious existentialism – a belief in dialogue as the defining act of human existence.

Across the road from Buber's old house Ashraf opens a small gate and we walk down a path around the side of another old house. Ashraf is still bemoaning the conversion of Talbiyeh's villas into luxury flats, but when we come to the garden beyond his talk trails to a halt. I prepare myself for yet one more encounter with yet one more extravagant Jerusalem resident.

'What larger-than-life figure are we going to meet now?' I say.

But in the silence that follows I realise that Ashraf has come to a different kind of encounter, a personal encounter with his own past. We've arrived at our afternoon's destination.

'No one larger than life, but someone from another life,' he finally confirms. 'I used to live here.'

I glance around. The old stone house is Palestinian-built, nowhere near as large or luxurious as some in the neighbourhood, and of a simple charm. There's a broad first-floor balcony with balustrades of Arab geometrical design, a covered outdoor terrace with chairs and climbing vines for shade, and a garden where lemon trees grow. Just beyond the terrace, on a piece of carved, circular stone that looks like the lid of an old well, a cat is stretched out in afternoon sunshine. The place is a picture of quiet, modest, domestic bliss.

'I used to love reading out here on the terrace,' Ashraf says, crossing it to look in through window blinds at a white-tiled kitchen. He is moved. 'I had another existence then, saw the future another way. It was a long time ago.'

He seems sad, or at least touched by a kind of nostalgia I don't usually see in him. 'Sometimes we're tempted to dwell too much in the past,' he reflects. 'But I need to come back to it from time to time. It's a way of holding the different pieces of life together.'

I think of all the places, and not just in this city, where this singular man has lived... Dacca, London, Zurich, Paris, Leipzig and a dozen more. I think of Ashraf's Muslim father, his Christian mother, of a life devoted to Jewish thought. It seems natural, in the midst of an impermanent, always-changing existence, to want such a return. Who doesn't have a need to patch the past together, to fit the pieces into a coherent pattern? I think Ashraf is wrong. I think he *is* a larger-than-life figure, a man who in his many different and disassociated parts is a perfect expression of the city. If Jerusalem strikes a sympathetic nerve in him, if year after year he keeps returning, it is because he and the city share a common need. Like Jerusalem itself, he is looking for a unifying narrative.

We sit for a while on the terrace, playing with the cat in the sunshine, then start walking back to East Jerusalem. The afternoon has left me with more than just a sense of rupture and discontinuity. It's given me the desire to try to patch the bits together – more than ever I want to fit the different pieces of my own Jerusalem into a whole.

Soon it will be Christmas, and time to return home. But before I do I want to stand back from Jerusalem again. I want to try one last time for that perspective I've been seeking from the start. I've looked towards

Jerusalem from many directions, but now another comes to mind. What place could be quieter and calmer, more conducive to a final, undisturbed contemplation of Jerusalem, than an empty place, a desert waste? By the time we've walked back through the gates of the Maison d'Abraham I have decided on one final trip. To the south lies the Negev.

Seventeen

Not far from Beersheba on Highway 40 the last of the greenery finally gives up and the desert takes over. Gone are the dark, rich soils, the citrus groves, the fields of newly sprouted winter wheat that blanket the land further to the north. Gone, too, are the prosperous little Israeli farming towns, tidy bungalows laid out in neat housing-tract rows off the highway. The land is now brown and dry and gravelly, the towns spaced further and further apart until there are no towns at all and prosperity is as rare as water. In the Negev these are not two different things, but one and the same thing.

This is not a place of first choice, a countryside where anyone would take root through natural preference. Not true desert yet – this will come further south – it's flinty, marginal land. It's where people settle because there's no other choice, because there's nothing better left elsewhere. And its people, too, are flinty and marginal. When we stop at a small settlement twenty kilometres from Beersheba the seat beside me is occupied by a seventy-year-old Jewish immigrant from Belarus. He limps down the bus aisle leaning heavily on a cane and sits with effort and pain. He is followed by a wife who hunches into the seat on the far side of the aisle opposite him, silent and stolid.

He hasn't spoken English in six decades. In laborious, near-forgotten words dredged from Soviet school English lessons, he tells me about radiation. He has been irradiated. His wife has been irradiated. When they lived in Belarus in the mid 1980s Chernobyl lay just a few kilometres over the Ukrainian border. They are both sick, and getting sicker. He had a factory job when he came to Israel and had to quit it. But it could be worse. He has a small pension. Medical treatment is free. They go to the outpatient clinic in the Beersheba hospital once a week – it's where they are going now. Life is difficult, the man says, smiling and raising his hands. Through the bus window he looks at the passing desert, the flat, stony ground stretching far into the distance, with the same stoic optic as he looks ahead at what remains of his life. Here we are, and it's tough. But what can you do?

The bus rolls on towards the biggest city in the Negev. Beersheba is a name that for me conjures up romantic desert visions. Perhaps it's because this was the place where the armies of Empire, pushing north against the Turks during the Palestine Campaign in 1917, conducted the last successful cavalry charge of British military history – using only horses and bayonets, lancers of the Australian Light Horse stormed Turkish trenches here and captured the desert wells of Beersheba. But there's nothing as romantic as plumed cavalry or strategic desert wells here now – as the bus heads into the city there's nothing to charge but mile after mile of dreary apartment-block suburbs. Nor, at the central station, are there any flamboyant Ottomans or dashing Australian subalterns waiting to board the bus. They've been replaced by the poorest of Negev residents – Ethiopians heading to even drearier Beersheba satellite towns and Bedouins on their way to homes further outside the city.

No exotic desert-dwellings, these. As the bus continues southwards into ever barer and more arid country, we stop to let off passengers at makeshift roadside camps. The Bedouin settlements are miserable, desolate places of tents and bare earth, flimsy tin-sheet huts, sheep and camel pens where livestock drink at rusty oil-drums cut in half and full of greenish water. Each time the bus door opens the smell of animals is strong. Each time the door closes and we move off again the bus is carrying an extra complement of buzzing flies.

But there is still odder camp-life in this desert. The Negev finds uses that other, richer land elsewhere is too valuable to be wasted on. On

Highway 40 we drive past the sprawling Nafha Prison, a turreted, walled, barbed-wire-enclosed complex where Palestinian prisoners are held. As the bus winds its way through low hills and wadis other installations come into sight. The Negev is also the playground of the Israeli Defense Force. Vast stretches of barren territory, much of it off-limits to civilians, are scattered with army bases, field-manoeuvre grounds, firing ranges, rest zones and other military terrain devoted to shadowy, unstated purpose. Not far to the east lies the town of Dimona, home to Israel's nuclear reactor and unacknowledged nuclear weapons research programme. Where in these desert sands the country's arsenal of nuclear missiles lie buried and waiting in underground silos is anyone's guess.

The Negev is a place earlier generations believed central to Israel's peacetime destiny as well. David Ben Gurion, father of the country, is also father of the Negev. About an hour south of Beersheba we pass the Kibbutz Sde Boker, site of the country's first and not entirely successful attempt to raise cattle in the desert. It is better known as the place where Ben Gurion retired from political struggle to pursue an even more challenging foe – the Negev itself.

'If the state does not put an end to the desert,' he once famously said, 'the desert might put an end to the state.' Ben Gurion was convinced the Negev had vast productive potential. Two things were needed to unlock it – technology and human energy. Not far past the kibbutz we pass another turnoff, the entrance to the Ben Gurion University of the Negev. Here, at facilities devoted to the study of desert hydrology, water engineering and Negev meteorology, the search for the technological farming fixes initiated by Ben Gurion goes on. Whether or not innovations developed there can stand up to Israel's irrigation-intensive agriculture and an ever-sinking water-table is uncertain. But there is no doubting at least one human being's energy. Even decades after his death and burial in the Negev the ghost of Ben Gurion is still hard at work: such institutions as the Ben Gurion University, the Ben Gurion Home museum and the Ben Gurion Tomb National Park continue the state effort to promote development in a hostile environment.

It's a tough sell. Government incentives and Ben Gurion's spirit not-withstanding, few Israelis have shown much willingness to spend their lives in the Negev development towns. And when in the late afternoon, 150 kilometres north of Eilat and the Red Sea, I finally step off the bus in the town of Mitzpe Ramon I understand why.

The towns of the Negev are the dullest, deadest places on earth. The only other people who get off the bus are three skinny Tel Aviv hippies. Nothing happens here, they tell me. Ever. The Negev hasn't changed since Moses and the Israelites spent forty years wandering around here lost and living on manna. They haven't got forty years, they tell me; they've only got a weekend. But they've also got tents, cooking gear and their own manna – a large stash of marijuana. It's Friday and they are going out into the wilderness for three days to camp, have fun and get bombed out of their minds.

When I ask about local accommodation they point towards a visitor's centre sitting on a gentle slope that rises away from the far side of town. 'Watch out for the step on the other side,' says one of them. At that the other two start giggling uncontrollably. I can only imagine they've already dug into their weekend's entertainment supplies.

I trudge through an assemblage of blocky houses and low, cube-like apartment complexes. It's a small, desolate and beleaguered-feeling place – from almost anywhere in town you can look out between buildings and see the empty rock- and rubble-strewn desert outside. The buildings look like they've been constructed elsewhere and fitted together here piece by piece. Started as a road-builder's camp fifty years ago, the whole town still has an impermanent, prefabricated feel. It's as if it's been plunked down in the middle of nowhere and is now waiting for the necessary people, jobs and a *raison d'être* to animate it. I still can't see what that reason might be.

The streets are deserted, the whole place silent and eerie. Then, far up the road, I see a sign of life. It appears to be a small deer. It is thin-legged and tawny-coloured and agile. It jumps a four-foot retaining wall with ease. But its horns are all wrong for a deer – they are massive, and instead of branching outwards they curl up and around in a wide arc until they are pointing to the back of the animal's ears. First there's one of these animals on the sidewalk, then two or three nibbling dead weeds in an empty lot, then an entire small herd walking down the middle of the main street. They are Nubian Ibex, and they have taken over the town-centre.

Ibex are not the only exotic inhabitants of Mitzpe Ramon. At the top of a sloping street, newly paved and smooth, I come across a group of small black American children on roller-blades. They are waiting to take turns rolling down the empty tarmac. 'Y'all! Y'all! Lookit!' a little girl with pink skates shouts to her friends as she trundles down the slope. The voice is Deep South. These could be kids from any small town in Alabama or Mississippi. What are they doing in *this* Deep South?

But Mitzpe Ramon keeps its greatest secret hidden behind that gentle rise on the far edge of town. There are signs for a Visitors' Centre, and a path and concrete steps leading up the rocky incline. It's only when I am almost at the top that I see what lies beyond – thin air. The land suddenly falls away and only resumes again far, far below. I am looking at vacant space, a vast volume of emptiness that is forty kilometres long, eight kilometres wide and 400 metres deep. From one side of the earth to the other a wide void fills the entire visual field. I've seen sheer, thousand-foot cliffs before, but none that give on to anything quite so desolate and unfurnished. It's all smooth, worn rock, but there's nothing here to give a sense of scale at all. The desert highlands that begin again on the far side of this gigantic hole might as well be a cardboard backdrop in a photo studio.

It's only at this point that I identify Mitzpe Ramon's *raison d'être*. Back in Jerusalem Frère Pierre must be laughing by now. I'd asked him about quiet desert places, but there's nothing of the serene, monkish retreat in this recommendation – it's primeval, a howling wilderness, the world not long after its creation. I can see why outsiders are attracted to Mitzpe Ramon, why there's an impressive visitor's centre, a youth hostel, an upscale tourist hotel. I can understand why giggly Tel Aviv dope-smokers are drawn here. The Ramon Crater is hallucinatory. I've never seen anything like it. In its immense size, in its bizarre rock formations, unearthly colours and sheer lunar weirdness it is a spectacular and unnerving sight.

The guide behind the counter at the visitor's centre wears glasses and a patient, pedagogical air. She's got plenty of time to talk, for the place is empty. Everyone makes the same mistake, she tells me. It may be called the Ramon Crater in English but it's not actually a crater at all. The Makhtesh Ramon (its Hebrew name) is the world's largest erosion cirque. It's a rare geological formation, and to explain it she uses rare geological terminology. There are bits about friable Senonian limestone deposits, differentiated angling of strata slants, the formation of the Ramon asymmetrical anticline and the vigorous sandstone erosion of the Ramon Ridge. The longer the guide talks, the more technical her explanation becomes.

It's far too complex for me to make any sense of, but what I do latch onto is the fact that there are walking trails that lead down the cliffside and out onto the floor of the crater. It's too late to leave today, the guide tells me – the hike is stiff and the conditions are harsh. I should leave at dawn, and will need at least six hours to get down there and back. Stay at the youth hostel, she advises – all the walkers leave from there. She looks through the window at a sun now dipping towards the crater's edge. The stone sides of the Makhtesh Ramon have turned blood red and the distant floor below lies in darkness. If I hurry, she says, I'll just have time to buy lunch to take on my hike. After sunset everything closes – it's Shabbat eve.

Can the laws of Shabbat apply even here? By day the town is hardly a riot of activity, but the guide is right. In the fast-sinking twilight Mitzpe Ramon, already dwarfed into insignificance beside its deep, dark trench, becomes the loneliest place on the planet. I walk back through streets deserted even by Nubian Ibex. It's suddenly grown cold and the black kids, too, have disappeared. The shopkeeper in the little corner-store I find is reluctant to let me in, and locks his premises tight the moment I leave. When I finally open the door of the youth hostel and find warmth and light and human voices it feels like coming home.

It's a bright, modern place and a large youth-group from a farming kibbutz have just arrived for the weekend. They fill the place with lively chatter and I like it. I don't care if there are bomb-shelter signs pointing to the basement or a receptionist who wears a pistol on his hip. I don't care if we're in a border area and Israelis feel threatened and defensive. I want human company.

It comes in the person of Dieter, the hiker I'll be sharing Dorm Number Four with for the night. He's already in the six-bunk room when I arrive, cleaning up after a long walk to prehistoric rock cisterns behind the town.

Dieter – at least I call him Dieter here, for I prefer not to use his real name – is German. He's in his mid-thirties, clean-shaven, well-mannered, well-spoken, and meticulously tidy. He is an organised traveller. When I arrive he is unfolding and refolding clothes that have been creased in his backpack. No matter that he's moving on to a dive-site near Eilat in a day or two. His outdoor gear is carefully arranged on hangers, his clothing is sorted and stacked in individual piles, then neatly put away in bedside drawers. The empty backpack, brushed clean, is stowed in a locker. Dieter also has a nifty nylon roll-up toilet bag with separate webbed compartments for different items. Unrolled, it's about four feet long, contains every travel convenience and personal hygiene-aid known to man, and already hangs from its own plastic suction cups on the back of the bathroom door.

We sit and chat as we wait for dinner. Dieter is on a two-week holiday, relaxing from a job that keeps him on the run for most of the year. It's a demanding job, he says, and he needs open spaces and exercise to unwind. I ask him what he does.

'I am a senior administrator for a global company that delivers clinical-trial packages to pharmaceutical firms,' he says. His English is as precise and organised as his clothes-folding.

What does that involve, I want to know.

'Everything,' he says. 'I am contracted to provide trial protocols, patient permissions, medical personnel selection, hospital release authorisations and so on... the entire legal and logistic framework that pharmaceutical companies require to conduct trials of untested drug products on human beings.'

Dieter talks on about his job. A model of multinational modernity, he sees himself as a manager, a supervisor of technological progress. He is cool and efficient and unemotional. Most of his work involves cancer victims – he establishes the conditions by which terminal cancer patients are permitted to use unproven drugs as a last resort in a losing battle. It is, of course, an exercise fraught with unimaginable anguish for the patients involved. They are desperate, Dieter tells me, and willing to sign on to any programme that offers even a sliver of hope. But I'd be surprised, he adds, how many variants of new drugs actually fail before a successful, marketable product can be developed.

'But what happens to all the volunteers?' I ask, taken aback by the reasoned calculation of it all.

'Well, they die, of course,' says Dieter. There's barely a flicker of expression on his face. He looks at me as if, despite his excellent English, I've failed to understand what he's been telling me. He seems untouched by the personal drama that he daily unleashes, unmoved by the thought of a distant and impersonal corporate hand which extends hope and then just as abruptly withdraws it. With the same regard he might show for a signature on a release form, he looks at the arrival of death with clinical equanimity.

'But aren't you affected emotionally?' I ask. 'Don't you ever think about the suffering? About death? You live surrounded by it every day, you are complicit in it, even. And it doesn't bother you?'

Dieter shakes his head. 'That would be unacceptable,' he says. 'I am a professional.'

Dinner begins at seven o'clock sharp, and is served as a vast buffet. At the head of a large, well-lit dining-room a long table groans with fruits and cheeses and yoghurts, chicken, beef and breaded schnitzel, a dozen different kinds of salads and endless cakes and dessert pastries. Most of the room is taken up by rows of long tables at which teenage *kibbutzim*

are seated. Freshly washed and changed after their bus trip, they are all dressed for Shabbat eve, boys and girls alike, in immaculate white. Dieter and I sit at a small table in the corner and are joined by Ami. Well-travelled, erudite and an amateur historian, Ami hasn't come to the Negev on holiday. He's an Israeli tour-operator and he's scouting sites for next year's foreign tour-package offerings. The Americans, he tells us, have yet to discover the Ramon Crater; when they do they'll find it as grand as their own Grand Canyon.

'But at least some Americans have discovered it,' I say. I tell him about the black American children I've seen playing in the streets of Mitzpe Ramon.

'Ah, yes, the Black Hebrews,' Ami nods. 'Most live in Tel Aviv, but there are many in the south as well. There are a few here in Mitzpe, and more than a thousand in Dimona. You're right, they *are* Americans. But actually they'd prefer to be Israelis.'

The Black Hebrews, Ami tells us, come from a religious sect that was founded in Chicago. Many of its members are from the Deep South. The men have adopted the last name of 'ben Israel' – son of Israel; the women 'bat Israel' – daughter of Israel. They proclaim themselves Jews, and have unconventional ideas about the past. They believe that Abraham, Moses, Jesus and other Jews of biblical history were black, and that they themselves are descendants of the original tribe of Judah. Exiled in the Jewish Diaspora, they ended up in Africa, from where they were then taken as slaves to America and the Caribbean. Now they have come to Israel to claim their right to return to their land of origin. They do not smoke, drink or practice other corrupting habits. Vegetarian, they have their own dietary rules. Polygamous, they observe their own marriage rights. They are, all things considered, a most particular group.

'Chapter and verse, they will cite you biblical proof of Jewish negritude,' Ami is saying to Dieter as I return with a plate-load of schnitzel. 'According to them the Song of Solomon, the books of Revelations and Daniel all show that it is black people who are the true Jews today. Not all black people, mind you – just the black tribe of Judah. Of course this doesn't make white Israeli Jews too happy.' The Black Hebrews, he goes on, began arriving in Israel in the 1970s, and claimed the right to stay under the Jewish Law of Return. But the Israeli state wouldn't recognise their Jewishness, and wouldn't grant them citizenship. After much controversy the Supreme Court finally gave them the right of residence, and many moved into Negev towns desperate for new citizens. But still today they live on the margins of Israeli society.

'They are very much on their own,' says Ami, raising his voice over the growing clamour. 'Most Jews want little to do with them, and they have little to do with us. They claim to be a tribe, and they live like one.'

It's getting hard to talk in the dining-room because the tables in front of us are growing festive. Ever since the meal began we've been hearing some of the happier, less inhibited Shabbat-celebrators breaking out into short snatches of song. Now they unite in singing in confident, concerted fashion. Swaying rhythmically back and forth on each side of their long tables, everyone joins in until the room is filled with single, united, jubilant voice. Given flowing steins of pilsner, we could just about be celebrating a beer-festival in a Munich cellar.

'They are kibbutz songs,' says Ami, almost shouting now. 'Religious songs, happy songs. A lot of *kibbutzim* are secular, but not these ones.'

'Do they always sing at dinner?' I ask.

'They sing when they are happy, and they're happy when they're together.' Ami sits for a minute, listening, and then leans forward to be heard. 'Jews don't like to do things on their own. They think it's abnormal. If they can avoid it, apart from sex they don't even like to do things as couples. They are at their happiest when they are in big, extended families, everybody doing everything together.' He halts once more, reflecting. 'Maybe they prefer even larger groups,' he says finally in a gap in between songs. 'I was saying the Black Hebrews think and act like a tribe. Of course, they aren't the only tribe around.'

Dinner over, the kibbutzim repair to another room for evening prayers and Torah reading. It's too soon to turn in, so Dieter and I put on jackets and head outside. It's pitch black and silent along the edge of the crater, but a short stroll into the town takes us to the Ramon Inn – Dieter has seen Friday evening music advertised there.

In the end I prefer the kibbutz songs – the hotel performers, an Israeli folk duo with an electric organ, are as dire as any lounge-act I can remember. They're more insipid, even, than the peppermint tea most residents at the Ramon Inn are sipping. The Negev, it seems, saves splendour for nature and not much else. When we finish our own peppermint tea Dieter suggests we go outside to see the desert sky. It's not like any night-sky elsewhere, he promises; it's so clear and untroubled by the light of human habitation that on some nights he's seen entire showers of shooting stars.

Dieter is right. Back near the lip of the crater we sit on a low stone wall. As our eyes adjust to the darkness we see a brilliant sky, more bright stars billowing out in thick clusters across the firmament than I've ever seen before. The Jerusalem sky seen from the roof of the Maison d'Abraham, so bright in my memory, suddenly dims by comparison.

But why, I ask Dieter as we sit there looking heavenward, has he chosen this particular desert in this particular part of the world for star gazing? If he's looking for escape and relaxation there are other deserts, equally bright stars in much less troubled parts of the globe.

'But it's not escape I'm not looking for,' Dieter says. The voice is quiet, but there's more emotion, more intimacy in it now. Is it our dark surroundings, our sitting on the edge of nothing that encourage him? 'I come here because of the trouble. I am part of the trouble,' he says. He swivels back to look at the lights of Mitzpe Ramon. 'Why does this place exist if not for what for Germans like me have done to Jews like these? For this I have come to Israel many times.'

Here, abruptly, is an unexpected side to Dieter, a side that doesn't fit in with that cool, controlled manager of technology. It throws me, and I remain silent so long in the dark that Dieter finally tries to explain more clearly.

'We Germans have a word, *Autoritarismus*,' he says. 'We use it when we want to talk about our respect for authority, which is sometimes too much respect for our own good. We don't like to go against our fathers or our bosses or our leaders or the state. We like to be like everyone around us. *Autoritarismus* has allowed us to do many things in the past. Some of them we are not so proud of today.'

Now it's Dieter's turn to remain silent. What has that got to do, I ask, with his decision to come to Israel?

'Everything,' he says. 'But it's not easy to explain. I, also, am subject to a kind of *Autoritarismus*. I impose it on myself. I work hard, I forget the past and I am proud of being a German. But sometimes my emotions do not obey and then I feel bad. I am a German who feels responsible for the Holocaust, responsible for the German murder of six million people. I cannot forget the Jews who died, and I cannot forget the Jews who didn't. I come here to try to make it better with them.'

Dieter was not alive when these things happened. How can anyone so personally disassociated from so distant an act assume such responsibility? Confessions are as difficult for those who take them as for those who make them, and I'm content to let Dieter keep filling the night's silence.

Many years ago in Germany, he tells me, he joined a church youth organisation, a Christian group seeking ties with Jews and dedicated to the reconciliation of two religions and two peoples. 'With such groups we try not to forget what happened,' he says. 'We try to make sure anti-Semitism will not come back to Germany again.' But it is also important, Dieter tells me, for Jews to know that Germans can feel contrition and remorse. 'How can they know this, given the past, unless we show them?' he asks.

And so he made his first trip to Israel with the same religious group – an unofficial goodwill ambassador on a personal mission. Later, he made subsequent visits to Israel by himself, working on kibbutzes or simply traveling around the country. Always the aim is the same – Dieter seeks to make amends for crimes committed not by himself, but half a century ago by earlier generations of Germans.

I am still looking out at the night sky over the Ramon Crater. There *are* comets out there, bright, fleeting things with long tails. But they don't do anything to help illuminate matters for me. Are Dieter's visits to Israel intended for the benefit of Jews, or for his own benefit? For it's clear that somewhere deep inside, for reasons that I, and probably he too, cannot understand, a massive sense of personal guilt continues to eat away at Dieter.

It is no longer simply collective; he's seeking expiation for a painful, intimate kind of guilt. When Dieter was a boy, he tells me, he entered a children's photo competition. His submissions were not like other children's – as his theme he chose the burial sites of Nazi slave labourers who perished in camps near his home. Since then, I surmise, those feeling have only fed on themselves and grown. They have affected his whole existence. Does even Dieter himself know why he became involved in the clinical testing of the sick and the dying? The arbitrary granting of life and death to last-hope patients, it seems to me, is a kind of delayed replay – ultimately it's not so far removed from the power of life and death exercised in the camps themselves.

And so the punisher punishes himself. As we walk back toward the hostel I find myself thinking that in the end Dieter is no model of clinical equanimity at all. Twisted from the start, his life turns in a spiral around death. In the end Dieter is consuming himself with his own cancer.

Now it's certainly the result of all the talk beside that vast black hole in the middle of the night, but when Dieter and I return to Dorm Number Four the oddest of impressions comes over me. After we switch out the lights and are lying there, I in a bunk by the window, Dieter in a bunk by the door, I notice a strange odour drifting from his direction. Even with the window open it is noticeable. It is not the rank smell of sweat or the stale smell of irregular bathing – quite distinctly, it's a sickly, sweetish odour, a whiff of bodily rot and decomposition. In his personal habits Dieter is the cleanest of people, and I suppose it's only the heavy walking boots he has placed neatly beneath his bed. But nonetheless that smell is there, and I feel troubled and haunted enough to tell myself that it is nothing other than the smell of death. In an end-of-the-world place like Mitzpe Ramon you can tell yourself anything you like and half-believe it.

And there's not only that. Once Dieter has fallen asleep he frightens me even more. All through the night he tosses and turns sporadically, muttering to himself through clenched jaws. There are faint moans and shudders, muffled gasps of surprise and protestation. And he talks, too – his is speech is disjointed and rambling, his words indistinct. What is he saying? I don't speak German. What pictures are playing through his mind? I don't want to think about them. But I know they are not all sweetness and light, and hours pass until at last I fall asleep.

It's six-thirty, the sun is just up, and Dieter has already left the dormitory without my hearing him. Again there is a vast buffet spread out on the dining-room serving table and I eat a sustaining Israeli breakfast of corn-and-tuna salad, tomatoes and olives, cottage cheese and boiled eggs, almost alone. The garrulous *kibbutzim* have departed on their own hike already, and I don't mind. This is the kind of walk I'd prefer to do in silence.

Outside the youth hostel the new day is still cool and quiet and the town sleeps on. It's not all silence, though. As I cross the street and approach the rocky edge of the Makhtesh Ramon I see a dozen or more figures gathered. There is nothing but the depthless, bluish hue of early morning air behind them and they seem to teeter precariously on the crater's edge, a step away from nothingness. The sunlight now hitting it from the other side, the crater is not the same in the morning as the evening, and the colour in the rocks is colder and harder. But it is as overpowering as ever, and for the moment it is being used as dramatic backdrop. Three men stand side by side in front of the crater. They wear heavy, untrimmed beards and are dressed in flowing white robes. White skullcaps adorn their heads. I know nothing about them but I've spent long enough in Jerusalem to know what their regalia signifies: unmistakably, they are spokesmen of God.

The little congregation the three men face are equally distinctive. Both men and women wear the vivid colours of the tropical forest – bright greens, flaming reds, strident yellows. They carry no prayer books, sing from no hymnals, but stand there rapt, listening intently. I know of no Christian church, have heard of no Muslim mosque, have seen no Jewish synagogue with worshippers like these. But I know who they are. They are Black Hebrews, and on this Sabbath they have come to the yawning mouth of the Ramon Crater to celebrate their maker.

Following the path that leads along the edge of the precipice I come close enough to hear what's being said. In the rich, robust accents of the American South the robed man who stands on the cliff-side flanked by two others is making some kind of invocation. Waxing and waning in volume, rising and falling in pitch, it is a prayer that alternates between a preacher's affirmation and his congregation's response.

At first I hear something of the high exaltation of Martin Luther King in the rolling, forward-driving voice. But then there is something else. 'And when they came to the Promised Land,' it intones, 'they were full of joy and jubilation, and gave thanks to the Lord, shouting WOW!'

It is a loud, sharp exclamation. 'WOW!' shout the two men on either side of him.

'WOW! the members of the congregation cry in ragged, happy unison.

'And they fell down before Him, and made offerings at His altar, and sang songs of praise, hollering WOW!'

'WOW!' call out the two aides again.

'WOW!' trumpet the congregation once more.

The Black Hebrews pay no attention to me; their prayer-cycle continues as I make a broad detour around the little group and carry on to the head of a steep trail. Marked with small flashes of green paint, it plunges earthwards in a series of short, tight zigzagging switchbacks. Down and down I go, hearing as I descend those jubilant, repeated WOWs! They continue to float downwards long after I lose sight of the white-robed figures on the crater's rim, and only slowly do their echoes become fainter and less distinct. They finally fade away entirely when I am close to the foot of the cliff.

I would like to say that I am thoroughly at ease in the world that stands revealed at the bottom of the Ramon Crater, but I'm not. The sky above is a depthless blue, hard and enamel-glazed. Bouncing off smooth, time-scoured rock, the sharp light penetrates every indentation and crevice in the earth. It glances off the crater wall that stretches behind me, picking out striated earth-colours I've never seen before – magentas and bronzes, puces and cinnabars, siennas and maroons. The whole place is stunning, but it's also a little frightening.

What scares me is not the rock that lies above and behind. The solid, material things I can deal with. It's what lies in the crater ahead of me: nothing. For as far as I can see there's a total lack of anything at all. There's not a human, not a tree, not a blade of grass. Except for those occasional green flashes of paint, the rocky surface of the crater floor that stretches away is absolutely empty and runs on forever. It's like seeing infinity for the first time.

Why nothing, rather than something, should be frightening I can't say, unless it's that we're unused to such complete absence – perhaps we fill our lives with activity and movement, objects and distraction simply to cover up the great resounding void that lies behind them. There are none of those things here. There's just vast emptiness, and silence.

As I walk on minute after minute the noiselessness is so total that for the first time I discover what silence really is. Never before have I heard the cotton arms of my T-shirt rubbing against my sides. Every sound seems magnified – I hear every inhalation and exhalation of my breath, every step I take on the crater floor. If I inadvertently kick a loose rock as I'm walking I register the exact sound it makes as it bangs into other rocks. Some resonate with the dull chink of glass; others ring with a sharp metallic clang.

So stark and bright and alien is this place, so acute is any response to its slightest stimulus, that soon I'm wondering if my senses can actually be trusted. If I walk for a minute looking down at my feet and then raise my head I know what will be there, but still it's an unexpected surprise. It's difficult to believe my surroundings at all.

How much of this, I begin to wonder, can anyone take? I imagine other, longer trips in this desert. Never mind the forty minutes I've just spent walking here. How about forty years? How long would it be before hyper-reality began transforming itself into mirages, delusions, poetic dreams, spiritual visions, psychotic episodes? How long would it take, for instance, before you began to see burning bushes? How long might it be before you were ready to follow pillars of cloud by day and pillars of fire by night? Directionless, with no points of reference in this desolate place, you might finally be prepared to follow any sign, any unexpected portent at all. If man is so utterly absent from this place, where else could such strange things come from but God?

Puffing with exertion, the sun growing stronger by the minute, I walk on for an hour and arrive at a fork in the path. One branch, with paint flashes marked in red, turns south, heading across the middle of the crater. I am not tempted; it leads to the far side of the Makhtesh Ramon and then onward over ancient trade routes into Jordan – if Israeli border patrols didn't get you vultures would. I continue eastwards on the green-marked trail, skirting the towering wall of the crater and heading towards the rock formation known as The Prism.

Another hour passes and I arrive in the blinding light of a sun now standing high in the sky. The Prism, a pile of hexagonally shaped limestone columns that protrude from the crater floor, is disappointing. I was expecting a kind of Giant's Causeway in the Negev; these small columns are short, lopsided and dull in colour. But I'm happy to have followed the route nonetheless, for once again there's human company – sitting in a small, dark patch of shade by the rocks are Dieter and Ami, our tour-operator dining companion.

They've already eaten lunch, and while I use falafel bread to dig into the plastic tub of hummus I've brought they continue on, deep in discussion.

The theme doesn't surprise me, but in his obsessive preoccupation with the intertwined lives of Germans and Jews Dieter has steered the conversation in unexpected directions. What finally happened, he is asking Ami, to the Jerusalem Germans interned in camps during the Second World War?

They've been discussing, I learn as I listen in, the changing fortunes of the Templers, the community of German Protestants who emigrated to Palestine in the 1830s. Founders of the German Colony in Jerusalem, they remained highly successful until war changed their prospects overnight. With one out of five Templers a Nazi party member and many more active sympathizers, the British Mandate rulers of Palestine declared the entire community enemy aliens and shipped them off to detention in Australia.

All Israel, Ami is now saying, was caught up in impassioned debate over the Templers when independence came. In post-war agreements Germany had agreed to pay financial reparations to Israel for Nazi crimes committed against Jews. The question was whether the Templers were eligible for reparation too. After all, just like the Jews, they'd had their businesses and property taken away, their land confiscated, and themselves arrested and summarily deported. Some Templers, even though they were non-Jews, also demanded the right of return to the place they'd lived for generations.

Ami reviews the case in detail, going over the claims and counter-claims, the technical and emotional aspects of a prolonged legal contest. 'In the end,' he says as I scrape the bottom of the tub with a scrap of bread, 'the Templers won. The Israeli Knesset decided that a portion of the German reparations going to Israel would be channeled to them. But the whole issue was contentious and sensitive. It wasn't just the question of Jewish blood-money being awarded to Nazi sympathisers. If non-Jewish Templers could be awarded restitution and return, why then couldn't Palestinian Arabs? They, too, had lost land and livelihoods and property. They too had been chased out. It was feared the Templer settlement would establish a precedent.'

We rise and dust ourselves off, preparing to leave. And as we do Ami tidies up the Arab question in a couple of sentences. 'Of course,' he adds, 'the situation was totally different. We weren't at war with the Templers, but we were with the Arabs. And in war there are always refugees. It is only natural. So adjudication in favour of the Templers, then, and case closed.'

Sunglasses on, hat-brims shading our eyes, we begin our return trudge towards the cliff-side and the steep climb back to Mitzpe Ramon. My head down, my concentration turned to putting one foot in front of the other, I'm walking slowly and at the same time turning Ami's little story over in my mind. Without noticing it I allow my two companions to get further and further ahead of me. Soon they are mere dots beneath the rearing wall of the crater and I am trudging alone in the bright sun.

And then as we approach the crater's side something odd and unaccountable happens. All around me I hear a faint, repeated noise. WOW! WOW! WOW! it reverberates in every direction, a sound of human voices that seems to have no human source. Is it a Black Hebrew echo, a vestige of supplication that's hung suspended in the still, clear desert air since early morning? Or is it something even older and more portentous still – a manifestation of those divine guides who bring lost biblical wanderers safely through the desert? It is neither – eventually I realize it's the distant voices of Dieter and Ami, magnified and deformed, bouncing off the crater wall towards me.

Perhaps though, I think, those voices are biblical voices after all. Even today there are bands of men wandering through the wilderness, tribes looking for deliverance by a heavenly hand. You don't even need to be lost in a desert to look for that. Any unfamiliar ground, an unresolved border between two nations, say, will do. Nor do you have to belong to an officially constituted tribe. Everyone in the Middle East belongs to one tribe or another, and WOWs for God are ringing through the heads of them all. For such wanderers divine myth and symbol is still everything. It might not matter for the individual, but the question 'Who was here first?' remains crucial for the tribe. 'Who was here first?' can be more important, even, than settling the quarrels of two tribes who've been wandering so long they've both forgotten when or why they arrived in the first place.

I continue thinking about it until we can see the Visitor's Center observation platform high above us, and begin climbing towards it. And the closer we get the more it seems to me that we three hikers are indeed members of tribes. Dieter continues to suffer remorse for the wrong committed by his tribe. Ami sees no no need for remorse for he sees no wrong committed by his tribe. And I, member of a third group, have little means to understand how those who suffer wrong at the hands of one tribe can fail to see their own suffering in another. Despite attempts to step back and see things clearly, I am no closer to the answers I've come looking for. We may have pitched up in civilisation again. But as far as I'm concerned, on matters of wandering all three of us are still lost far out in the desert.

Eighteen

I'm lucky with timing. A little after five o'clock, running hard from the youth hostel to the bus-stop on the edge of town, I make the Eilat-Jerusalem express. It stops just once more, in Beersheba. Then, the aisle crowded with soldiers on leave, we roll on northward through the dark without stopping. By eleven o'clock I have passed through the IDF baggage checks at the exit-doors of the Jerusalem bus station, and am walking down the Jaffa Road.

After Mitzpe Ramon Jerusalem, for once, seems what I took it to be in the beginning – the centre of the world. It's a Saturday night, less than a week before Christmas, and if Jews and Muslims aren't getting ready to celebrate the birth of a saviour a festive spirit seems to have bubbled out all over town anyway. Central Jerusalem is in energetic, party-going mood.

King George Street, Ha Histadrut, Zion Square and other thorough-fares are jammed with young people. The pedestrian mall on Ben Yehuda is even more crowded – you have to shoulder your way from one street spectacle to the next.

There's something for everyone. Half-notes quiver delicately in the night air as a string quartet of women in elegant black evening gowns plays *Ein Kleine Nachtmusik*. A few metres away a Brazilian duo in baggy white trousers, their chests bare and sweaty, is performing a ballet-like demonstration of *capoeira* fighting. Celebrating the immanent return of the deceased Rebbe Schneerson, a band of happy, singing, black-hatted Lubavitchers are pulling supporters and bystanders into a spinning, dancing, ever-growing circle. Further on there's a guy with a saxophone, and past him a Marcel Marceau clone in white grease-paint. At the top of the mall a Christmas choir of touring Chinese Christians, two dozen men and women with fixed smiles on their faces, are massed in ascending tiers of benches singing 'O Come, All Ye Faithful.'

On the Jaffa Road college students, young Americans come to Israel on Jewish study programmes, are behaving more like weekend bingers than devout Jews. They've had too much to drink and are hanging around outside the Leonidas chocolate shop, laughing, falling about and cluttering the sidewalk. One is blocking it altogether. Supine, resisting his friends' attempts to pull him up, he too is caroling. In his rambling, off-key version of 'The Twelve Days of Christmas' most of the words are missing, but at the end of each verse, cackling with laughter, he shouts '... And a pa-aar-tridge in a pear tree!'

Not far past him the counter of the Coffee Time bagel shop is lined three-deep with customers, as is the pizza take-out place beside it. There's a djembe drum player who's set up on the corner, and as a party of bagel-eaters emerge from the shop and head down the sidewalk they link up in a conga line, jiving from the shoulders and pumping from the knees. Straight out of the silence and empty spaces of the Ramon Crater, it's all a bit too much for me. I spot a bar sign down the street and duck in.

It's not a local watering hole, but an expat bar full of tourists out on the town. It's hardly quieter than the street outside, but there's a just-vacated stool at the bar. To one side of me a girl is lobbing pretzels through the air into her boyfriend's mouth. To the other a man is trying to locate one of his mobile phones by dialing it with another. In a corner at the far end of the bar a plasma-screen TV is tuned to the evening news – there is footage of Red Crescent ambulances pulling away from the scattered wreckage of a street-side explosion. It's just one more bomb. It might be Iraq, Gaza, Pakistan or any other troubled eastern place; the sound is turned down and no one is watching. Behind the bar a bartender is mixing up batches of specialty drinks one after the other for a roomful of noisy Christmas drinkers. They've discovered his name. 'Gilli! We're thirsty!' 'Gilli! Another round over here!' Gilli, working at top speed, has no sooner filled one order than the waitresses are pressing him with three more.

'Brandy Alexanders, can you believe it?' Gilli mutters half to me, half to himself, as I sit watching him assemble a tray of cream-filled cocktails. 'Who for God's sake wants Brandy Alexanders these days?' Between the table-waitresses and the crowd pressing around the bar he can barely keep track of who wants what. Finally he picks up a pack of Marlboros, shouts 'Nat, take over for a minute!' to a colleague washing glasses at a sink, and stomps out of the back door of the bar for a cigarette.

I sympathise with Gilli. After a few months in Jerusalem I know how he feels. Like him, I am less capable than ever of keeping track of who wants what. There are too many people in this city clamouring for too many specialty mixes.

'Religion, can you believe it?' I want to say. 'Who for God's sake wants Bible-belt Methodism these days? Or Wahabi Islam? Chabad Lubavitch Judaism?' But of course all sorts of people do. Jerusalem is the biggest religious-specialty establishment in the world, an entire city with a vast spiritual thirst. And as long as that thirst for completion exists, there will be holy men to tend the bar and keep serving up every exotic cocktail variety of faith known to man.

My own thirst for completion remains unquenched. But in just a couple of days I, too, will be walking out the back door. And unlike Gilli, I won't be returning to the confusion and overheated tumult anytime soon. It wouldn't matter if I returned to the city a hundred times – Jerusalem will always leave me perplexed.

The beer that Nat finally gets around to serving me is good and cold and washes down the last of the Negev dust. Still in my hair and eyelashes, the fine powder is as persistent as my memory of the desert itself. The Negev's great empty space is still in my head, and with it the faintest of echos. 'WOW!' It's an exclamation at the sheer strangeness of creation. But the noise of the bar and its distractions muffles such noise – by the time I have finished my beer and slid off my barstool the echoes have grown fainter still. And by the time I have walked down the Jaffa Road to the New Gate and the walls of the Old City they have disappeared altogether.

There is nothing on the far side of the high walls but silence. If an ancient, sun-blasted desert offers vague and tantalising hints as to how it all started here, these dim alleys offer no clue about how it all might end. However clamorous its inhabitants usually are, no one in this still, dark midnight is saying a word. The Old City is dead to the world – its streets are deserted, its windows barred, its metal shopfront blinds lowered and padlocked.

The Maison d'Abraham lies on the far side of the city walls. As I worm my way through the labyrinth of passages and alleys I try to stick to broader, safer thoroughfares. But without crowds and noise to follow I'm not sure of my way. There is none of the tinny music, the cluttered display of domestic wares, the persistent market-chatter that by day makes the Old City seem homey and familiar. In the silence and emptiness even places I know look strange and threatening. There are sudden rustlings and rattlings as frightened cats jump from piles of refuse, brief sightings of obscure figures vanishing down ill-lit passages, the nasty surprise of dead-ends that shouldn't be there but are. Most eerie of all is the sound of my own solitary footsteps hitting the stone flagging with regular monotony.

I'm lost. But as long as I keep heading downhill I know I'm moving in the right direction. So left and right through the alleys below St Francis Road I turn, descending any stairways I can find. On and on it goes, a looped dream whose scenery keeps repeating itself. Just occasionally there's an encounter – there are, after all, Jerusalem denizens abroad in the murky night. But our meetings are hardly reassuring, and the people I pass in the dark are as anxious as I am.

Once, near the Greek Patriarchate, I come across a Orthodox monk, his head lowered, his bushy white beard folded flat on his chest. I might be the devil himself – he crosses himself three times in rapid succession as we pass each other. Near the Al-Attarin Souq and the road leading to the Jewish Quarter I am overtaken by a worried-looking *Haredi* sloping along at high speed, his side-curls swaying vigorously as he steams past me. In the Muslim Quarter I approach a man smoking in a doorway; by the time I am abreast there is nothing left of him but drifting smoke and the smell of tobacco.

But finally I have my bearings again. I come to the Austrian Hospice, turn right on the Via Dolorosa and arrive at last at the Lion's Gate. There is an Israeli army checkpoint there, an IDF jeep with a blue flashing light and a pair of soldiers in dressed night patrol gear. One is a woman – her hair is wrapped in a khaki scarf and she is stamping her feet on the ground against the rising cold.

And then, relieved, I am through the gate at last, away from the Old City and out into the open night. A half-moon has risen and illuminates the Kidron Valley in a pale wash of light. In daytime it is thick with diesel exhaust, but now as I cross the hollow by St. Mary's Tomb and start up the Mount of Olives on the other side the night is crisp and clean. The grove of olives opposite the Garden of Gethsemane stands clear and silvery in the moonlight and the Jewish cemeteries sprawled across the hill are wind-sculpted fields of snow. In the unfamiliar moonlight I am seeing Jerusalem again for the first time.

But the wonder of these thing fades before another, brighter wonder. Just past the Russian Church of Mary Magdalene I turn back towards Old City. And there, rising above its walls, looms the great hemisphere of the Dome of the Rock. It is not, like everything else in this night, touched with a cold, white luminescence. Spotlit from below, it glows as I first saw it glow in the bright light of day, warm and burnished and golden. It glints and shimmers, as if powered by some living source inside. A beacon out-shining everything else, the Dome becomes the city itself, a central point for everyone looking to Jerusalem.

And in its brilliance what it makes me think is this: we've got it all wrong – Jerusalem does not lie at the centre of the world.

I think back to the day I bought a Jerusalem Cross, that carved, olive-wood representation of the city that even now sits zipped in the pack hanging from my shoulder. For millennia such symbols, Jewish, Muslim and Christian, have placed the city at the very middle of things. Priests and imams and rabbis all endlessly affirm it, but now I know it is not true. It is not God's divine nature, emanating outwards from the city, that determines man's fate across the world. It's the other way round. It is man's earthly nature that determines God's fate in Jerusalem. Jerusalem is not our starting point – it is our culmination, the end-product of all our acts and beliefs. This, perhaps, is the one, simple thing I have come at last to realise in the city. How can you explain a heavenly Jerusalem if you can't explain the human world that surrounds and makes it what it is?

Maybe it is not God's symbols – crosses and crescents and six-pointed stars – which best indicate the real position of Jerusalem on the earth. Perhaps it is we, human individuals, who do that job better. If I must have four surrounding points on my Jerusalem Cross, they will not be Antioch and Alexandria, Constantinople and Rome. Neither will they be Spain, Italy, Germany and France, nor Matthew, Mark, Luke and John, still less the pierced hands and feet of Christ. They will be the many aspects that make up all of us, the human character that in its entirety has formed the city.

I turn away from the Dome to gaze for a moment at the Church of Mary Magdalene. Fast asleep or lost in prayer, but in any case returned to the grace of nuns and candle-lit meditation, Frère Pierre is somewhere there in the darkness. The midnight-blue Jetta is safely parked behind the church, *Le Petit Guide de la Terre Sainte* is stowed back in the shelves of the convent library, and it may be some time before the monk heads north once again on the road to the Holy Land. Nonetheless Frère Pierre, mystic adventurer and plumber of the depths of divine mystery, remains for me one of the four figures that surround the city.

And what of Jesse Rosenfeld, not far to the east of Jerusalem? There is no question of his being fast asleep in Ramallah on this Saturday evening. I see him at a noisy party instead, deep in conversation, arguing a hypothetical future for the land he has returned to. No matter that those around him at the music- and smoke-filled party are content to imagine action – Jesse takes it. He conceives it, writes of it, pushes it upon the world, even if the world is not certain it's entirely ready to receive it. Jesse, too, wields the kind of energy with which Jerusalem has been, and will be, built.

What, on the other hand, of Barry Gilbert? He's no more likely to be sleeping on this clear, cold winter midnight than Jesse is. As I stand on the Mount of Olives is he standing not far to the west on a stage by the sea, lulling a Tel Aviv crowd with *A Whiter Shade of Pale*? Rocker, sybarite, unwilling witness to blood and horror, he's neither a mystic nor a man of action. But he, too, is a seeker. He's the man with the appetite for life, the consumer of its pleasures and its pastimes, and he only wants more. And Barry Gilbert, too, is another side to our collective self – the side which exonerates itself, refuses to see it has anything to do with Jerusalem or its conflicts, and ends up paying the price.

But there's no need for me to conjure up Dieter and the desert wastes of the Negev to the south – a long night's sleep-slurred recriminations are still fresh in my ears. Of all the figures who stand on the Jerusalem horizon it is Dieter who perturbs me most. Is he really Death? Of course not. But unlike the musician on the stage in Tel Aviv, he has not sought to disassociate himself from Jerusalem's pain – he has sought it out. There is much that is dark and disturbing in his guilt, something that acknowledges a genuinely guilty element that is dark and disturbing in each of us. Why is it, century after century, that we continue to treat each other in the appalling way we do? And this culpability, too, is part of the Jerusalem that belongs to us all. In the end I realise I am starting to look at the city itself as some sort of person, as an individual who has come to despair of ever integrating the different and conflicting parts of his own self.

But that leaves a fifth figure, one who sits neither to the north, south, east or west of the city. Nonetheless he looms larger in my mind than any of the others. Ashraf Noor occupies a place in Jerusalem itself, a place barely visible yet, but which might one day become its vital, living centre. Neither Jew nor Muslim nor Christian, yet something of each, it is he, of all the pilgrims I've met, who best inhabits the city.

Will there be others like him? It depends on our willingness to acknowledge the human elements, the shared narratives, that are common to all Jerusalemites. Perhaps that, in the end, is the heaven that Jerusalem has been seeking for so long – the room we make for each another here on earth. But I have no doubt: all of us, travellers from every point of the compass, those already arrived and those not yet departed, are part of the making of Jerusalem. And we all carry a map to get there, a Jerusalem Cross of our own construction.

It is late, and like that Israeli soldier's feet, my feet, too, are cold. I take a last glance at the Dome of the Rock, pull my pack more firmly onto my shoulders, and start walking again. There, not far away on the flank of the Mount of Olives, lies the Maison d'Abraham.